Process Drama for Second Language Teaching and Learning

Also available from Bloomsbury

ESSENTIALS FOR SUCCESSFUL ENGLISH LANGUAGE TEACHING,
Thomas S. C. Farrell and George M. Jacobs

Inspiring Writing through Drama: Creative Approaches to Teaching Ages 7–16, Patrice Baldwin and Rob John

Performative Language Teaching in Early Education: Language Learning through Drama and the Arts for Children 3–7, Joe Winston

Teaching English to Young Learners: Critical Issues in Language Teaching with 3–12 Year Olds, edited by Janice Bland

Teaching Listening and Speaking in Second and Foreign Language Contexts, Kathleen M. Bailey

Teaching Literature in Modern Foreign Languages,
edited by Fotini Diamantidaki

Using Graphic Novels in the English Language Arts Classroom, William Boerman-Cornell and Jung Kim

Using Literature in English Language Education: Challenging Reading for 8–18 Year Olds, edited by Janice Bland

With Drama in Mind: Real Learning in Imagined Worlds,
Patrice Baldwin

Process Drama for Second Language Teaching and Learning

A Toolkit for Developing Language and Life Skills

Patrice Baldwin and Alicja Galazka

BLOOMSBURY ACADEMIC
LONDON • NEW YORK • OXFORD • NEW DELHI • SYDNEY

BLOOMSBURY ACADEMIC
Bloomsbury Publishing Plc
50 Bedford Square, London, WC1B 3DP, UK
1385 Broadway, New York, NY 10018, USA
29 Earlsfort Terrace, Dublin 2, Ireland

BLOOMSBURY, BLOOMSBURY ACADEMIC and the Diana logo
are trademarks of Bloomsbury Publishing Plc

First published in Great Britain, 2022

Copyright © Patrice Baldwin and Alicja Galazka, 2022

Patrice Baldwin and Alicja Galazka have asserted their right under the Copyright, Designs and Patents Act, 1988, to be identified as Author of this work.

Cover design: Toby Way
Cover image © Klaus Vedfelt, Getty Images

All rights reserved. No part of this publication may be reproduced or transmitted in any form or by any means, electronic or mechanical, including photocopying, recording, or any information storage or retrieval system, without prior permission in writing from the publishers.

Bloomsbury Publishing Plc does not have any control over, or responsibility for, any third-party websites referred to or in this book. All internet addresses given in this book were correct at the time of going to press. The author and publisher regret any inconvenience caused if addresses have changed or sites have ceased to exist, but can accept no responsibility for any such changes.

A catalogue record for this book is available from the British Library.

Library of Congress Cataloging-in-Publication Data
Names: Baldwin, Patrice, author. | Galazka, Alicja, author.
Title: Process drama for second language teaching and learning : a toolkit for developing language and life skills / Patrice Baldwin and Alicja Galazka. Description: London ; New York : Bloomsbury Academic, 2021. | Includes bibliographical references and index. |
Identifiers: LCCN 2021010166 (print) | LCCN 2021010167 (ebook) | ISBN 9781350164758 (hardback) | ISBN 9781350164741 (paperback) | ISBN 9781350164765 (ebook) |
ISBN 9781350164772 (epub)
Subjects: LCSH: Second language acquisition. | Drama in education. |
Drama–Study and teaching. | Language and languages–Study and teaching.
Classification: LCC P118.2 .B34 2021 (print) | LCC P118.2 (ebook) | DDC 401/.93–dc23
LC record available at https://lccn.loc.gov/2021010166
LC ebook record available at https://lccn.loc.gov/2021010167

ISBN:	HB:	978-1-3501-6475-8
	PB:	978-1-3501-6474-1
	ePDF:	978-1-3501-6476-5
	eBook:	978-1-3501-6477-2

Typeset by Integra Software Services Pvt. Ltd.

To find out more about our authors and books visit www.bloomsbury.com and sign up for our newsletters.

Contents

Acknowledgments	vi
Introduction	1

Part I Introducing Process Drama — 5

1 What is Process Drama and How Can it Help Language Learners and Learning? — 7
2 Using Process Drama to Develop Twenty-First-Century Skills — 25
3 How to Introduce Process Drama to a Class and What is Expected of the Teacher? — 41

Part II Process Drama Strategies and Conventions for Use in the Second Language Classroom — 49

Part III The Drama Units — 75

Unit 1: Bullying — 77
Unit 2: The Great Fire of London — 84
Unit 3: Refugees — 91
Unit 4: Conservation or Change? — 100
Unit 5: Beowulf — 108
Unit 6: Over the Top—The True Story of Annie Edson Taylor, the "Queen of the Mist" — 116

Appendix: Resource Sheets — 132
References — 142
Index — 147

Acknowledgments

Every effort has been made to trace copyright holders and to obtain their permission for the use of copyright material. The publisher apologizes for any errors or omissions in the above list and would be grateful if notified of any corrections that should be incorporated in future reprints or editions of this book.

INTRODUCTION

Global society has been going through massive economic and technological transformation. Rapid change has affected organizations worldwide and shifted employers' expectations of employees, and this has led to new demands and requirements of the educational system (Dede, 2010). A new skill set, termed "the twenty-first-century skills," has now been deemed necessary to succeed in educational workplaces, businesses, companies, and organizations. The twenty-first-century skills and abilities are certainly needed by students graduating from higher education institutions, if they are to become sought-after, skilled employees, able to create and produce what organizations require and able to adapt within the constantly changing environment of a modern workplace (Dede, 2010).

All educationalists and teachers must explore how to adapt their teaching for a new era of constant and potentially overpowering changes. To deal with this effectively, we may need to develop different personal and social skills. Teaching second languages (especially English as a foreign language) has been one of the most rapidly developing sectors in education. However, language is an essential medium for teaching other subjects, as well as ways of thinking and for developing students' social and emotional skills.

Learning and innovation skills that best prepare students for increasingly complex lives and work environments in the twenty-first century are being identified and recognized as crucial. There is a focus on creativity, critical thinking, agility, communication, and collaboration, which are all essential when preparing students for the future. A twenty-first-century education must give students opportunities to think deeply and critically together about issues, solve problems creatively, work collaboratively and work productively in teams, communicate clearly, and use a variety of media in appropriate and discerning ways. Education needs to be less about giving and getting the "right" answers back from students and more about stimulating them metacognitively and developing their ability to ask the right questions.

Second language teaching is a complex process, requiring students to shift into a different mental world that involves different thinking, feeling, acting, and cultural understanding. It involves a total, holistic form of engagement on a personal, social, cognitive, physical, and emotional level.

There have been many theories and much research on second language acquisition (SLA), which has tried to explore, understand, and explain the complex process of both language learning and teaching in the light of linguistic, educational, and psychological research evidence. Many different approaches have been applied to try and make the process of SLA increasingly effective. One of the most significant is the sociocultural theory, which is based on constructivism. This closely corresponds to the way that Process Drama can be used in language education. Sociocultural theory claims that humans are better able to understand information that they have meaningfully constructed themselves. Learning can be considered as a social advancement that involves language, real-world situations, and interaction and collaboration among and between the learners themselves. Social constructivism sees each learner as a complex and multidimensional individual with unique needs and backgrounds. Social constructivism not only acknowledges the uniqueness and complexity of the individual learner but also encourages and uses it, as an integral part of the learning process (Wertsch, 1998). It provides a psycholinguistic explanation as to how language learning can be fostered effectively, through interactive pedagogical practices. It emphasizes that language learning takes place in a sociocultural environment and learners are actively involved in the learning process. They construct their own understanding, look for meaning, and discover principles, concepts, and facts for themselves (Ackerman, 1996; Brown, 1989; Von Glasersfeld, 1989). Process Drama enables students to actively find and make meaning autonomously. It provides shared experiences and enables human interaction and social communication, all of which are necessary, when learning and using languages.

Also, the recent development in research on interpersonal neurobiology and social neuroscience (Adolphs, 2003) has been trying to explain the process of learning within the context of human relationships. "Interpersonal neurobiology assumes that the brain is a social organ built via experience" (Cozolino, 2014). The relationships we have with other people change the neural pathways in our brains and create a new neural architecture. Cozolino stated that "the brain is capable of change at any time and social interactions are a primary source of brain regulation, growth and health."

Language teachers have been trying many different methods and techniques to make language lessons efficient, effective, interesting, and enjoyable for students. As language teachers learn more and more about the ever-growing findings of neuroscience and psychology, the whole field of SLA has shifted accordingly. The teacher's role is now increasingly seen as being that of facilitator and mediator of the students' learning. The idea of more autonomous learners, independently searching for knowledge and interpreting and explaining reality, according to their own perceived needs, has gained prominence.

Language teachers are facing new professional challenges and need to come to terms with their multiple, ever-changing roles in the classroom. This book sets out to explain to language teachers how Process Drama can help them and how and why it can work highly effectively, as a way of learning and teaching foreign languages. This book will also help teachers to help students develop their twenty-first-century skills within compelling, emotionally engaging, social, and relevant contexts. The theory and lessons in this book can be generally used in second language learning and teaching, although English as a second language is most prominent within the examples and lessons provided.

Using drama for SLA is becoming increasingly popular and there is research that explains and supports its use. The studies conducted by Kao (1995) and Kao and O'Neill (1998) were an early example of the successful application of Process Drama in SLA.

This book explains how Process Drama started and evolved, what it currently is, and what it offers students and teachers now. Process Drama consists of much more than "drama games," which are already used by many second language teachers. It also differs from performative learning through theater. Process Drama is an immersive, "whole class" learning and teaching medium and a shared, imagined, collaborative experience. The drama is co-created by the students with their teacher, and the teacher facilitates and mediates the intended and unexpected learning experiences.

The book explains how to set up and sustain a Process Drama with students and how it can work well, for learning and practicing languages within meaningful contexts. Process Drama offers structures for learning and practicing second language skills in an integrated, cross-curricular way, while also helping students to acquire and develop their twenty-first-century skills set. We are sure, that once you have tried this drama approach and seen the enjoyment, engagement, and learning outcomes, you will soon be using the strategies in your work and planning your own drama lessons.

The book is divided into three parts. Part One consists of three chapters that explain what Process Drama is, how it links to and develops twenty-first-century skills, and what it offers second language teachers. Part Two of the book provides a substantial practical toolkit for language teachers, which consists of drama strategies that can be used to structure lessons and are explained as pedagogical tools. Part Three of the book contains six detailed drama units (each of which can be subdivided into several lessons). There are also ten resource sheets that can be used with the lessons provided but can also be used more generally by teachers.

The first chapter explains what Process Drama is and gives a brief background of its development. It explains how drama links with the learning process and how it can specifically help second language learning. It explains why drama works as an enjoyable, social, and emotionally engaged way of learning languages and how it provides motivating contexts and structures for learning receptive and productive skills in SLA. Long-term memory and learning recall are extremely significant in second language learning. Process Drama involves learning in a multisensory and embodied way that makes the learning memorable and retrievable in various ways. Process Drama offers a learning medium that can be used across the curriculum, and it is an excellent way of approaching content integrated language learning (CLIL). A research-based rationale and relevant psychological and neuro-didactic theories that support the use of drama for SLA are presented.

Chapter 2 briefly presents the twenty-first-century skills and demonstrates how they can be developed through drama. Drama can be used as a teaching and learning medium to help students acquire and develop not only necessary linguistic skills but also the full range of literacy, media, and life skills.

Chapter 2 also explains how Process Drama stimulates and requires critical and creative thinking and inter-thinking, imaginative problem-solving and decision-making within socially meaningful contexts. It explains too how Drama involves actively participating and collaborating in co-created, imaginary situations and contexts, and how these inevitably link with (or are drawn from), the students' real-life experiences. Process Drama contexts and the drama strategies it uses give learners opportunities to think and inter-think deeply and motivate students to question, reflect on, respond, and communicate what they are feeling and thinking. They can be using their second language to do this.

The chapter goes on to explain how drama can be used to help support students' psychological well-being and strengthen their resilience. When "in role," students will sometimes express their personal, real feelings but as they are in role, they can remain safely distanced from personal judgment or criticism. Within a drama lesson, they might be helped to work on a personal issue or toward resolving a personal problem but they will be doing so "as if" they are a character, i.e., not as themselves.

Drama can offer a forum within which students may feel able to speak their minds and to release emotion and tension. It can help them learn to control and manage stress, develop empathy, and gain new perspectives.

Students learn and remember most effectively when they are interested, emotionally engaged, and actively involved in the learning. This chapter explains why and how drama gets and sustains students' attention, increases their levels of concentration, and aids comprehension, through immersing and empowering them within shared, imagined situations. This deepens their engagement with characters, situations, plots, and the subject matter of the drama.

Students enjoy dealing with and discussing real issues and problems, albeit within imagined worlds. They get satisfaction from collaboratively figuring things out, doing interesting activities, and experimenting together. Stress inhibits both communication and learning. As Process Drama is enjoyable and social, this helps reduce the stress levels of second language learners.

Chapter 3 explains how to introduce Process Drama to the language class and what the teacher needs to do with the students prior to and during a Process Drama lesson. It offers important advice about how teachers can prepare themselves and their students for Process Drama.

Most language teachers probably know and use some drama games already but may not feel ready to progress to Process Drama lessons with their language learners. This chapter will help build their knowledge and confidence to do so. This chapter starts by explaining how to negotiate and agree a "drama contract" with the students. This will establish the necessary protocols for working in and through drama together. The multifaceted role/s of the teacher during the drama process is also explained in some detail.

Part Two of the book is very practical. It presents a broad and flexible teachers' toolbox of drama strategies and explains in detail how to set each of them up and when they might be used in a lesson. Each strategy is explained 'step by step' in detail and examples are offered that link directly to the drama units that follow. It also explains how the various drama strategies can specifically be used and applied by second language teachers for the teaching of various linguistic skills and twenty-first-century skills. The authors are encouraging language teachers to try out different strategies and adapt them if they wish, to fit well with their own teaching situations and the learning needs of their students.

Part Three of the book consists of a series of six drama units that can be used with teenagers and adults who are likely to have varying levels of linguistic competency (A2-C2). Teachers are welcome to adjust the lessons, to ensure that they match well with their own students' levels of language proficiency. Vocabulary is provided for each drama unit and teachers may of course add more vocabulary if they wish. It is recommended that teachers introduce appropriate vocabulary before the students start the drama unit.

Each unit can be subdivided into several lessons by the teacher to fit with their own timetables and plans. The lessons are presented in grids, which clearly indicate which drama strategy is being used, how to carry out the activity, and what it offers the learning. The role and function of the teacher are also explained alongside each activity, and there are suggestions made sometimes for ways of simplifying or extending an activity. The grid approach used for the drama units may be helpful to teachers when planning their own "Drama for Languages" lessons in the future. Language teachers can use the drama units flexibly and may wish to select the most appropriate activities, to fit with the time available, the learners' needs, and the teacher's level of confidence. However, every drama unit is designed developmentally and offers much more than the sum of its parts. It is therefore hoped that teachers will try out a complete drama unit at some point and not just pick out certain activities.

The final column of the grid suggests some optional and additional writing opportunities that the teacher may wish to use with the students during, after, or between lessons (if the drama unit is being delivered over several lessons). Teachers will probably come up with their own writing ideas too, linked to the drama.

Any resources that are needed for a particular drama unit have been placed at the end of that drama unit, for easy access. Additionally, there are ten resource sheets provided at the end of the book which can be used with various drama strategies. They can be used with the drama units in this book but can also be used more generally by teachers, as they are graphic organizers that will help students to record their own thoughts and speech, as well as the thought and speech of characters.

The book will be of interest to any language teacher in either the public or private sector. The themes and subject matter of the drama units have been carefully selected to be of universal interest and relevance and to help students to acquire and use language within emotionally engaging and memorable contexts, while also developing their twenty-first-century skills.

Part I

Introducing Process Drama

Part I: Introducing Process Drama

1. WHAT IS PROCESS DRAMA AND HOW CAN IT HELP LANGUAGE LEARNERS AND LEARNING? 7
2. USING PROCESS DRAMA TO DEVELOP TWENTY-FIRST-CENTURY SKILLS 25
3. HOW TO INTRODUCE PROCESS DRAMA TO A CLASS AND WHAT IS EXPECTED OF THE TEACHER 41

1

What is Process Drama and How Can it Help Language Learners and Learning?

Chapter Outline

DRAMA IN SECOND LANGUAGE TEACHING	8
DRAMA IN EDUCATION	8
WHAT IS PROCESS DRAMA?	9
WHAT CAN PROCESS DRAMA BE ABOUT?	10
EMBODIED LEARNING	10
DRAMA, EMOTION, AND MEMORY	11
DRAMA, LANGUAGE, AND INHIBITION	12
DRAMA AND "SELF"	12
PROCESS DRAMA AS SOCIAL LEARNING	14
THE "ROLE OF THE ADULT" AND THE "ADULT IN ROLE"	14
THE BOUNDARIES BETWEEN REAL LIFE AND FICTION	14
PROCESS DRAMA AND LANGUAGE	15
TEACHING ENGLISH FOR SPECIFIC PURPOSES	15
PROCESS DRAMA, CLIL, AND SLA	16
DRAMA AS COMMUNICATION	17
CULTURAL LEARNING THROUGH DRAMA AND LANGUAGE	18
DRAMA FOR TALK	18
REASONS FOR SPEAKING AND LISTENING	19
THE DRAMA/TALK CONTRACT	19
TALK, ROLE, AND DISTANCE	20
DRAMA FOR WRITING	21
TEACHER AS SCRIBE OR CO-WRITER	22
USING DRAMA STRATEGIES AS "THOUGHT AND TALK" FRAMES	23
THE USE OF PERFORMANCE WITHIN PROCESS DRAMA	23

Drama in Second Language Teaching

The use of drama in second language teaching is not a completely new pedagogical approach. Drama has been used in language teaching since the late 1970s and has become an integral part of the communicative approach, which is increasingly used as a way of teaching and learning a second language. However, what teachers actually mean by "drama" and what they do with it will vary greatly. In the second language classroom, drama often consists of little more than drama games and some role-play activities. Drama games can be helpful. They are enjoyable and can help students to acquire and practice vocabulary and phrases but Process Drama can offer so much more. It enables students to practice using a language in both spontaneous and rehearsed ways within humanly meaningful and sustained contexts that are far closer to the way they will need to use language in real life.

Process Drama fits well with the increasingly popular and prevalent communicative approach in second language acquisition (SLA), a key aim of which is for students to become good communicators, able to use the target language appropriately and effectively within relevant contexts. For students to become proficient communicators, teachers need to provide foreign language/L2 learners with engaging contexts within which they can use, apply and practice the language they have acquired. We know that "traditional language classes limit adequate practice opportunities for each student" (Lee, 1999: 11). Learning and repeating words and phrases is one step but being able to use them appropriately and well, when necessary in real-life situations, requires students to take further steps. Process Drama can help move students along their language learning pathway.

Several books have been published on using drama for second language teaching and the research interest in this area has been growing steadily in recent years. The journal *Scenario* was created to specifically publish papers linked to using drama and theater in language education (Schewe, 2007; Schewe & Scott, 2003). There are also numerous academic publications on using drama in language acquisition, focusing on linguistic benefits and intercultural learning through drama.

Drama in Education

What some now refer to as "Process Drama" started out in the UK as "drama in education," mainly during the 1960s to 1980s. It was based primarily on the work of Brian Way, Dorothy Heathcote, and Gavin Bolton and developed further through the work of others, such as Jonothan Neelands (UK), Cecily O'Neill (UK/USA), David Booth, (Canada), John O'Toole (Australia) and Peter O'Connor (New Zealand), and others.

During the 1970s and 1980s, an unhelpful, ongoing debate emerged, about whether drama in education could really be termed "Drama" or not. There were years of counterproductive "Drama as Theatre" (product) versus "Drama as Pedagogy" (process) positioning. Theater educators such as David Hornbrook (1989) and drama in education teachers became unhelpfully polarized by this issue. Process Drama uses the art form and its associated techniques and strategies but for learning purposes. When practiced by teachers who have knowledge and understanding of both learning and drama, deep, memorable learning and good drama can result.

Over time, drama in education started to be referred to in various ways, for example, as "Experiential Drama," "Drama for Learning," and later as "Process Drama" (Ackroyd, 2004; Bowell & Heap, 2001; O'Neill, 1995; O'Toole & Dunn, 2002). During the late 1980s and early 1990s, when "thinking skills" were becoming a clear focus in schools, "Dramatic Enquiry" and "Dramatic Inquiry" started to become terms used for drama in education and the dramatic contexts were increasingly being steered toward a need for the students (in role) to get involved in "enquiry based learning."

Drama in education gradually spread from the UK to other countries, such as New Zealand, Australia, Canada, Jamaica, Norway, Finland, Sweden, Iceland, Turkey, Greece, Singapore, South Korea, and the United States. This often happened because those who trained with Dorothy Heathcote (and others) in the UK, then emigrated to (or returned home to) these countries, as teachers, initial teacher trainers, and researchers into the field of drama in education. Degree and postgraduate courses in drama in education started to appear and international communities of drama, theatre and education practitioners emerged and many flourished.

Process Drama has more recently started to be taught and developed by some universities in Poland, China, and Spain. Whether Process Drama has flourished or diminished in various countries has been influenced greatly by changes in governments and shifts in national and international, education agendas. Internationally, however, the use of Process Drama as an effective and enjoyable, context-based way of teaching second languages seems to be steadily growing, for example, in South America, China, and most European countries. Certainly, the drama methodology fits well with Content and Language Integrated Learning (CLIL).

Dorothy Heathcote created and used her own terminology for the various drama strategies and conventions that she used. Some are known by different names nowadays and also new drama strategies have been created, named, and developed by other drama for learning specialists (e.g., Neelands and Goode, Baldwin). When the UK and other countries started to produce official national curriculum documents which contained drama terminology, schools started to use that terminology. This book uses the drama strategy terminology which is most commonly used now.

There are some drama specialists that are highly prescriptive about the way that "drama for learning" strategies and conventions can and "must" be used. This is not a helpful approach to take. Second language teachers should not feel held back from adapting drama approaches and strategies to meet their own teaching purposes and the language learning needs of their own students.

What Is Process Drama?

Process Drama is a whole class activity, which involves everyone working in role together within an imagined time, place, and situation. It is not about rehearsing and performing scripts for a theater performance and does not involve performing for an external audience. It does involve the students improvising scenes and sometimes sharing them with each other. However, when Process Drama includes performance, it will be the class performing to each other during the lesson and for a learning purpose.

Many of the drama strategies and conventions used in Process Drama will be familiar to actors. In Process Drama however, the strategies are being used primarily as pedagogical tools by teachers. Used sequentially, they can help to build and sustain a whole class drama while also stimulating, scaffolding, and deepening student's thinking, inter-thinking, talk, and learning.

The theme and learning intentions of a Process Drama will have been decided by the teacher, who will also decide which language opportunities to plant within the drama and which drama strategies to employ, to best support language use and development. At times during the drama, the teacher will place themselves in role, alongside the students. At other times, the teacher will be operating out of role. Either way, the teacher can operate as a model, learning facilitator and mediator, provocateur, storyteller, and guide, for both the learning and drama processes.

The teacher has responsibility for ensuring that learning happens and that students' skills are developed. They will be constantly observing and listening, deciding when to make their next "teacher move" (in or out of role), when to introduce the next drama strategy, and which to use.

Well-timed teacher comments, interventions, and strategies will help to

- focus the students' attention on what matters for the learning and the drama,
- deepen and scaffold the students' thinking and inter-thinking,
- shift the cognitive and linguistic demands,
- help the students to explore and consider key moments and situations from different viewpoints,
- move the narrative of the drama forward,
- shift the drama's time and place.

The teacher might, for example, decide to "freeze" the drama and invite the students to suggest what the different characters might be thinking at this precise moment, or what they might say or do next. Alternatively, the teacher might hold a moment still and ask the students to comment on what is happening in the scene, "as if" they are just an eyewitness, who happens to be passing by.

Once the drama has generated content, words, and images, these can be used in various, purposeful ways by language teachers.

Language teachers using Process Drama do not need to be drama specialists. They are language teachers first and foremost and are not being expected to teach drama as a discrete subject. Drama is providing the context and content for the language teaching, and language teachers can easily learn to use some of the main drama strategies as pedagogical tools.

Language teachers are likely to initially use published lesson plans for their whole class drama lessons and then might start to adapt them or create their own after a while. They will be using drama as a learning and language medium, which enables a second language to be used by their students within stimulating, meaningful, and relevant contexts. Being able to create imagined worlds with students, within which they are highly motivated to speak, listen, and respond, will be helpful to both L2 teachers and their students.

Inclusive practices aim to remove barriers, so that all students have equal chances to contribute and to learn successfully (J. Kormos, 2008), and Process Drama is an inclusive and collaborative activity. It can help strengthen the students' sense of belonging and provides them with equal opportunities, status, and rights as active participants. It is not surprising that Process Drama is increasingly being recognized and valued as a highly effective medium for language teaching and learning.

What Can Process Drama Be About?

Process Drama can be about anything. It can provide infinite contexts, within which students can enjoyably explore and practice any second language. A whole class of language students can be helped to imagine that they are a different group of people, in a different place, at a different point in time (past, present, or future). They can engage with and become fictitious characters and deal "in role" together with imagined and re-created situations and/or events that require and compel them to speak in and/or out of role, in various ways, for various purposes and audiences.

For example, students in role could become people who are deciding whether or not to leave their homes and become refugees (Drama Unit 3). Later in the drama, they might change roles and become border guards or the people who might accept or reject these refugees. Changing roles enables students to explore situations from different people's viewpoints and they often need to change their language register and style to fit with the different roles, situations, purposes, and imagined audiences.

A Process Drama lesson can be linked thematically to one or more subjects or academic disciplines. A lesson can be based on either truth or fiction (or often on truth, veiled as fiction). Whatever the drama is about, it needs to be of interest and relevance to the students, hooking them in at the start and keeping them interactively engaged and motivated to speak and listen.

Every Process Drama lesson will have specific vocabulary and phrases that are relevant to the theme and/or subject matter and all lessons in this book have pre-lesson vocabulary suggestions. Teachers might decide to use drama and language games to help their students interactively learn the useful vocabulary and practice speaking it, in advance of the Process Drama lesson. Drama games are already very common in language teaching and can be used to help students acquire, practice, and play with specific words and phrases, which they might then be able to recall and use within meaningful Process Drama contexts and use again, thereafter.

Embodied Learning

Process Drama intentionally provides multisensory, embodied learning experiences. Drama is full of sounds, speech, still and moving images, gestures, actions, reactions, interactions, expressions, and movements. The students are engaged, visually, auditorily, kinesthetically, and often tactilely.

When students are experiencing learning in embodied, multisensory ways, the learning is being tagged in the memory across multiple areas of the brain and this helps students to recall the learning. Words and phrases are often taught in ways that get students to say a word aloud, while making a particular gesture or movement. When the student makes that movement again (or even when they are imagining that they are), the physical movement (real or imagined) will help them to recall the word or phrase. They are literally "re-membering" the words and phrases that they previously associated with that movement. Conversely, just saying the words and phrases can trigger an involuntary, associated physical response.

Each student's brain is unique and not all brains process information in the same way. This is a challenge and opportunity for teachers. They need to create and/or strengthen the neural pathways of all the students they teach and therefore need to teach in a range of ways. Different ways of learning will help to build and strengthen new neural pathways and this will help second language learners to remember a language and use it appropriately in different contexts. Drama is congruent with the interactional model of understanding learning differences (Frederickson & Cline, 2002; Norwich, 2008). It caters for neurodiversity in the language classroom, providing a safe environment for pupils who have different strengths, personalities, and models of mind.

Drama, Emotion, and Memory

Repetitive rote learning methods are predictable and can all too easily become dull, boring and contextually meaningless to students. Such teaching and learning methods all too easily lose students' attention and put them off learning a language. Rote learning can help students acquire knowledge of words and phrases, but they need to be able to then practice using them spontaneously within meaningful contexts that are interesting and personally relevant.

Humans give their attention to what arouses them emotionally. Learning that involves emotional experiences is more memorable and therefore more easily retrieved. Neuroscience suggests that emotions are integral to learning:

> Learning is dynamic, social and context dependent because emotions are, and emotions form a critical piece of how, what, when and why people think, remember and learn … It is literally neurobiologically impossible to build memories, engage complex thoughts or make meaningful decisions, without emotions.
>
> (Immordino-Yang, 2016)

Process Drama stimulates and sustains emotional engagement and fosters learners' understanding (Bolton & Heathcote, 1999; Craig & Bloomfield, 2006). Heathcote described her early drama in education work as being about a "Man in a Mess." She hooked the students in emotionally, working with them in role, to enable and support them, as they tried to get the man out of the mess. Characters and situations in a Process Drama are usually fictitious but the students' emotional engagement and empathy they generate are real. They feel motivated, empowered, and able to deal with the problems and messy situations happening within the drama.

By its nature, a Process Drama lesson will be unpredictable. The drama is happening and unfolding "in the moment" and the language and action it generates are frequently improvised and spontaneous. The students' emotional engagement helps keep them alert and focused. It helps them feel compelled to speak, listen, act, respond, and behave appropriately "in role," using their second language. They will be verbally improvising for much of the time but will also have opportunities to select, try out, and refine various linguistic choices at times (e.g., when devising and performing a short scene).

When working in role, students have the opportunity to "walk in someone else's shoes for a while." They can meet characters and situations that invite and encourage empathy. In drama, they are simultaneously operating betwixt and between two worlds, i.e., real and imagined worlds. This "in-betweenness" can be linked to what Plato termed "Metaxis." Theater directors, such as Boal (1997), have made connections between their own theater work and metaxis. The ability to use a second language might also be seen as opening up another world for students, within which a different "self" (including an emotional "self") might be safely revealed and explored.

The teacher is often a co-participant in role during a Process Drama and working in this way with language students can help create and strengthen emotional bonds between language students and their teachers. This strengthening of teacher–pupil bonding can then positively influence students' attitudes to learning (Birch & Ladd, 1997; Hamre & Pianta, 2001).

Students learning within emotionally supportive classrooms report greater interest, enjoyment, and engagement with their learning (Curby et al., 2009; Marks, 2000; Rimm-Kaufman, La Paro, Downer, & Pianta, 2005; Skinner & Belmont, 1993; Wentzel, 1998; Woolley, Kol, & Bowen, 2009). The role of affect in foreign language learning has been emphasized by many researchers (Dorneyei, 1998; Stevick, 1980).

Drama can provide a safe forum within which students can speak their minds in role. It can enable them to feel and release emotions and to relieve and resolve tensions. It can also help them to learn to practice controlling and managing stress, to develop empathy, and to appreciate the perspectives and viewpoints of others. It sometimes leads to students shifting their own, real-life viewpoints. People need to be able to express their ideas and feelings and being able to do so in or out of role can help them to understand the emotions and thoughts of others and to form and develop positive personal and professional relationships.

Drama, Language, and Inhibition

Students often have difficulty speaking a foreign language, even when their level of grammar competence and knowledge of vocabulary are sufficient. They are sometimes blocked from speaking competently by a high level of anxiety and may be too focused on their linguistic mistakes and imperfections. There is a specific anxiety known as "foreign language anxiety," which is related to using a second language (Horwitz, Horwitz, & Cope, 1986). A low level of linguistic self-esteem and lack of security make second language learners unwilling to talk. They are afraid of giving a negative image of themselves and being mocked by others. Collaborative learning situations, such as those provided by Process Drama, can help individual students feel less personally exposed than more traditional L2 classroom situations.

Students may also not be sufficiently engaged, motivated, or interested enough in a task to talk about it. Process Drama is likely to sustain the interest of students more than a series of decontextualized language tasks. The drama hooks the students in socially, emotionally, and cognitively. It can motivate them to talk and complete tasks because there is a dramatic purpose in doing so (not just a linguistic purpose). The students become immersed in a drama that has tensions, problems to solve, human dilemmas, conflicts and situations to explore and deal with. They feel the urge to speak and make a difference in role, to the drama itself. They want to communicate and contribute their ideas and feelings and to try to influence others in the drama and help shape the dramatic outcomes. The drama itself compels them to experiment with a real language enjoyably and purposefully and in doing so, they will gain more confidence and proficiency when they use the target language in the real world.

When a positive emotional environment is created in the language classroom, this encourages positive interactions and can provide students with an increased sense of competence and confidence, which helps learning to occur (Skinner & Belmont, 1993). When students feel safe and in a state of "relaxed alertness" with "high challenge and low threat" (Caine & Caine, 1991/1994, 2010), they are more likely to become deeply engaged in the language learning process, feel less anxious, and be more inclined to speak. When students are in role, they are speaking as different characters and personalities and this too can help free students, as their level of need to communicate can outweigh the level of anxiety they feel about speaking publicly in a second language.

Drama and "Self"

The notion of the self plays a crucial role in SLA and it is important for teachers to understand this and create a positive emotional environment in the classroom. Emotions are relevant not only to a student's relationship with their teachers and peers but also to their emotional relationship with "self." Research on the notion of "self" in relation to second language learning, has focused on various aspects and components of "self" and considered whether these correlate with student success and failure, in acquiring a language. The aspects of "self" considered, include

1. self-efficacy,
2. self-esteem,
3. self-concept,
4. self-image,
5. self-confidence, and
6. self-evaluation.

(Dorneyei, 2005; Gałązka & Trinder, 2018; Pinol, 2007; Puchta, 1999; Williams, Mercer & Ryan, 2015)

"Self-efficacy" is a term which focuses on a students' belief that they are able to do something successfully. It is closely connected with the notion of "locus of control" (LOC), which is derived from Rotter's theory of social learning (1966). Individuals with internal locus of control believe that they can control their lives and their choices, whereas those with external locus of control perceive themselves as victims of external circumstances. A study conducted by Madeline Ehrman, & colleagues (2003, 321) proved that one of the essential components of a highly motivated learner is an internal LOC and also that learners with high levels of internal attribution have a strong sense of self-efficacy and correspondingly higher levels of achievement (Hsieh & Schallert, 2008). Additionally, Williams & Burden (1997) place LOC within their complex motivational mechanism alongside goal setting and locus of causality, echoing Ehrman's claim that an internal LOC is an essential constituent of high motivation.

For second language learners, self-confidence seems to be of particular importance. A student's belief about their own linguistic competence has a significant impact on their achievements. Students with low linguistic self-confidence have a high level of anxiety and can be totally blocked when it comes to speaking and performing in a target language. They might come to their first Process Drama lesson, having already developed a negative self-image due to previous language learning experiences. They may not be expecting success. However, they will soon find that working in a drama situation is a very different way of learning and using a second language. Working and talking in role in an immersive and compelling drama can enable some students to overcome their anxiety, as they start to feel a strong need to influence the evolving drama. The immediate need to speak purposefully can become stronger than their level of anxiety about speaking. When what they say has a positive impact in the drama, this will be rewarding and can help to reduce their anxiety about speaking again (both during and after the drama). The feeling a student gets from being successful in an imagined situation is real, highly motivational, and can remain with them after the lesson. If you achieve a successful outcome, using a second language in an imagined scenario, then you will feel more confident about doing so in real-life situations too.

In drama, students are working together in role, often imagining, acting, and responding in role, "as if" they are already successful and competent in various contexts and situations. Dorothy Heathcote's "Mantle of the Expert" approach (see pages 57–58) can help raise students' self-esteem and improve their notions of self-image and self-efficacy. In a drama that uses Mantle of the Expert, the students are often running or working for an imaginary, successful business or enterprise. They will be in role and will be expected to talk and behave "as if" they already are proficient, knowledgeable, and skilled professionals with work-related tasks to complete. A "Commission Model" is often used with the students talking and working on task-rich commissions for external "clients" (often played by the teacher in role). With everyone sustaining the fiction, the students get a real feeling of being valued experts and will work hard at delivering what their client requires. They will be trying to ensure that their language use and behavior are appropriate. By doing this, they are rehearsing being successful and improving their performance levels. They are working in role but the linguistic gains will be real and lasting, as will their raised levels of self-esteem.

A popular model of self-esteem is that developed by Reasoner (1982). His model includes five components:

1. security
2. identity
3. belonging
4. purpose
5. competence

Process Drama (including Mantle of the Expert), can clearly help enable, support and develop each of these five components of self-esteem. In any Process Drama, the students will be working with a drama contract in place. This gives them a shared understanding and a sense of security. They will all be immersed in and belong in the same drama and will be working purposefully together to sustain and develop it. They will be collaborating to competently deal together with whatever situations arise in the drama. Everyone remains personally protected throughout, as they will be working and talking "in role" within a fiction.

The drama provides contexts and opportunities for thinking, talking, and working together and doing so successfully will help increase the students' confidence and linguistic competencies.

Process Drama as Social Learning

Humans are social beings according to Vygotsky (1980) and language learners will benefit from learning and using language within social contexts (Kuhl, 2003, Edutopia). Process Drama is an inclusive, social learning experience. The whole class is involved and works as a community. They interact to create, sustain, and develop the drama. The students belong not only to their class during the drama but also to the community that the drama is about, for example, a fictional community of refugees or the employees of an imaginary company.

As Process Drama is a social learning medium, most students will find it enjoyable. Language benefits greatly from being learned and practiced within socially meaningful and emotionally engaging contexts. This is evident within early dramatic play, when children start imitating and mimicking what they have seen people do and heard people say. They then move beyond imitation and mimicry and start to verbally improvise and enact more diverse roles. Young children naturally talk and interact with imaginary characters and real playmates (including willing adults). They re-enact familiar stories and will then start to change them and mix them together and create their own stories. Within their imagined worlds they feel in control and practicing real language and other skills. They are speaking, listening, and interacting during dramatic play and find it rewarding. Children can play in make-believe worlds for surprisingly long periods of time and all the while, they are learning. They are practicing using language in various contexts (alone and with others) and are rehearsing a range of important skills that will help them in both imagined and real worlds.

As children get older, the time they spend playing dramatically decreases (particularly once they start school), but they retain this powerful neurologically significant ability to "pretend" alone and with others and to learn in this way. Process Drama rekindles, uses, and develops these natural, important abilities and language teachers can use them effectively and enjoyably, in an age-appropriate way during Process Drama lessons.

The "Role of the Adult" and the "Adult in Role"

Parents and carers often join in with young children's sociodramatic play, as do early years teachers and assistants at school. Learning opportunities can be intentionally planted within dramatic play scenarios by adults who want to maximize the learning opportunities that dramatic play provides. Many adults will see learning and language opportunities arise naturally too and make use of them. The adult might, for example, intentionally use particular words and phrases that they know the child is not yet familiar with. They will be enabling the child to hear (and maybe use) appropriate and contextually relevant words and phrases within the dramatic play's context. Adults with a bilingual agenda for a young child might choose to do this in either a first or second language. The adult can model speech, adjusting their vocabulary, register, and style to help the children to practice talking within a range of play scenarios. L2 teachers can do this too with their students within Process Drama scenarios. The teacher can model different forms of speech and adjust the linguistic demands that the drama (and teacher) is making on the students. The teacher might do this in role as a co-participant or out of role by selecting and using various drama strategies at various points in the lesson.

Adults can add complications, introduce problems, build tension, and "up the stakes." A parent pretending to be customer in a young child's pretend café, might unexpectedly say that they have lost their purse, having already eaten the imaginary meal. The child will then need to respond spontaneously in role as the café owner and maybe find a way to deal with the problem. Teachers in Process Drama lessons also can be in role and "up the stakes" during drama lessons. The Process Drama units in this book contain many examples of situations that require students to realistically solve problems in role. In Drama Unit 2, for example, the teacher is in role as the Mayor of London in 1666 and is refusing to knock down houses to create a necessary firebreak. The students need to use language to reason, explain, justify, and persuade the Mayor to change his mind. If they are not able to use language effectively and get the Mayor to destroy houses, then London is likely to burn to the ground!

The Boundaries between Real Life and Fiction

The language teacher in an L2 educational setting is not working as a drama therapist and Process Drama lessons are not intended to become psychodramas. However, drama sometimes does trigger some personally sensitive issues and memories for individual students and teachers need to be aware of this and should always keep within the safe, fictional boundaries of the drama. Drama deals with universal human issues and situations and this helps hook students in. Whatever the theme of subject matter of a drama, it is likely to have some personal resonance for most students. For example, a drama about Bullying (Drama Unit 1) is going to resonate in some way with most students. They will probably have experienced bullying as victims, bystanders, and/or as bullies. The students cannot help but bring their real selves to the drama, although they may not always be doing so consciously or openly. The drama unit about bullying is dealing with the issue safely, in a distanced way, through a shared, imagined, reflective experience in role. However, if any drama triggers unfortunate and painful memories for some students, the teacher will need to use their professional judgment and be prepared to deal with this. It is rarely necessary to stop a drama to deal with a personal, individual student response but a teacher might decide sometimes, to discretely talk with and support the student after the drama.

Process Drama and Language

In many countries "Drama" is already popular and commonly used during the teaching of foreign languages. However, where it is being used, it too often consists of little more than drama games and role-play activities. Drama games are enjoyable and can help students to acquire and practice vocabulary and phrases, for example, but an evolving Process Drama can take L2 students much further and deeper. It enables them to practice using language in both spontaneous and rehearsed ways within humanly meaningful and sustained contexts that are closer to the way they will need to use language in real life.

Process Drama as a way of learning and using foreign languages fits well with the increasingly popular and prevalent communicative approach in SLA. A key aim in second language/L2 acquisition is for students to become good communicators, able to use the target language appropriately and effectively within meaningful contexts. For students to become proficient communicators, teachers need to provide foreign language/L2 learners with relevant contexts within which they can use, apply and practice the language they have acquired. Learning and repeating words and phrases is one step but actually being able to use them appropriately and well, when necessary in real-life situations is what is truly needed and Process Drama can certainly help students to move enjoyably along this path.

Teaching English for Specific Purposes

Teaching English for specific purposes (ESP) can be traced back to the 1960s but interest in English as a second language (ESL) has grown in recent years. Researchers have emphasized that ESP responds more directly to learners' real needs and can also be used to explore different disciplines and subjects (Dudley-Evans & Tony, 1998; Hutchinson & Waters, 1987).

English is recognized as a necessary language for those wishing to have international careers. Process Dramas can be set up that will give specific opportunities for students to work in role "as if" they are already professional employees in any type of work or business environment. For example, they can work in role as employees or owners of companies and can be required to present innovative ideas, to consider and discuss various development possibilities, to chair or attend work meetings, to deal with and report to imaginary clients, to create advertisements, to prepare press releases, conduct interviews, and complete work tasks, and so on. As already mentioned, Dorothy Heathcote's "Mantle of the Expert" approach and "The Commission Model" have become increasingly popular, as education seems to have become increasingly aligned to and shaped by the perceived needs of industry. The dramatic tension in this type of drama tends to lie mainly in the students having to complete work tasks for external clients (often to deadlines).

Some teachers prefer to take a more flexible approach to Mantle of the Expert, using it for part of the overall drama lesson. This gives opportunities for students to take on various roles in the drama and not be primarily and repeatedly in role as expert workers. Using Mantle of the Expert more as one drama strategy also can more easily allow other dramatic tensions to be developed in the drama that are not work and worker related. In Drama Unit 4, for example, the students are in role at times, as experts who need to design a Holiday Park for a client. However, the students also at times are in role as the villagers whose lives will be affected by the proposed Holiday Park in various ways, if the planning permission is approved. Within this Drama Unit, the students do have work tasks to do as experts but they also attend a public meeting as villagers who feel compelled to speak in public, for or against the development. When they are villagers, they have a personal, rather than professional stake in the planning outcome. When they are in role as employed planning experts at a public meeting, the content, register, and style of their speech will need to shift, as villagers would speak differently. Changes of role result in different linguistic expectations and challenges. They also enable students to actively engage with different characters' viewpoints and situations.

Process Drama will always be helping students to develop their personal, social, cognitive, and emotional skills, which are important for both employment and life. Whatever the theme and content of the drama, the language students will need to exercise open-mindedness, flexibility, persistence, and willingness to compromise. They will be working individually but will also be practicing teamwork in pairs, small groups, or as a whole class. Both in and out of role they will be collaborating, interacting, cooperating, and communicating verbally and nonverbally. The skills being used and developed in any Process Drama lesson will always include many of those that are also valued and sought by employers and are also needed in personal lives.

Process Drama, CLIL, and SLA

When considering Process Drama in relation to second language teaching, we need to also consider CLIL, an approach that is becoming increasingly popular in second language education. "It is a dual focused educational approach, in which an additional language is used for the learning and teaching of both content and language" (EuroCLIC, 1994).

Process Drama can be used to teach any school subject in a second language, for example, biology, history, science, geography. Even one drama lesson or unit can be designed to involve learning in several subjects with students learning and using language (and more besides) in a cross-curricular way.

CLIL is primarily considered to be a form of bilingual education. It is often used when teaching English for specific purposes and disciplines, for example, medicine, law, technology. It is an approach which is responsive to what employers think they need and expect from their future employees, in the modern job market. It encourages students to be proactive and interactive, to enquire and to seek information, and to work together collaboratively in teams and produce outcomes. The students will need to learn specific vocabulary in the target language, to enable them to contribute appropriately and participate effectively in team discussions. They also need to learn phrases that will help them, when critically analyzing and communicating ideas and issues.

CLIL and Process Drama help develop twenty-first-century skills in the second language classroom. Both help increase students' intrinsic motivation and provide meaningful contexts within which both the language and the subject are being learned. Both enable students to learn and practice a language in a more natural and flowing way. CLIL and Process Drama enable students to acquire and develop skills through their immersion in the language, the context, and the content.

Recent research has already highlighted the fact that Process Drama and CLIL have much in common (Galazka & Muszyńska, 2016; Hillyard, 2012, Muszyńska, 2012). Both Drama and CLIL link the cognitive processing of language and culture learning. Language development is often defined as a "sociological event," a semiotic encounter (Halliday, 1978). In both CLIL and in Process Drama, social interactivity is happening within the learning setting and a foreign language is being used meaningfully, purposefully, and responsively.

CLIL lessons should include four elements according to Coyle's 4Cs curriculum (1999):

Content—Progression in knowledge, skills, and understanding related to specific elements of a defined curriculum
Communication—Using language to learn while learning to use language
Cognition—Developing thinking skills which link concept formation (abstract and concrete), understanding, and language
Culture—Exposure to alternative perspectives and shared understandings, which deepen awareness of otherness and self.

Drama integrates and develops all four of these elements and acknowledges the symbiotic relationship that exists between them. Language, cultural understanding, cognition, engagement, and thinking are all embedded in the content and contexts that are created within Process Drama and within CLIL. Both involve problem-solving and the use and development of higher-level thinking skills. Learning takes place with the students immersed in the content and the shared, dramatic experience.

Swartz & Parks (1994) describe the teaching of thinking through different subjects as "infusion." They claim that the infusion approach improves pupils' thinking, as well as enhancing the learning of any content. Both CLIL and Process Drama can motivate and engage learners holistically, allowing the integration of language, subject area knowledge, and thinking skills. They use a problem-solving approach that stimulates and develops both critical and creative thinking skills in ways that foster and enable student autonomy.

Process Drama is immersive and experiential. It involves much more than just giving students information and subject knowledge. It stimulates and gives form to the students' individual and shared ideas and imaginations. It invites and challenges them to think critically and creatively together, to make meaning of their world, in and through the art form of drama. Through working in role, they can enter and explore issues, events, and relationships in an emotionally compelling, cognitively challenging, safely distanced way. They can experiment individually and in groups, shaping and symbolically representing their individual and collective ideas and feelings. In role, they can speak and take actions safely and discover the impact and consequences of their words and actions. Throughout the lesson, the teacher is enabling and supporting the students, sometimes working alongside them in role, as a co-participant and sometimes pausing the drama, to move it forward in some way or to go deeper into the moment, using an appropriate drama strategy. Language teachers will be particularly aware of the many opportunities to focus the students' attention on the linguistic elements, opportunities, and demands of the evolving drama.

Drama as Communication

Drama is about communication. Within the drama, students will use language to express thoughts, ideas, and feelings. They will not just be practicing phrasal verbs and conditionals! In role-play and improvisation (and even in re-enactment), communication is important and unavoidable. In role, the students may need to explain, negotiate, or defend the position and viewpoint of their character verbally and nonverbally, in response to each other's arguments. Studies (Kuhl, 2003) suggest that students who learn a language in a defined social reality acquire it more efficiently than through just listening to their teacher or watching a film. Drama provides an imagined world and a social context, within which the students cooperate to establish interactions. The drama generates reasons to speak and experiment with a language.

Drama uses the body, mind, images, and emotions and so stimulates different areas of the brain simultaneously. It involves communicating verbally and nonverbally and students will become increasingly aware of how gesture, movement, facial expression, posture, tone of voice, and eye contact work alone and with words, for effective communication.

In teaching a second language it is important to use the knowledge that students already have. In drama, learners have opportunities to recall, use, and actively apply their linguistic knowledge, practice newly learned forms, and expand their linguistic abilities with a sense of continuity. The breadth and variation of the roles and relationships in the dramas leads to an expansion and variation in the students' language usage. Drama increases the range, fluency, and effectiveness of speech (Gałązka, 2008).

Pupils at any age will participate more willingly in language lessons, when topics relate to their interests. Drama brings real-life situations into the classroom that are not usually evident in typical language course books. When students are operating within unfamiliar drama contexts, they will also be taking on unfamiliar life roles. These roles will shift the students' relationships with their peers and the teacher, during the drama. In order to accommodate the newly imagined settings, context, roles, and relationships, students will feel compelled to grapple with and use, the appropriate language, and communication skills. The main focus of their attention will be on the drama. As they become preoccupied with working in role and responding to the dramatic situations, their anxiety about making mistakes is reduced and their confidence grows.

Drama pushes the students into using language for real purposes and this involves using a range of thinking skills. The students in a drama lesson are likely to speak more spontaneously and frequently than in traditional language lessons. The drama stimulates them to think, inter-think, and talk more, which improve their fluency and often their accuracy. They are talking purposefully and listening responsively, which can help language to flow in a more natural and even subconscious way.

Stern supports the notion that language development occurs through creative, active language use with "its continuing modifications" (1983: 20) and original combinations, as students want to express their thoughts and feelings in situations which require human interaction. To acquire a language, students need not only to be surrounded by rich language but they also need to want to use it, to express their personal intentions, feelings, viewpoints, and attitudes to others. In Process Drama students can play with language and manipulate and use it creatively.

Cultural Learning through Drama and Language

Language is not only a means of communication. It is a product of the thought and behavior of a society. Effectiveness in speaking a foreign language is directly related to understanding the cultural source of that language, its societal behaviors and culturally rooted customs. Communication is seldom culture free. It is now widely accepted that language learning and learning about target cultures cannot realistically be separated (Kramsch, 1993; Valdes, 1986). The interdependence of language learning and cultural learning is so evident that language learning could be considered as cultural learning and language teaching as cultural teaching. Foreign language teachers need to be aware of the place of cultural studies within foreign language teaching and the need to stimulate and develop students' cultural awareness and improve their intercultural communication skills and competences.

Drama allows language students to immerse themselves in a culture to learn and use the language within culturally relevant contexts. Drama is never culture free. The drama happens within an imagined culture that is usually based on a real culture. If the students create a culture for the drama, they will be bringing their own cultural knowledge and understanding to the task. The drama is conducted in a language that is also culturally rooted and the artistic forms that are used will be culturally rooted too.

Drama for Talk

Professor Robin Alexander (2017) recognizes and highlights the unique contribution that Drama makes to "talk" in educational settings:

> Children's capacities to use talk to reason, argue, explain, explore, justify, challenge, question, negotiate, speculate, imagine, evaluate, and in these and other ways to take ownership of their talking and thinking rather than merely answer someone else's usually closed questions. Such talk, unusual in the teaching of mainstream subjects, is actually not unlike that habitually deployed and encouraged in performance arts, for example in the kind of discussion that might be generated to support and explore improvised drama.

The devising process in drama fits closely with what Robin Alexander has defined as Dialogic Talk (2008), i.e., "Sustained stretches of talk which enables speakers and listeners to explore and build on their own and others' ideas to develop coherent thinking. The aim is to achieve a common understanding through structured cumulative questioning and discussion." In drama, the "common understanding" is sometimes encapsulated, given form, and communicated as a performance.

When a group of students are devising a short scene for performance (Small Group Playmaking, for example), it involves listening to the teacher's instructions, maybe questioning for clarification of the task, enabling everyone to share and explain their ideas and listen to everyone's ideas, justifying decisions, trying out and adapting some ideas, while rejecting others, giving and responding to directions, speaking in a performance, evaluating, and discussing whether the scene is clear and audible for the audience, verbally evaluating the quality and impact of the performance, and so on—all skills that students need and that are taught in the second language classroom.

Drama requires collaboration and the talk involved in the drama for learning process is congruent with what Neil Mercer (2008) has defined as Exploratory Talk, in which

- pupils listen critically but constructively to each other's ideas;
- the objective of this interaction is to reach an agreement;

- in the task, students must explore the different possible answers;
- they exchange ideas with a view to sharing information to solve problems;
- everyone listens actively;
- people ask questions;
- people share relevant information;
- ideas may be challenged;
- reasons are given for challenges;
- contributions build on what has gone before;
- everyone is encouraged to contribute;
- ideas and opinions treated with respect;
- there is an atmosphere of trust;
- there is a sense of shared purpose; and
- the group seeks agreement for joint decisions.

Reasons for Speaking and Listening

Reasons can be planted (or arise naturally) in a drama that require the students to talk for a range of purposes, to or with a variety of responsive audiences. A drama lesson or unit can be planned that will intentionally provide contexts, roles, and opportunities, for students to use language in specific ways, for particular purposes. The drama stimulates and emotionally engages the students and then provides them with compelling opportunities (both in and out of role), to verbally reason, argue, debate, discuss, question, negotiate, speculate, create, critically analyze, and evaluate. For example, when in role as refugees, the students might be asked to explain and justify to a loved one, why they need to flee their home now. Then, at a secret meeting with the people smuggler's agent, they need to listen carefully to what they are being told and then maybe ask relevant questions. They might try to negotiate a cheaper price for the journey. Next day, they might recount to a friend, what the agent said at the meeting and try and persuade the friend to come too. Together, they might speculate about some of the dangers of the journey. The teacher could then ask them to critically analyze and evaluate (and then present), the pros and cons of making the journey. Once they have made a decision, they might be asked to explain and justify it to a relative they love, who will not be going on the journey.

The Drama/Talk Contract

When groups or whole classes get involved in talking and creating collaboratively, there needs to be some sort of agreed contract in place, to ensure everyone gets a chance to give ideas to speak and be listened to. Before teachers use Process Drama, it is recommended that they first negotiate and agree a drama contract with their students (see pages 41–43).

Many of the activities in Process Drama are improvisational and spontaneous but some involve talking out of role, for example, creating, planning, and devising a scene or image collaboratively. It can be helpful to have some talk protocols in place, such as the following:

1. We will all talk together and say what we think we could do.
2. We will share what we know and think with each other.
3. We will ask everyone to say what they know and think.
4. Everyone will listen carefully to each other's ideas and suggestions and we will consider all that we hear.
5. We will give reasons for the ideas we suggest and be willing to explain and justify our suggestions.
6. We will decide what to do, once everyone has had an opportunity to speak and be listened to.
7. We will try to reach agreement about what we all think we should do.

Drama strategies may have different "ground-rules" and protocols in relation to "talk," for example, Eavesdropping and Conscience Alley allow students to speak only when the listener passes by, whereas Improvisation and Voice Collage allow students to decide whether and when to speak. Still Images are usually silent but the characters in them may be allowed to speak. Hot-seating allows just questions to be asked. Collective role limits the speech of each person in turn.

Different strategies also enable students to talk in groups of different sizes and constitutions (e.g., Small Group Playmaking). Some talk groups remain fixed during the activity and some are flexible with the students able to move around the room, listening and talking in role with anyone (e.g., Rumors). Sometimes a student will just be talking to themselves with no one listening (e.g., during a Thought Walk).

Drama can require the students to use different levels of formality in their talk, for example, talking in a marketplace (informal, spontaneous talk), a court (formal talk and rigid turn-taking). Mantle of the Expert often involves the students talking professionally to clients about work tasks and delivering presentations to clients.

Teachers are often in role alongside the students and talking with them during a Process Drama. This gives the teacher the opportunity to use language that is contextually appropriate and to model ways of talking and responding. The students can listen to the teacher using language appropriately and respond accordingly. The teacher in role is also interacting in ways that make linguistic demands and can shift their linguistic expectations of the students at different points in the drama.

Several drama strategies have names that suggest speaking and/or listening, for example, Rumors, Voice Collage, Eavesdropping, Talking Objects. However, any drama strategy can be used flexibly and adapted by teachers to stimulate and enable specific types of talk to be used. Drama strategies can function separately as "Talk Frames" in any subject lesson, as well as within drama lessons.

Drama strategies in L2 classrooms are also used as a way of generating and sharing relevant vocabulary, phrases, sentences, dialogue, questions, descriptions, explanations, ideas, instructions, and so on. The students will benefit from listening to each other's verbal contributions and ideas, as well as being able to communicate their own.

Talk, Role, and Distance

Different roles can be used to place the students at different distances, from a dramatic situation or event, in terms of time and/or space. For example, the students in role might be inside an event that is happening to them, at that exact moment, for example, "The fire is getting nearer and I am leaving my home now." Or the students could be asked to watch an event from a safe distance, as eyewitnesses, for example, "I am in a boat on the River Thames with Samuel Pepys. We are at a safe distance, watching the fire spread and the crowds gathering on the riverbank."

Also, the passing of time can be used to distance the participants from a dramatic moment, event, or situation in the drama. Once an event is over, the language about it will shift from the present to past tense. The teacher might ask the students to recount the event later, either to someone who was there too or someone who was not present. The drama provides a purpose and audience that should influence *what* is being said and *how* it is being said. If an event in a drama is about to happen (but has not yet happened), this too should influence the content, register, and style of what the students say in role.

What is the function of their role?	How distant are/were they from the event?
Participants	I am in the event and it is happening to me now
Commentators (eyewitnesses)	I am commenting on what is happening at this moment, as it unfolds before me
Guides	I was there and now I am recounting it for you
Investigators	I have the official authority to ask you questions about the event and find out what happened
Recorders/reporters	I am recording what you say about the event, for all time
Critics	I am critically analyzing and interpreting the event
Artists	I am changing the form of the event, interpreting it, and remaking it, e.g., a poet

L2 teachers will know what their students most need to practice and can shift the context and instructions of the drama task accordingly, giving opportunities for students to practice talking in specific ways. What the students and teachers roles are and how the drama/talk task is framed will significantly impact on the linguistic opportunities and demands being made. The different relationships between the various characters in the drama should also influence the content, style, and language register used by the students in role. For example, how a student in role talks about an event in the drama should change, depending on whether they are talking with a trusted friend or a child or an official.

Drama also gives many opportunities for practicing and rehearsing in advance, what is then going to be said in role, to others. In Small Group Playmaking, for example, groups of students prepare scenes that usually include dialogue. They might experiment with different dialogues and ways of speaking, decide what is most effective and then rehearse what they are going to say before they perform it to others. Through rehearsal, they can gain confidence before talking more publicly. When talking in role within the drama, the students will be trying to use the language and style appropriate to their role and the situation. When they come out of role, they will be talking in a different way.

There are also times in a Process Drama when the students (in or out of role) discuss and formulate what they are going to say to a character or a community within the drama, before actually doing so. They may start by saying something that they have prepared but might then need to improvise thereafter, for example, a group of students might be in role as planners at a public meeting. They might have already rehearsed the formal presentation of their plans to the public but will then need to improvise, when answering questions asked by members of the public (or press) afterward.

Drama for Writing

Writing is considered by many teachers to be the most difficult language skill to teach. Students often don't feel like writing and don't have anything they want to write about. They lack the motivation, stimulation, inspiration, and compelling reasons to write. Drama can provide these. Students who have been interactively immersed in a drama emotionally and cognitively will already have plenty of content to write about. The drama has planted the context, characters, dialogue, events, situations, and a plot in their minds already. If they are then given a relevant reason to write that connects with the drama, they are in a much better position to start writing, than if they were just being asked to do a piece of writing with no real purpose, context, reason, or support.

Compelling reasons for purposeful writing can be planned into a drama lesson and/or might present themselves naturally and unexpectedly, as a drama progresses. Different drama strategies can be selected and used to generate different types of talk that can subsequently underpin different types of writing. Several such opportunities are highlighted and suggested within each drama unit in this book.

Students do need to practice talking and writing in English, for specific purposes and audiences, using appropriate vocabulary. They also need to practice writing in different genres and forms, for example, formal and informal letter writing, descriptive writing, story writing, balanced arguments, instructions, emails, text messages. Teachers know the diverse range of writing types that their students need to practice and can soon start to create and recognize contextually based opportunities for writing in and about the drama.

Co-participants in a drama are also each other's uniquely placed, responsive audience for both talk and writing. When students are immersed in the same drama, then reading or listening to each other's writing in or about the drama becomes personally more relevant. When students writing is allowed to contribute to the content and direction of the drama, then this can be particularly motivating for them as writers.

Students might be in role sometimes, as actual writers in a drama, for example, poets, newspaper reporters, diarists. The teacher might ask students to "talk like a writer" (a verbal form of writing rehearsal which can be linked to aspects of Pie Corbett's "Talk for Writing" approach). "Talk for Writing" is a development of the second language work carried out by the psycholinguist Traute Taeschner at the University of Rome in the 1990s. It then was promoted through the National Strategies for schools in England and Pie Corbett continued to develop it, when the National Strategies ended. Pie Corbett and Patrice Baldwin worked together regularly between 2012 and 2017, combining their work as "Talk and Drama for Writing" across England and Wales. Teachers then learned how to use Process Drama in conjunction with "Talk for Writing." Patrice Baldwin used drama strategies and contexts to generate and gather words, phrases, and sentences during a Process Drama lesson. Pie Corbett then received these and used "Talk for Writing" methods with them, to show teachers how these written fragments could be used and developed into a finished piece of writing. The legend of Beowulf (Drama Unit 5) was used during some of their "Talk and Drama for Writing" training sessions for teachers.

During Process Drama, there will often be opportunities for writing individually or collaboratively in groups of different sizes and in whole classes. For example, the students could be asked to write individual letters to the council, giving their opinions about the proposed Holiday Park, or the villagers together could be asked to collaborate and draft a single letter, or different groups of villagers could draft letters to the council (Drama Unit 5). The teacher can decide which of these options are most beneficial for their students and adapt the task accordingly.

A teacher in role might commission a piece of writing from the students, who may be in role as professional writers. For example, the students could be newspaper reporters and the teacher could be their editor, who sends them to interview some eyewitnesses about an incident and then write a newspaper report, to a tight deadline. Or the teacher could be in role as a Holiday Park entrepreneur who needs the students (in role as professional planning consultants), to write a formal letter on his company's behalf, to accompany his planning application to the Council. This elevates the status of the students, who are being interacted with "as if" they are professional writers (which some of them might wish to become in the future).

Drama has characters, situations, and events. The students become characters in the drama and often talk with each other in role, thus generating dialogue. The dialogue can be scripted or inform other types of writing, for example, diary entries, narratives, official reports depending on the drama. As the drama progresses, information about characters is revealed and can be noted in various ways (e.g., Role on the Wall, see Resource Sheet 13). Notes about characters can be used to inform a written character study. Having immersed themselves in role, in the situations and events of the drama, the students can then be asked to recount them and write about them, for various imagined (or real) purposes and audiences.

Writing in role can be framed as "private" writing (e.g., personal diary entries) or as more public (e.g., letters to other characters or a newspaper report). In role, the students can be placed in the position of being eyewitnesses to incidents and/or people who overhear conversations. This can be a useful preparation for them then writing eyewitness accounts and reports about what they have seen and heard.

Teacher as Scribe or Co-writer

A teacher in role can act as a scribe, just writing down exactly what the students suggest. Alternatively, the teacher might choose to contribute to and guide the students' writing in role, for example, the teacher could be in role as a son, writing a letter to his elderly parents. The son says that the letter will be given to them after he has left with the people smuggler (Drama Unit 3). In role as the son, the teacher can talk with the students about their writing suggestions, read them out loud, try rephrasing some and explain why. The teacher and students are collaboratively writing in role together, for a particular audience and a dramatic purpose. The teacher is able to use the role, partly for linguistic teaching and learning purposes. The teacher in role as the son can make drafting and redrafting the letter, an interactive and emotionally laden experience, for example, "I need you to help me to get this letter exactly right. This might be the last letter that I can ever get to my parents. I will probably never see them again. I am sure that they will often read this letter and it really matters that I get the wording right. Please help me!"

Writing together collaboratively and purposefully can make writing enjoyable. It gives a collective sense of achievement and can help raise the self-esteem of students as writers. This can be a particularly positive and supportive experience for any student who has previously acquired a sense of failure as a writer.

Drama enables teachers to meaningfully integrate the language skills of reading, writing, speaking, and listening. A teacher in role can pretend that they are unable to write at all (or are not good at writing). They therefore need the students in role, to help them write within the drama. This raises the comparative status of the students as writers and lowers that of the teacher for a while. The students know this is a fiction but the pretence can evoke in the students, a real sense of empathy, writing competence, and compassionate responsibility.

Drama often uses authentic texts. The words and phrases in any text will become more memorable once they have been spoken and brought alive through drama. In drama, the students can be literally "re-membering" and "making sense" of text together. In a drama lesson they might also be improvising at times and generating new words, phrases, and actions that can then become the basis of new texts.

Using Drama Strategies as "Thought and Talk" Frames

Process Drama provides contexts and opportunities for critical and creative thinking, meta-thinking and inter-thinking, for imaginative problem-solving and decision-making. Students bring their current knowledge, skills, and understanding into new, shared imagined situations and contexts and can practice using necessary skills and a target language during the drama process. While using a target language "in role," they will be focusing together on real universal problems, dilemmas, and situations (albeit within a fiction).

All drama strategies can be considered as visual, auditory, and/or kinesthetic thinking and talk frames. They offer a unique way of stimulating, organizing, and sharing students thinking and inter-thinking. The names of some drama strategies are clearly connected with thinking, for example, Thought-tracking, Passing Thoughts, Thought-walks, and Conscience Alley, however, all strategies can be used as thinking frames. Teachers can intentionally stimulate and scaffold different types of thinking and different types of talk, depending on the drama strategy they choose and the instructions they give with it. The choice of strategy and the way it is set up will result in different cognitive and linguistic demands and expectations being made of the language students. For example, when students are talking to a character who is passing through a Conscience Alley, they are often expected to use persuasive speech. They are usually persuading the character to take (or avoid), a particular course of action. However, the teacher could give alternative instructions that would change the types of thought and talk required, for example.

As the character passes by,

- speak the character's thoughts "as if" you are the character;
- speak your "in role" thoughts about the character;
- speak "in role" to the character;
- speak out of role about the character;
- say (as the character) what you are wondering;
- say "in role" (as the character) what you have noticed;
- say "in role" (as the character) what you are remembering; and
- say "in role" (as the character) what you are feeling.

The teacher can join in with the drama strategies alongside the students, contributing ideas and modelling the type of thinking and language expected. The teacher will need to judge when it is most helpful to lead and model and when it would be more helpful to hold back and follow on from students' contributions.

Always setting up drama strategies the same way is likely to reinforce the same types and patterns of thinking and talk. When teachers change instructions and adapt strategies, they can intentionally stimulate their students to think in different ways and more deeply. Drama strategies can help students to build up, slow down, hold still and/or dismantle, significant moments in any drama, to think and talk about them together.

Teachers must give students the opportunity and time to think creatively and critically about relevant issues, to solve problems together, to work collaboratively in teams, and to communicate clearly, using a variety of media. Interpersonal skills, thinking, and inter-thinking skills help students to be flexible and adaptable, and this helps prepare them for their real lives, employment environments, and future careers.

The Use of Performance within Process Drama

Process Drama is not about teaching theater as a subject and/or performing for an external audience. It is not about actors being directed. It is about participants in role immersing themselves in an evolving, shared fiction, discovering and learning, thinking, talking, making, performing (for each other), and responding (in and out of role). It is about using drama and a target language, as a learning and communication medium with peers and the teacher.

During Process Drama there are times when the students will be creating short scenes or images to perform to each other. The process of making an image or scene in a class drama has value and it is not only the "theatre"-type outcome that matters. The devising process gets the students thinking, inter-thinking, talking together, creating, collaborating, and communicating with each other in their target language and nonverbally. They need to talk about what matters in the drama and decide what they need to do and say, to communicate what they want, in the scene or image. Each student gets a chance to be part of a performance and to watch and listen to each other's performances. The teacher might then ask for evaluative feedback or comments afterward (maybe focusing on the language and the learning and not just the theatrical elements).

It helps if the teacher sets clear, realistic expectations for the students as performers and as audience. The students will be expected to speak and communicate clearly and stay aware of their audience when they are presenting or performing. A clear performance is going to be more satisfying, memorable, and effective than a careless one for the participants and the audience. They need to pay attention to the content of what others say but they also should pay attention to the way it is said. Performing in drama lessons is good practice for presenting clearly and confidently in real life, in other educational settings, in interviews, and in places of employment. Process Drama is intended to be helpful for all students and is not being aimed at would-be actors!

2

Using Process Drama to Develop Twenty-First-Century Skills

Chapter Outline

TWENTY-FIRST-CENTURY SKILLS	25
LEARNING SKILLS—THE FOUR C'S	27
CRITICAL THINKING	27
CREATIVITY	29
COMMUNICATION SKILLS	30
COLLABORATION	30
LITERACY SKILLS IN THE TWENTY-FIRST CENTURY	31
LIFE SKILLS IN THE TWENTY-FIRST CENTURY	33
SUSTAINABLE DEVELOPMENT AWARENESS—A Global Skill for the Twenty-First Century	39

Something massive, unpredictable, and potentially overwhelming is happening fast in the world. Institutional systems from global means of trade and information webs to the personal network of connections between friends, families, and colleagues are changing because they need to. Such changes may well require a new language to describe them and will require new ways of thinking, learning, and teaching.

Current education systems were created for different times. Global pandemics and lockdowns have highlighted the need to reconsider and re-evaluate the skills that are most needed by students and the ways in which they might need to learn in the future. Education needs to become less about students getting the "right" answers and more about students asking the right questions. It must help them develop the skills they truly need for living and working in the twenty-first century, including a strong focus on developing their personal and social skills as well as their employment skills. Education programs at all levels, from primary to tertiary, need to focus not only on twenty-first-century competencies but also on academic learning goals that focus on knowledge and content. Gaining knowledge is not sufficient. They also need to be able to use and apply that knowledge in the future. Process Drama offers engaging contexts within which students can practice twenty-first-century skills and use and apply their current knowledge (including their linguistic knowledge).

Twenty-First-Century Skills

There has been a paradigm shift in language teaching over recent years. The most evident shift came with the advent of the communicative approach in the 1970s and 1980s. This was a shift from a more structured, content-based approach (Hymes, 1972). The employability of students became a major factor that needed to be considered in SLA (Canale & Swain, 1980). Globalization and increased career mobility have also led to changes in expectations and needs, and this too has impacted on language teaching and led to the introduction of the twenty-first-century skills approach to it.

Teachers, education experts, and business leaders came together to design a framework which outlines the competencies and the skills that twenty-first-century students require to be successful at school, at work, and in other walks of life (Framework for 21st Century Learning, 2007).

The term "twenty-first-century skills" is now very familiar to language teachers. These skills are abilities that have been categorized and defined in various ways with many different classifications. Put simply, they are the skills that our learners need to equip and prepare them for their adult futures (Puchta & Williams, 2014). The skills themselves are not really new. Most have been present in education since ancient times but there seems to be more urgency about the need to acquire and develop them in our more rapidly changing, unpredictable world.

In most publications the twenty-first-century skills are categorized as

1. Learning skills,
2. Literacy skills, and
3. Life skills.

A case can be made for now adding a fourth category (A. Galazka):

4. Global sustainable development skills.

It is likely that second language teachers already enable their learners to practice and develop these skills but Process Drama can offer particularly engaging and memorable contexts within which to do so.

Learning Skills

These can be described as cognitive, mental processes which are activated in order to adapt and improve upon a modern work environment, as well as develop the agility to adjust to changing requirements. There is a focus on metacognition skills in the classroom and the stimulation of students' self-reflection processes. These skills are often referred to as the four C's, i.e., critical thinking, creativity, communication, and collaboration (Centre for Curriculum Redesign, 2015; Davila, 2016; Eaton, 2010; Halverson, 2018; Herrmann, 2015).

Literacy Skills

This focuses on how students can gather and process information, using modern technology but also on their reading and writing abilities. Literacy skills include information literacy, media literacy, and technology literacy (IMT).

Students must learn how to select information in the modern, digital world. They need to be able to determine trustworthy sources and find factual information. They need to be able to separate authentic information from the misinformation that is so readily accessible online. In the language classroom, literacy skills also refer to the development of a range of reading and writing strategies and the ability to select and process information that is spoken or written in a target language for a target audience as well as the ability to understand and convert different types of text.

Life Skills

These are the skills such as flexibility, leadership, initiative, productivity, social skills, interpersonal and intrapersonal skills (often abbreviated and referred to as FLIPSI). Self-confidence, well-being, and resilience are also critically important to students in their everyday lives and in their work lives. Life skills are of prime importance to young people when dealing with the pressures of modern life.

Sustainable Development Skills

These focus on students' ability to be responsible, global citizens who are environmentally aware and active. These skills also help to develop cultural and intercultural empathy.

Learning Skills—The Four C's

The learning skills are often referred to as the four C's and are particularly important for academic achievement and employment.

The four C's are as follows:

1. **Critical Thinking**: convergent thinking, analyzing and selecting information, drawing conclusions;
2. **Creativity**: divergent, lateral thinking, generating ideas, thinking "outside the box," fluency and flexibility of thinking;
3. **Collaboration**: team building, working with others, problem and conflict resolving, negotiation;
4. **Communication**: verbal and nonverbal messaging, interpersonal skills, talking to others.

(based on New Vision for Education, 2016)

Language teachers need to keep the four C's in mind when teaching a second language. In any Process Drama students are likely to be using and developing all "4 C's" but teachers can choose to adapt a drama activity to intentionally give greater emphasis to one or more of the "4 C's."

Process Drama and Critical Thinking: As a Process Drama lesson develops, the students are often required to think and inter-think critically about situations, events, and characters, analyzing and evaluating their responses to them. The drama strategies used can function as critical thinking frames, enabling students to share their critical thinking verbally and/or nonverbally.

Process Drama and Creativity: Making drama involves creative processes and leads to creative outcomes, for example, plots, improvised dialogue, characters, scenes, and images. The drama produces contexts and situations that can stimulate creative thinking and inter-thinking, and drama strategies can be used to scaffold it.

Process Drama and Collaboration: Process Drama relies on collaboration and cannot work without it. The students must work together as a team to make the drama come alive and to sustain belief in it. In and out of role, the students are often problem-solving together as they work their way through the dramatic situations, conflicts, and dilemmas that the drama contains.

Process Drama and Communication: Drama focuses the students' attention on both verbal and nonverbal ways of communicating meaning and on understanding what is being communicated by each other. This process requires and develops interpersonal skills and the drama provides many contexts and opportunities for students to communicate with and respond to each other, both in and out of role.

Critical Thinking

Teachers need to help learners to shift from using lower-order thinking skills to also using higher-order thinking skills. Bloom's Taxonomy (1956) categorized thinking skills that educators need to help develop in their students. According to Bloom's framework, lower-order thinking skills include remembering and recalling knowledge to identify, label, name, or describe things. Higher-order thinking skills enable learners to use, apply, analyze, and/or synthesize knowledge when they receive new information or come across unfamiliar concepts and new situations. Drama can help make the familiar unfamiliar and vice versa. It can provide countless situations, within which students are stimulated and supported to use both lower- and higher-order thinking skills.

Higher-order thinking skills need to be used when information or concepts need to be broken into parts to understand more fully or to put ideas together to form something new. The systematic use of drama strategies clearly enables this as they can be used as deep thinking frames to explore and consider characters, situations, moments, events, and so on, in a range of ways at any point in the drama.

Bloom's framework and categories can be used as a starting point for L2 teachers to plan language lessons and "drama for language" lessons, although Bloom's Taxonomy may not be directly applied to all the cognitive processes that are involved in learning a second language. Some of the thinking processes used in second language learning may differ from those we use when learning and using a native language.

Bloom's Taxonomy (Revised)

Creating
Evaluating
Analyzing
Applying
Understanding
Remembering

Teaching thinking in drama and/or SLA requires teachers to set up cognitively challenging tasks that stimulate and support students to think in a sustained way about an issue or problem. They need to know, understand, and use of a range of thinking styles and patterns and to accept that there may not be just one right answer or solution to a problem or situation. In drama, situations can be replayed in various ways, which can result in different outcomes (e.g., in Forum Theater, see page 73). Teachers need to judge when to intervene (in or out of role) and when it is most appropriate and helpful to ask questions, challenge, support, or extend pupils' thinking and inter-thinking. The timing and frequency of teacher interventions are going to vary, depending on whether a student is using their native language or their second language, and in Process Drama lessons, the teacher will also be judging when it would be best to intervene in relation to the drama too. Language teachers using drama might also be debriefing pupils on their solutions to a drama task and the strategies they used to carry it out. They can also help them to make connections between the language required and the thinking involved in achieving the drama task as this encourages the transfer of knowledge and skills.

Working in different roles in a drama will bring different challenges, require different thinking patterns and responses, require the use and application of different knowledge, require different use of language, and can sometimes require different languages to be used.

Linking Bloom's Taxonomy, SLA Practice, and Drama

Remembering—This is the most basic thinking skill. When language students read or listen to a text, it requires them to retrieve, recognize, and recall information they have learned before. In second language learning, students are also required to describe, find, identify, label, or list some facts that lie within a text and they are asked to match two halves of a sentence.

An example of a drama strategy that requires students to remember would be "Role on the Wall" (see pages 68–69), as the students need to jot down and gather what they know about a character and place it around an outline of that character. It is a way of visually organizing and recording what they remember.

Understanding—When students read a text (or listen to it), they try to understand it. This is not as easy to do in a foreign language as in a native language. Language teachers know that it sometimes takes longer, especially at lower levels of proficiency, and that sometimes the teacher needs to support the process by asking additional, clarifying questions.

In drama, students are communicating their understanding of a text when they are enacting it.

Applying—In the language classroom, after students have read or listened to something, they usually have to answer some comprehension questions or decide if the statements are true or false. They often are expected to fill in the missing parts of a chart or table. They are just being asked to complete the task, using the newly acquired information, to show that they have understood.

In drama for language learning, a teacher could ask students to role-play a situation together to show that they remember what they have learned and can apply it dramatically. For example, Student A (or the teacher) could be in role as someone who works in a language school abroad. Student B could be in role as someone considering enrolling in a course at that language school. Student B is, however, very anxious about doing so and the role play can be used to reveal what Student B is anxious about and why. This gives Student A the opportunity to try and allay Student B's fears and enable him/her to then enroll happily on the course.

Analyzing—Language students use the process of analyzing when they become more critical and, for example, start to question the information that they have read or heard and/or when they consider the value of information they have been given. Analyzing in the language classroom often involves comparing and contrasting information. An activity in pairs might require two students to study and analyze two language courses that are being offered abroad. They can be asked to compare and contrast the two courses on offer and to justify choosing one over the other with reference to criteria such as price, living conditions, extra attractions, and size of groups.

Activities can also be set up in ways that require the students to synthesize. For example, students can work in small groups and create their own ideal summer language course. They need to consider and discuss what constitutes a good course and what they consider to be most important to have within a course. This will lead them into discussion, debate, and reasoned argument. They will need to decide what they think is essential on a course and what is just desirable, and this will lead them into evaluating and prioritizing.

In drama, students are sometimes asked to analyze a character and then physically position themselves in relation to the character. They have to justify and explain their positioning. This is called "proxemics."

Evaluating—Evaluation is a key "higher-order" critical thinking skill that needs to be employed in the second language classroom. Students need to evaluate the validity and relevance of the information they have acquired through reading or listening. In the second language classroom students might be asked to consider whether information they have read is evidence and research based and whether it would be valid to use it for their writing or speaking task. Evaluating is quite complex and challenging for many language learners as it requires a good command of language skills and a critical mindset.

In drama, students are often expected to evaluate the content, quality, and effectiveness of their own drama work (e.g., scenes they devise and perform). At times, they can be asked to evaluate each other's contributions to the drama.

Creating—Creativity is one of the subskills of critical thinking and a twenty-first-century skill. In the second language classroom, students are often asked to think creatively when speaking or writing. They can use and apply what they already know to produce an original piece of writing as an outcome or to make up and tell a story, using vocabulary that they have learned. They are using what they already know to create something original.

Process Drama happens in imagined worlds that are co-created, and during drama lessons, students are thinking, talking, and acting creatively for much of the time. Groups often devise their own scenes, for example, which are often shared with other participants. Target languages can be creatively used during this drama process, for example, for improvising and as rehearsed speech.

We can link the process of language acquisition to different types of thinking skills, which enable learners to process, generate, and communicate information in a variety of different ways. The research and rationale for teaching thinking skills with the teaching of language were outlined by Puchta and Williams (2014). They pointed out that in the language classroom, we focus mainly on language acquisition and often the cognitive and intellectual challenge of the tasks is significantly limited to make the tasks linguistically easier to understand. Learners are unlikely to be intrigued by boring, simple, repetitive activities that are designed for (and limited to) the learner's linguistic level as opposed to being designed around their actual interests and cognitive potential. Process Drama can provide challenging, interesting linguistic tasks which are cognitively and affectively engaging and require students to use and develop their higher-order thinking skills.

In second language teaching and in drama, students need to use and develop both convergent and divergent thinking. Divergent (lateral) thinking implies open and playful forms of thinking that generate new ideas, and convergent thinking stimulates and enables logical reasoning and consistent analysis. Creativity is central to the making of drama, and during a Process Drama lesson, different drama strategies can be employed and specifically honed to help stimulate and scaffold any type of thinking.

Creativity

Drama clearly involves and requires lateral thinking and the generation of new ideas, which can lead to creative outcomes that are shared. Creativity skills can be developed during tasks that provide learners with the freedom to use whatever language they have at their disposal to get their message across (Nunan, 2011). Creative thinking enables learners to make new connections and communicate meaning and new understandings in a variety of new ways and forms.

Drama is a creative learning and teaching medium, and the students are required to generate and try out ideas and express what they know and think in creative and often aesthetic ways. They have opportunities to use a target language creatively within exploratory, imagined contexts. The students' focus and attention will be on the message and the tasks they are completing, rather than on the correctness of linguistic form and structure (Nunan, 2011).

It has become essential to develop the skills of "Learning to Learn" and "Thinking about Thinking" (metacognition). Students need to perceive themselves as good thinkers (including in the target language), and proficiency in a second language includes being able to think and reflect in that language. Process Drama brings an inquiry-based, metacognitive learning model and method to the classroom, offering many opportunities for using and developing high-quality thinking skills, both in and out of role.

Communication Skills

Communication involves interchanging ideas, information, or messages between people and places, using verbal and/or nonverbal signs that both parties can understand. This could almost be a definition of drama. Students learn a second language mainly because they want to be able to communicate with other people from different parts of the world. It is also essential for international institutions and organizations to be able to communicate clearly to work well together. It requires active listening and the effective transmission of information and ideas. How well students can do this is going to have a huge impact on both their personal and professional lives.

The way people communicate is influenced and determined by many factors, including their personality type and their previous communication experiences. Some people seem to have a natural gift for communication and are expressive, outgoing, and energized by communication with other people. Others find it more difficult to communicate openly with others, and needing to communicate can be a source of stress for some people. However, everyone needs to work at improving their verbal and nonverbal communication skills as they are the foundation of all human relationships.

Communication is the *process* of transferring messages to one another whereas language is a *tool* of communication. Drama involves both process and product. Making drama involves a process and the tools used during the drama for learning, and/or drama-making process can be verbal and/or nonverbal. During drama, attention will be given to verbal and nonverbal aspects of communication, for example, silence, sound, tone, volume, gesture, movement, and stillness.

Communicating in a second language is challenging, and language students need to develop their communicative competences within situations that involve them working together to improve their receptive and productive language skills.

In drama the students speak and listen to each other for much of the time, sometimes in and sometimes out of role. Newly learned structures, vocabulary, and grammar can be used, practiced, and reinforced within meaningful contexts and situations. The second language becomes the medium that the learners need to be able to complete the drama task, and the students feel the urge to contribute to the content and direction of the drama. At times in the drama, there is opportunity for language to flow, for example, during improvisation, and at other times there will be opportunities to formulate language carefully to rehearse speech and then present verbally to others, for example, rehearsed monologues and scenes arrived at through "small group play-making." The teacher still needs to pre-teach some context-appropriate language and then support the students to use it during the Process Drama lesson.

Process Drama can also be used as a way of revising together, offering a more enjoyable, active and inter-active way of revising than decontextualized and solitary revision.

Collaboration

Collaboration can be defined as the ability to work with others. Social interaction plays a fundamental role in the process of cognitive development, and in a language classroom, there are many opportunities to work together. Whole class Process Drama can only be successfully sustained if and when the students work together collaboratively. Language learning classrooms and Process Drama lessons use pair, group work, and whole class activities to help develop speaking and listening skills and help students collaborate to reach shared goals and outcomes. Whatever size group students are working in, they will be sharing knowledge, ideas, expertise, and different ways and styles of working. This has a synergistic effect. Each group member shares responsibility for (and pride in) the outcome and/or product that the team generates. Group work can help students learn content (Kagan & McGroarty, 1993) and can help them acquire language (Mackey & Gass, 2006). At times, group members may be given different types of talk roles and responsibilities, for example, instigator, builder, challenger, clarifier, prober, summarizer (as suggested by the Voice 21 Oracy Project).

Collaboration requires students to be able to assert and clearly express their personal opinions, thoughts, and emotions, while also being able to compromise, for the sake of the whole team. In drama, students are talking in role for much of the time and will be expressing the opinions of the characters, whose opinions may be different from their own.

Scott (2012) explains that learning is a social process and therefore, when collaborating, learners should be encouraged to interact in one of the following ways:

1. through the teacher conversing with the learners
2. through a whole class discussion
3. through a small group discussion
4. by means of peer-to-peer discussions.

Process Drama lessons will involve interacting in all these ways, sometimes "in role" and sometimes "out of role."

Literacy Skills in the Twenty-First Century

Literacy skills are a category of twenty-first-century skills. Digital literacy skills and e-learning skills became increasingly important during the global pandemic, as many teachers had to transform and transfer teaching to online lessons and needed to communicate with and teach their students within a virtual reality. Drama teachers also had to find ways to adapt to online teaching. This was particularly challenging for Process Drama, which relies so much on human interaction and multisensory communication. During the pandemic, many drama lessons in schools needed to ensure social distancing between students, and teachers soon found themselves adapting drama strategies to enable this. Working online is not necessarily the best option for truly interactive teaching and learning, but nonetheless, it can help teachers and students to become more conscious, critical, creative, and effective in their use of media.

Information Literacy

Information literacy is an essential foundational skill. The whole world communicates now, mainly through digital media. We have new sources of information and new ways of exchanging and interacting with it. Teachers and students need to learn and adapt to these. Language teachers need to be able to create stimulating, technologically engaging tasks for language learners, which require them to search online for relevant information to complete linguistic tasks and projects. Young people nowadays are often referred to as "digital natives" but they still need to learn how to select, analyze, and interpret any information they find. They need to learn how to interrogate and understand the plethora of "facts" and data they find online and how to judge their authenticity and relevance. They will need to use and develop their critical thinking skills to separate facts from lies and avoid falling victim to sophisticated, well-constructed lies in an age of chronic misinformation and fake news.

Information literacy also requires students to become familiar and skilled at receiving information texts in different digital formats and become adept at reading various digital texts and getting to the subtexts.

Students can access and select authentic information online that will be helpful to them during various dramas. Students (and teachers) might search online for images of the Great Fire of London, eyewitness recounts, and diary excerpts when working with Drama Unit 2 in this book. They might search and select from photographs and old newspaper reports about Annie Edson Taylor when doing Drama Unit 6. Historical dramas often benefit from further online research, as do dramas that place students in role as "experts" of some sort. Students can search for authentic information online that will help them complete their tasks and presentations "as if" they are experts. For example, in

Drama Unit 4, when they are designers creating a Leisure Park, they might look at real Leisure Park Websites to select and present some design ideas and images to their client (usually the teacher in role).

Media Literacy

Students need to understand how media works and how to evaluate its content, credibility, reliability, and real value. They need to learn to look critically at the structure, meaning, and ways of interpreting and presenting through various media. The challenge for teachers is to find ways to implement and develop critical thinking skills in media literacy and raise students' awareness to help them to become discerning consumers of, and responsible contributors to, media. Drama can offer safe, distanced ways of doing this within imagined worlds. Although Process Drama is not deeply, digitally rooted, it can nonetheless be contextualized and planned in ways that can help raise students' awareness of how language is used and manipulated to persuade and influence people through various media.

Media literacy requires students to learn to access and critically evaluate media messages in and across a range of media. They need to learn that people respond differently to the same media messages and that the messages have been carefully and purposefully constructed to promote certain values and manipulate the feelings and opinions of the recipients. Students can be "told" this and can "know" it but drama enables them to experience it in interactive, memorable ways. They can come to understand media manipulation in engaging yet safe contexts. The drama can provide reasons for them to create and manipulate various media themselves and to practice using it for a range of imagined purposes that reflect the way it is used in the real world.

Students need to learn to identify media bias, and misinformation within the real-world working in role, within a drama world, can help raise and heighten their awareness of this. In drama, they can have opportunities to create media images and texts in role as media creators and manipulators. Within the drama they can be working in role for power and/or profit and can create and/or receive false news and misinformation. They can become the perpetrators and the victims of media manipulation. The learning and skills used during the drama experience will stay with them in the real world long after the drama finishes. For example, in a Process Drama, they could be asked to write newspaper reports about the same newsworthy incident but from very different viewpoints and perspectives. The students might all be "in role" as journalists but some might intentionally mislead the reader whereas others might report accurately. Some might create and publish false information and others might present the "truth" but with a deliberate bias. Following different instructions as newspaper reporters can help raise their awareness of the reasons and ways in which the media sets out to manipulate readers. The drama can provide a fictional and shared experience of this that can then be discussed, analyzed, and evaluated.

In Drama Unit 4, the teacher is in role as a company owner and the students could be employed as "expert spin doctors" who are being commissioned to create favorable materials, sound recordings, short films, and other media releases about the proposed holiday park development. They might even be asked to publish them on a restricted online platform (e.g., the school's own Website). The students in role could be asked to manipulate public opinion in favor of the planning proposal and might then become publicity and marketing professionals, should the plan be approved. They could change roles at times and become responsive members of the public, who receive their media messages. The students will be using and applying their media literacy skills within the drama and will be learning and recalling some of the ways in which the media sets out to manipulate public opinion.

Unfortunately, cyber-bullying and cyber-mobbing can be intensely present and problematic in the digital world. Drama can be used as a way of helping prepare students to cope with these. For example, Forum Theater as a structure (see Drama Unit 1) can be used effectively as a way of helping students to become increasingly confident and competent at dealing with various forms of oppression.

Students enjoy going online and playing games, watching films, and listening to music. Films and music found online by teachers or students can be appropriately used within a Process Drama, for example, during Drama Unit 6 a film loop of the Horseshoe Falls could be projected as a backdrop to some scenes. During Drama Unit 5, soundtracks from the Beowulf film could be found online and played at appropriate points during the drama. When films and soundtracks are used with drama, they can be replayed later and re-evoke the associated feelings, ideas, and experiences.

Technology Literacy

It is difficult to imagine learning and teaching in the future without computers, cloud programming, and mobile devices. Students (and teachers) need to learn how various devices work to master them and not feel intimidated by them. There are already many e-learning platforms and digital tools, which enable teachers to provide online lessons and courses, some of which are outstanding, and the global pandemic inevitably led to a surge in online learning. Publishers have produced many materials for different devices and students are becoming increasingly adept at exploring and experimenting in the digital world. Interactive whiteboards are now considered as a basic requirement in many classrooms worldwide.

Drama can provide meaningful contexts within which technology can be used enjoyably and purposefully by language students. For example, a group of students could be asked to devise a street incident that they would not want filmed. Another group can then become passers-by who actually film it (maybe using a real mobile phone). The film clip can then be shown to a third group (who did not see the incident themselves). Group 3 can then question the eyewitnesses to get further information. The third group might be in role as they ask the questions, for example, as friends, police officers, newspaper reporters, or they could be just asking the questions in a more detached way, which Heathcote described as being in "shadowy role."

Life Skills in the Twenty-First Century

Life skills are essential in personal and professional lives. Researchers and practitioners tend to focus on five subcategories of life skills, i.e., flexibility, leadership, initiative, productivity, and social skills. These skills are often referred to as FLIPS. However, a case has been made for adding intrapersonal skills and expanding it into FLIPSI (Galazka, 2020). The global struggle with the COVID-19 pandemic has highlighted how intertwined and essential all these life skills are for teachers and their students.

Flexibility

The first subcategory of life skills is flexibility, which can be defined as one's ability to adapt with agility to significantly changing situations or circumstances. Flexibility is not a speedy process. Agility on the other hand is the ability to move cognitively and affectively quickly with relative ease. It involves remaining calm and productive during periods of change and being able to access necessary information and take action as and when new and unexpected opportunities arise. In education, agility can involve seeking new learning opportunities, making sense of unfamiliar and complex situations, internalizing learning experiences to become more self-aware, to connect with others, and to react appropriately in new situations and to be curious. Flexibility requires a growth mindset and remaining open-minded to possible solutions and opportunities.

Agility requires a quick reaction, for example, language students might need to quickly find the most appropriate word or phrase in a social situation (and in improvisational drama situations). Language students should humbly accept that they always be learners who are trying to master their language even when they have become very experienced and proficient at using it. Drama can be intentionally set up to provide gradually more linguistically challenging situations for students at any level of competence.

Flexibility is necessary for long-term career success. Knowing when to change, how to change, and how to react *to* change is a necessary skill for success in work and life. The pandemic revealed the need to have an "agility mindset" and the ability to adapt, cooperate, trust, and be flexible. People found they were unexpectedly having to work differently, take on different roles, and change familiar work and life patterns to successfully meet the new challenges.

Process Drama gives many opportunities for language students to practice agility and flexibility. In a Process Drama they can use and apply these skills while using their second language in a range of roles and situations that often demand spontaneous responses, both to their peers and to the teacher in role.

There are different types of agility (Figure 2.1) and in SLA these include the following:

1. Cognitive agility
2. Interpersonal agility

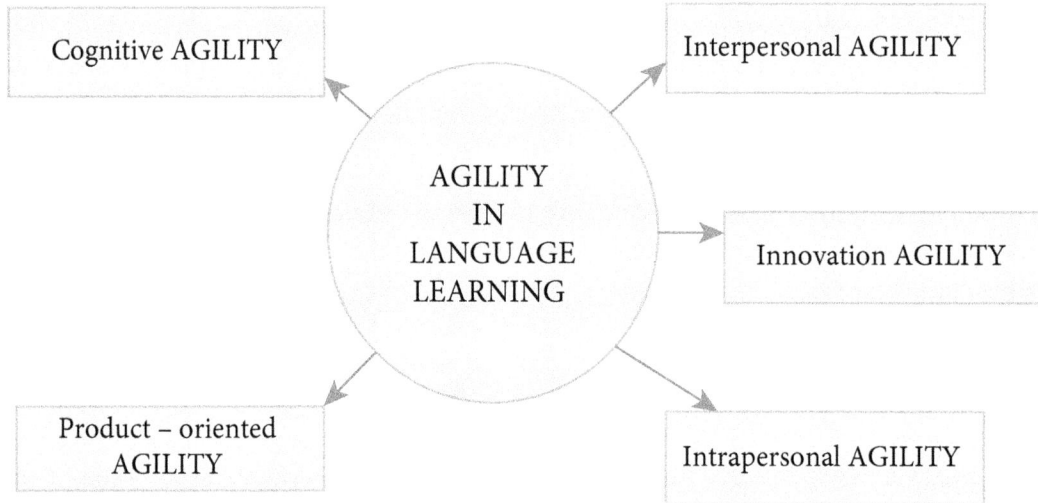

Figure 2.1 Agility in language learning.

3. Innovation agility
4. Product-oriented agility
5. Intrapersonal agility (Galazka, 2020, based on Korn Ferry's concept of learning agility)

Cognitive agility can be displayed by second language students through their curiosity. They often work quickly to identify linguistic patterns and the usefulness of new information. They can scan information quickly, find the most relevant facts, and use them appropriately to fulfill the given task.

Interpersonal agility. Language students with interpersonal agility connect easily with others emotionally, feeling and displaying true empathy. This helps them to communicate more effectively with different people, value their differences, combine different perspectives, and work through and resolve conflict. Seeing a situation from the perspective of others, can be of great benefit to the development of cultural and inter-cultural empathy. Language learners who are interpersonally agile are more likely to enjoy group debates, group projects, and teamwork and may well enjoy participating in Process Drama. Certainly, Process Drama can provide diverse and challenging situations, within which interpersonal agility can be required, practiced, and improved.

Innovation agility involves seeking and accepting new challenges. Language students and teachers who are "innovation agile" will be open-minded and keen to try out new approaches and methods of learning such as Process Drama. Innovation agile students will not be afraid of improving their language within different environments and contexts and won't feel anxious or inhibited about it. Indeed, the thought of trying something new is more likely to interest and excite them. Likewise, innovation agile teachers will be keen to try teaching through Process Drama. There will always be new strategies to try new methods to experiment with, and no matter what the immediate outcomes are, they can see that there will always be something worthwhile and new to be learned in any situation.

Product-oriented agility means being motivated by the final result by the prospect of success and the outcome. Students who are product oriented often work with a sense of urgency to complete their assignments and achieve the outcome. With a successful outcome in mind, they care deeply about the academic grades and are likely to consistently give of their best. In a Process Drama lesson, it may be that product-orientated students particularly enjoy the presentation and performance activities, which require clear outcomes that are then shared, for example, small group playmaking.

Intrapersonal agility is an important element of emotional intelligence. Students who have a deeper insight into their own thoughts and emotions and know their own strengths and weaknesses perform better and can better manage and use their cognitive and affective potential. A strong awareness of "self" and the ability to hold regular internal monologues with oneself are vital to the growth of personal resilience, the maintenance of well-being, and furthering oneself career-wise. Students working in role in a Process Drama inevitably bring their real selves and emotions to the drama but can rise to the challenge and consciously present a different or other "self" when they are working in role.

Leadership

Some language students will end up in leadership positions in the future, maybe within a company or organization. They may be required to build and lead teams and/or lead different projects and initiatives.

Leadership is really a combination of several different skills working together, rather than a single skill and is not just about being charismatic. A leader needs to be able to motivate others to complete tasks, according to stated expectations, and be able to lead themselves as well as others. They need to set challenging and achievable goals for themselves and others and be able to realistically plan the necessary steps to achieve those goals.

Process Drama can provide students with many contexts and opportunities, within which to practice and demonstrate their leadership skills and abilities. Indeed, businesses sometimes hire drama specialists to work with their "would-be" leaders to help them decide which people to recruit and/or which to promote in their companies. Leadership skills and styles are frequently being revealed and demonstrated within drama contexts. Drama can also be used to highlight how good various individuals are at working in teams and being led by others.

Mantle of the Expert often involves students in role as employees and some may be given leadership responsibilities and tasks and have small teams to manage within the fictitious enterprise or company. This can enable students to try out different leadership styles and try working with different types of leaders. The importance of creating a positive and motivating work environment will become evident and the students as leaders will need to make decisions and exercise flexibility and agility to keep their teams motivated and achieve successful outcomes.

Good leaders need to have strong personal values such as honesty and integrity. Ethical choices can help a company or institution to acquire and maintain a positive public image and will get and keep the respect of its employees.

Rather than overtly set up a work-related drama to give leadership practice and/or explore ethical choices with students, teachers might covertly use drama with stories such as traditional tales to help students to actively reflect on personal values and ethical choices in a more distanced way. Traditional tales often carry important messages about the importance and rewards of behaving with honesty and integrity. When students explore values and behaviors through drama, it can help them to gain a clearer sense and understanding of their own, and this can lead to small, real-life changes that contribute toward them becoming better as leaders.

Leadership involves building relationships and being able to create and maintain a strong and collaborative team of individuals, who are all working toward the same goal. Effective team building requires leaders to have good communication skills and be able to problem-solve and resolve conflict. Leaders need to be able to deal with issues that arise within the team and the work. Clearly, students will benefit from being placed in situations that enable them to safely practice dealing with issues while working in and/or leading teams.

Process Drama can provide language students with many opportunities for practicing working within teams and groups. It can also give opportunities for practicing leading within the drama. Drama focuses on human tensions, conflicts, and difficult situations and the students in role work together to resolve these.

Effective problem-solving requires leaders to stay calm and identify a step-by-step solution. Leaders need to be able to make quick decisions, resolve obstacles with and for their team, and ensure that tasks and projects are completed on time. Good leaders think more about how to make their team work well than they do about themselves. In the language classroom there are opportunities for students to support and mentor each other. In drama they need to be able to give and take constructive criticism from each other at times to reach a collectively agreed and shared outcome.

Initiative

The modern world needs people who are "self-starters" and have the courage to think and work "outside the box" to show initiative and take responsibility for their work. Process Drama always has many opportunities for the participants to use their initiative and try out their own ideas, for example, during improvisations and when creating images and scenes to present. The students are working both independently and within teams and have a shared ownership of and responsibility for the drama, to which they are all expected to contribute their ideas and share their outcomes.

Productivity

Productivity in education and the workplace requires an understanding about implementing ideas effectively within time limits and how to solve problems during the production process. Students need to be able to complete tasks in an appropriate amount of time. In professional life, it is called "efficiency" and is a skill much needed and appreciated by employers.

In language and Process Drama lessons, teachers will often give strict time limits for the completion of certain tasks, for example, preparing a presentation or devising a scene for performance. Some of the drama strategies are time-limited, and if students don't contribute promptly, they lose the opportunity too, for example, Hot-Seating (see pages 66–68) only carry on as long as the character stays present and available for questioning. Also, when involved in a Conscience Alley (see pages 62–63), the student must speak only when the character passes by them, or they lose their opportunity to speak. When a student knows that they have a strictly time-limited opportunity, then they usually become more efficient because they do not want to miss out. Teachers need to stick to the work deadlines they set and not always be willing to stretch them.

Social Skills

Humans are social. They want to interact and make meaningful connections in both their personal and professional lives. Good social skills will help students to establish long-lasting relationships and build networks. Social media has significantly altered the nature of much human interaction, and many of today's students seem to possess high levels of social skill in the virtual world but are often less able to sustain social interactions in the real world.

During recent pandemics, real face-to-face social interactions were highly restricted, and language and drama teaching and learning had to adapt to this. Work and relationships had to be increasingly conducted using "online" platforms. This was functionally necessary but felt very different (and often less satisfying) than being in the same physical space together. Slight body signals are easily lost in a virtual space.

Intrapersonal Skills

Schools can play an important and often pivotal role in the prevention and/or reduction of student's mental illness, which can have serious adverse consequences for students' well-being, achievement and attainment. Students' engagement with school can be strengthened by "positive education" interventions such as mindfulness and self-compassion programs. These have been shown to have a positive impact on student's attention, memory, cognitive performance, problem-solving, resilience, stress management and their ability to cope with emotional problems. The pedagogy of positive education takes a holistic approach to education and focuses on "educating the whole person." It has both well-being and academic mastery as the goals of learning and teaching (White & Kern, 2018) and can have a positive impact on students, teachers and others within the education community. Student well-being is not just about how a student is feeling on a particular day or week; it is about an individual's balanced development and growth and about them becoming healthy, contributing members of society with growth mindsets.

Drama is a holistic, inclusive learning and teaching medium. Positive psychology and Process Drama both focus on the learner's strengths and potentials and what they can do, rather than focusing on their weaknesses. Process Drama for learning (including in the second language classroom) can enable teaching and learning to become more social and positive. Success in a drama can help develop the real "psychological capital" of the learner.

Forum Theater methods can offer a way of looking collaboratively and responsively at the intrapersonal difficulties of fictional characters in a distanced way. The characters' realistic difficulties are often linked to some form of oppression they have become victim to, such as bullying (Drama Unit 1). Forum uses theater and "simultaneous dramaturgy" to collaboratively help people to take actions, which might then positively change aspects of their real lives. However, using drama to directly deal with someone's real-life difficulties and problems is the domain of psychodrama, which is a specialist area professionally and requires training and accreditation. Language and/or drama teachers who are not trained and accredited psychotherapists and/or psycho-dramatists should stick with fictitious characters and safely distance their students by using fictional situations and roles.

Well-Being

Well-being can be considered from various perspectives such as individual, social, and economic (Prescott, 2010). The World Health Organization defines mental health as

> "a state of well-being, in which every individual realises his or her own potential, can cope with the normal stresses of life, can work productively and fruitfully, and is able to make a contribution to her or his community." (WHO, 2001d, p.1)

Another definition of well-being is *"optimal human experience and psychological functioning"* (Ryan & Deci, 2001).

Process Drama offers students a drama community and an imagined community within which they have opportunities to productively contribute. Any drama will also have characters in it that the students can become or can interact with. The well-being of characters in the drama can be explored and considered collaboratively. Each Drama Unit in this book provides opportunities for teachers to look with their students, at various characters' well-being and the ways they might be coping (or not) with their work, stress, emotions, relationships, problems, and dilemmas. The students might make their own connections with the mental health and well-being of the characters and can maybe find ways to support them. They might find that they are concerned about the well-being of Annie Edson Taylor (Drama Unit 6), who is risking her life to clear debt. They might feel an active concern for the well-being of the victim of bullying (Drama Unit 1). The students' attention in the drama can be intentionally focused by the teacher on characters' well-being, resilience, and self-compassion.

Working through the medium of drama can be helpful to a student's own sense of well-being, as they will be working socially, collaboratively, productively, enjoyably, and their personal contributions are contributing to the whole. Some components of well-being such as optimism, positive emotions, relationships, engagement, meaning and life purpose, vitality, self-determination, self-esteem, and resilience are particularly important for learners' own well-being and can be helped to develop through the drama process.

It is important to reduce the levels of student stress when they are learning and using a second language. Stress can have a detrimental effect on the well-being and inhibits communication and learning. As many students will find learning through drama novel, entertaining, and enjoyable; it can help reduce stress levels. Students can feel more relaxed and be able to deal with a character's issues and problems, as they are happening within the safety of a shared, imagined world. Students may empathize with characters and realize that they too may have similar problems in their own past, present, or future lives.

Resilience

Resilience is important for maintaining well-being. It enables people to "bounce back and carry on" when faced with very stressful and difficult situations in life. According to the American Psychological Association (2014),

> [r]esilience is the process of adapting well in the face of adversity, trauma, tragedy, threats or significant sources of stress—such as family and relationship problems, serious health problems or workplace and financial stressors.

Resilience is one of the key constructs of positive psychology. It can be focused on the following areas: social skills, internal protective strengths, and the ability to maintain positive emotions (Carbonell et al., 1998). It reflects an individual's mental capacity for adapting and recovering after experiencing life challenges (Ryff et al.,1998). According to some scientists, resilience requires negative emotional experiences or adversity (Block & Kremen, 1996). Resilience is the reason why some people continue to reach their goals, maintain well-being, and achieve positive personal and professional outcomes, despite the negative situations that they face (Yates & Masten, 2004). Being resilient does not mean that a person does not experience difficulty or distress but that they are able to overcome it well enough to "bounce back."

The drama units in this book each place students in role together, in situations that would be (or have been) stressful, tragic, threatening, and/or traumatic for people in real life. Drama builds individual and collective belief in the

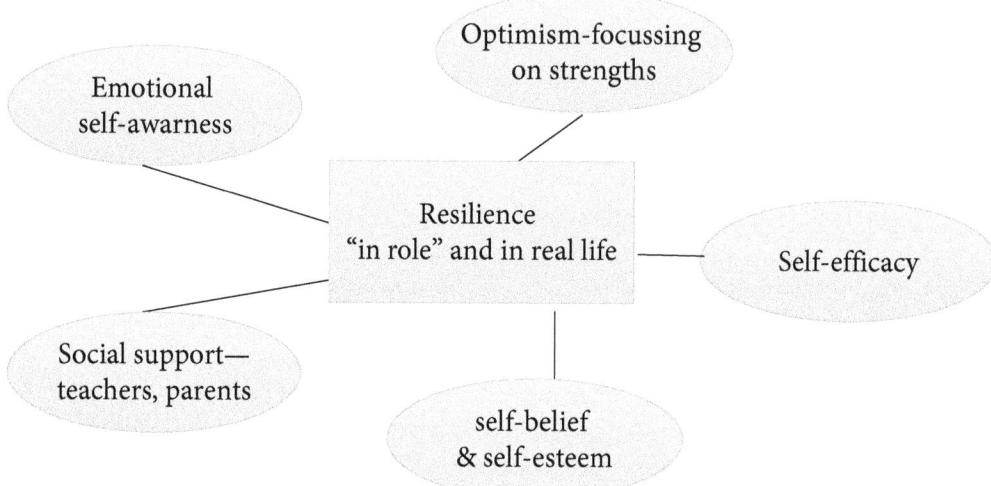

Figure 2.2 The elements of resilience.

fiction and places the students in tense situations together, in which they can use, demonstrate, and reflect on human resilience.

Resilience is built through focusing on one's strengths, developing self-efficacy, self-belief, and self-esteem. Resilient individuals also draw their strength from their social networks. The availability of social support reduces anxiety and stress. After all, it feels easier to face adversity when you have a close friend that you can rely on. When you have strong social support, you don't have to use as many of your own personal resources to cope with adversity. Drama develops resilience "in role" and in real life (see Figure 2.2).

In real life, becoming more resilient is a gradual process and a person may go through much emotional stress and distress on the way. Becoming more resilient involves changing behaviors, thoughts, and actions in ways that can be learned and practiced. Process Drama can provide contexts and scenarios, within which resilience can be exhibited, practiced, and reflected on. As characters in role the students can together be given opportunities to solve problems, cope with work and relationships challenges, and move on positively from negative events and feelings. The active, imagined experience can be helpful to them when they need to be resilient in their real lives.

Language teachers who also focus on teaching resilience can make a positive difference to their students' lives, and levels of resilience can also have a significant impact on students' academic performance and on teachers' ability to cope with stress (Galazka, 2019, 2020). High levels of resilience help lower student's levels of anxiety, distress, and depression and this can lead them then to perform better in education generally and certainly in SLA.

Traditional language teaching methods are heavily focused on memory and recall. This approach is less helpful for developing students' resilience than learning and using languages within personally, socially, and emotionally supportive "live" contexts such as those that Process Drama can provide. Schools and teachers can stimulate and support students to become more resilient through the ways in which they teach and respond to students, especially as individuals. Just one teacher can make a significant difference to a student's resilience, well-being, and life pathways. Werner and Smith (1989) found that "[a]mong the most frequently encountered positive role models in the lives of the children outside of the family circle, was a favorite teacher."

Process Drama for language teaching helps students to develop supportive relationships with each other and with their co-participating teachers in role. The students have opportunities to work to their combined strengths, collaboratively, as they complete any tasks that the drama requires. They are working together but can be developing resilience individually through doing so.

Drama focuses on what Heathcote described as "[a] man in a mess" (Heathcote & Bolton, 1995). In role, the students explore challenging human situations, conflicts, and/or dilemmas together. The teachers and students are dealing with real-life problems together, albeit within a dramatic fiction. They can be using a target language to do this. Both in and out of role, the language students and their teachers can discuss a character's resilience and can practice resilience within dramatic contexts. This can in turn have a positive impact on the actual resilience of the students in their real lives.

Mindfulness and Self-Compassion

The inclusion of mindfulness principles, theories, and practices in education has been growing steadily in recent years. "Mindfulness means being present here in non-judgemental way" Jon Kabat-Zinn (1994). It can help students to calm down, focus their attention, and extend their spans of concentration. This can have a positive and lasting impact on their interactions with other people, in school, and in life. Mindfulness can help students personally, socially, and emotionally to become more self-aware, self-regulated, self-compassionate, empathetic, and communicative.

In the language and drama context, practicing mindfulness can become a routine at the start of the lesson as preparation for learning. Mindfulness exercises often require the students individually to use their imaginations, to be still and "in the moment," to imagine themselves in another place, to imagine they are exploring something with attention to all their senses, and so on. Drama lessons often start with activities that support the students to focus deeply and "center" themselves before shifting together into "drama mode."

Students can learn the vocabulary connected with practicing mindfulness and discuss the advantages and challenges of various exercises. They can also do this with various drama exercises that are intended to aid them in terms of concentration and focus. Mindfulness will be more effective if teachers practice it themselves with the students and if it is embedded in the school culture. Again, there are parallels with Process Drama as teachers often join in alongside pupils as they shift into drama mode and willingly distance themselves from the distractions of the real world around them.

Mindfulness is closely linked to the concept of self-compassion (introduced by Kristen Neff). It is about being kind and understanding to oneself when dealing with personal failure and not being over-critical or judgmental. This is not the same as self-pity, egocentricity, and selfishness. Self-compassion enables the individual to see how their own experiences are connected to what other people also experience. Drama too helps individuals to feel less isolated and more at ease with themselves.

Three components of self-compassion:

1. Self-kindness
2. Common humanity
3. Mindfulness (see Neff, 2011; Gilbert, 2009)

The concept of self-compassion is helpful in education. Students of foreign language often hear their critical inner voice telling them how poor they are at a language and this can inhibit them and make them feel embarrassed when speaking that language. There are activities that can help language students become kinder to themselves, for example, they can write a positive and supportive letter to themselves, "in role" as their best friend. Within dramas, students (and teachers) can model and practice being kind "in role," for example, when a character in the drama is personally and emotionally struggling, they could be invited to walk through a corridor of voices (made up of two lines of students, facing each other). Each person in the line says something positive, kind, and restorative to the character as he/she passes by.

Sustainable Development Awareness—A Global Skill for the Twenty-First Century

We need to ensure that we and our students have lifestyles and behaviors that ensure a sustainable future for our planet and for those who will live on it after us. Education for sustainable development goals include ensuring "inclusive and quality education for all and promoting lifelong learning opportunities for all" (SDG 4). Sustainable development issues need to become embedded within teaching and learning for students to learn about climate change, disaster risk reduction, biodiversity, poverty reduction, and sustainable consumption. It requires participatory, interactive teaching and learning methods that motivate and empower learners to change their behaviors and take positive actions for sustainable development. Sustainable development cannot be achieved through only technological solutions, political decisions, or economic tools. It requires all people across the world to positively change the way they think and act. Learning for sustainable development needs to happen in interconnected, social contexts and the ways students learn about its needs to reflect this.

Language education and drama can separately and together offer a common platform for exchanging ideas, discussing issues and problems, generating actions, and contributing to solutions. Drama and SLA can enable and support the global exchange of information and the generation of ideas and actions concerning sustainable development. Many course books contain topics linked to sustainable education, and Process Drama can bring such topics alive and enable the students to think together, have meaningful dialogues, and act together. Meaningful dialogues and actions linked to sustainable development issues can happen within the drama, which can raise the students' awareness of the issues and possibilities, then leading toward taking positive, real-life action after the drama. It is worth remembering that among today's students are the leaders of tomorrow.

3

How to Introduce Process Drama to a Class and What is Expected of the Teacher?

Chapter Outline

SETTING UP A "DRAMA CONTRACT"	41
DRAMA CONTRACT	43
ARE THEY READY TO START?	43
PLANNING A DRAMA LESSON	44
OPENING ACTIVITIES	44
PAUSING THE DRAMA	45
MOVING THE DRAMA ON	45
DEVIATING FROM THE LESSON PLAN	45
SHARING OWNERSHIP AND RESPONSIBILITY	46
WORKING TOGETHER IN GROUPS	46
SETTING TIME LIMITS	46
CLOSING THE LESSON	46
AFTER THE LESSON	47
NEXT LESSON	47

Traditional teaching methods used in language education place teachers as the "givers of knowledge" and the students as the passive recipients. Traditionally, the students sit still, listen, and recall on demand the knowledge that has been delivered to them. However, teachers who use Process Drama for language teaching have a more flexible, social, and holistic approach. Not everything is best taught through drama. Language students will also need to gain knowledge of a language and linguistic skills in other ways but once acquired, the language can be used and applied meaningfully within many socially and emotionally engaging contexts that Process Drama can provide. During Process Drama, the students will be stimulated and motivated to think, talk, respond, interact, and sometimes write for a range of compelling reasons, purposes, and audiences (using the target language).

Teachers can decide whether and when to work in role alongside their students. They can step in or out of these imagined worlds, whichever is going to be most beneficial to the drama and the students' learning. The teacher will have clear learning intentions and linguistic goals for their students and can structure and guide the drama toward the students achieving these. The teacher will be working alongside the students, both in and out of role at various times as a facilitator, enabler, and mediator of the drama experience and of the learning.

Setting up a "Drama Contract"

Teachers need to ensure that certain protocols are in place before embarking on Process Drama with a class as the students may not be familiar with this way of working. The protocols can be referred to as the "Drama Contract." Even classes that are familiar with learning through drama will sometimes need to be reminded of it during lessons. A drama contract benefits from being negotiated with the class, rather than just given to them. A "Drama Contract" is a set of talk and behavior protocols that everyone agrees to abide by during the drama. It will be most effective, when negotiated, agreed, and co-owned with the students, rather than simply imposed on them by their teacher, and it could be negotiated and prepared with them in a second language.

Students bring different personalities, levels of confidence, and linguistic competence to the drama. When entering a Process Drama, they need to understand what is expected of them in terms of talk protocols and behavioral expectations. This will help them feel secure enough to contribute and respond in role without fear of embarrassment or derision.

Second language learners will probably have participated in drama games, acted out some scripted scenes, and maybe improvised short role-play scenarios before encountering Process Drama. Most students will be keen to take part in a Process Drama but some may initially be a little hesitant. Most students will probably be thinking about drama as acting and theater performance, rather than immersing themselves together in role within co-created imagined worlds. Of course, theater also involves working in role but it is usually scripted, directed, and rehearsed for an external audience. Process Drama is closer to socio-dramatic play. It does make use of some theater conventions and techniques but to focus and deepen the learning for the participants. It reawakens and uses dramatic play skills in more targeted and aesthetic ways.

When setting up a Drama Contract, teachers can begin by asking students what they think drama is. Their answers are likely to include "plays," "acting," and "theater." Students are less likely to say that drama is "working in role together" or "pretending" unless they have already experienced Process Drama as a way of working. The teacher should begin by accepting all reasonable definitions of drama before moving on to say, "Now I'm going to ask you three questions. If your answer to a question is 'yes', then just raise your hand."

The teacher then asks:

"In real life ...

1. Do you ever pretend to be someone else? (*Character*)
2. Do you ever pretend to be somewhere else (in a different place or time)? (*Setting*)
3. Do you ever pretend that something is happening when it isn't really?" (*Plot*)

The teacher might then go on to say, "So, let's agree to call that 'Drama'. Drama is happening, when we are all pretending to be someone else, somewhere else, with something happening that is not really happening."

This will resonate for most students, as most students will have pretended to be someone else, somewhere else, with something happening (that was not really happening) but they might not have considered it as "drama" before. Most will recall having played dramatically as young children and many might still pretend sometimes (although they might not wish to admit this publicly). It is interesting for teachers to see which students do not raise their hands to any of the three questions. A few students might never have "pretended" and this might indicate that they are on the autistic spectrum and might require some targeted support during the drama. Process Drama is an inclusive activity and the whole class should take part. All students need to be included in the drama and must stay present but without being put under pressure to contribute. No students should be just sitting out and watching, as this creates an external audience and changes the whole class dynamics. It also makes it harder for them to then re-enter the drama. The deal is that everyone stays present in the drama throughout and no one will be forced to contribute and put "on the spot." Anyone can signal "pass" at any time and remain silent if they wish. This also helps reduce the fear that some students may have acquired, of being made (rather than invited) to perform in front of classmates.

The teacher can then go on to ask, "What stops a 'pretend' from working? What *messes* up a 'pretend'?" Responses are likely to include "It doesn't work if someone laughs at you or says that the drama is not real," "It does not work if someone is messing about and not taking it seriously," and so on. The teacher can move on to positively reframing the students' suggestions as the basis of the "Drama Contract" by saying, "So what can we all agree that *we will do*, which will help us to keep the Drama going?" The teacher can reframe, record, and maybe add to the student's suggestions, ending up with a contract they have contributed to. Below is an example of a Drama Contract, which is framed positively, rather than being a list of "don'ts."

The students, having helped shape the Drama Contract, co-own it and will be more inclined to comply with it. The teacher must take account of the contract too and model a serious approach to working in role. This will help the students to feel more secure about talking and reacting in role too. If the teacher is embarrassed or reluctant to work in role, then some students are more likely to feel uncomfortable about doing so.

Drama Contract

We all agree to

- try to keep pretending that what is happening in the drama is real;
- try and stay in role during the drama;
- never deliberately say or do something that risks breaking the pretend for others;
- try and contribute if we can and only signal "pass," if we don't feel able to contribute;
- not comment if other people "pass";
- accept that what someone in role says and does belongs to the character and not to the person who is pretending to be that character.

Process Drama needs everyone working together in a serious and committed way to help achieve deep engagement and deep learning. Once a drama lesson is underway, if any students are not complying with the drama contract, then they may need to be reminded of it by fellow students or the teacher.

Are They Ready to Start?

The following "Drama Balloon" game can be used to help teachers to judge the readiness of a class to enter an imaginary situation together. The teacher should join in too with this activity.

The Drama Balloon

The teacher stands in a circle with the class. The teacher explains that he/she will pick up an imaginary balloon. The teacher then mimes doing so and explains,

> "This is the Drama Balloon. Soon, I am going to throw this balloon to someone in this circle and they will catch it and then throw it to someone else. We are going to see if everyone in the circle can get a turn at catching this balloon, without anyone dropping it. We all need to try to keep "the Drama Balloon" in the air. We will only be able to do this if we all work together and concentrate. Let's try."

This activity relies on whole class concentration, collaboration, and a willingness to accept and mime using an imaginary object. Once this activity has been carried out successfully, it can then be referred to as an example of the "Drama Contract" in action. The teacher can say, "Well done, everyone. We all managed to keep 'The Drama Balloon' up in the air together. At any moment, anyone could have stopped us all believing in that balloon but because we worked as a team, we managed to keep the 'pretend' going." During a subsequent drama lesson, the teacher might simply say, "Balloon" as a quick way of reminding a student to keep to the Drama Contract.

Often teachers use drama games and/or warm-up activities at the start of a lesson before moving into the main drama. Drama games can be an effective way of getting the students focusing and working together at the start but do not need to be used routinely to start the lesson. Drama Games are usually fun, familiar, and are rule bound and keep a teacher and class well within their comfort zone. However, they can become too time-consuming in relation to their worth and need to warrant the time they take within the lesson overall. Teachers can select and adapt drama games to fit closely with the lesson's theme and the intended learning. They might choose and adapt games that introduce and/or practice vocabulary (maybe linked to actions) that are of direct relevance to the Process Drama lesson.

Planning a Drama Lesson

A drama lesson can be about anything. The teacher knows what their language students need to learn, understand, and practice, and the drama can provide the stimulation, motivation, and contexts for doing so.

Second language teachers planning a drama will want to provide opportunities for their students to talk in different registers and styles for different purposes and audiences. The students may need to learn some relevant vocabulary before the drama, to recall and practice using it, within the meaningful context of the drama.

When planning a drama lesson for language learners, the teacher's learning intentions will influence their choice of drama strategies and their positioning within the lesson. Teachers will gradually become increasingly knowledgeable about what each drama strategy offers and more adept at selecting the one that will be most helpful for achieving their intended language learning outcomes.

It sometimes helps if students have some pre-existing knowledge of the subject matter of the drama. This is particularly true for historically based drama lessons, such as "The Great Fire of London" (Drama Unit 2). It will be easier for language students to be in role seventeenth-century London residents, if they know something about seventeenth-century London life and the streets of London before the drama starts. They could already have been asked to search for authentic images and historical information online before the drama starts. They might then be asked to look at the images and information and share one thing that they have noticed (and maybe noted). When they share this with the class, they can be asked to start their sentences with the referential sentence stem, "I notice …." Everyone can have more than one turn but no one should offer two sentences in a row. The teacher can then change the sentence stem to " I wonder … " or "I know … " Different sentence stems encourage different ways of thinking and enable students to practice corresponding sentence patterns.

Opening Activities

There is no right or wrong way to start a drama lesson. The teacher needs the students' full attention and ideally wants the class in a state of "relaxed alertness." Warm-up activities and drama games are not always going to be necessary and are often overused, taking up too much of the lesson time. They can often be amended to link with the lesson's theme and can be used as an active way of learning and practicing vocabulary and phrases that the students might then choose to use within the subsequent Process Drama.

A useful and adaptable opening activity that can be linked to the theme of any drama is "Move if …." (see Drama Unit 3).

Move If …

The class stands in a circle with the teacher. The teacher calls out a sentence, starting with "Move if …." Whenever the sentence is personally true for someone, they move across the circle. The teacher then calls out the next sentence starting again with the sentence stem "Move if …."

This activity can be used to help students make personal connections with the theme of a drama from the outset. The teacher just needs to have a few "Move if … " sentences ready, which connect with the lesson theme.

"Teacher in Role" (see pages 55–57) is often used as a highly effective and compelling way of starting a Process Drama. It gets the students' attention immediately and enables them to meet characters and get information of importance early in the drama. The teacher in role can stimulate and intentionally provoke responses to help get the drama underway (e.g., Drama Unit 6).

Pausing the Drama

Once the drama is underway, teachers can pause it whenever they think it will be helpful to do so.
For example:

- to invite individual or shared reflections "in the moment" about a character's thoughts and/or actions
- to stop and consider "in the moment" or situation from different characters' viewpoints
- to gather and share what the students are all thinking "in role" at this moment in the drama
- to move the drama forward in time (as it has already achieved what the teacher intended)
- to move the drama back in time to recall or review afresh what has already taken place in the drama
- to invite the students to predict what might happen next in the drama (gathering alternatives)
- to enable the teacher to offer additional information or vocabulary at an appropriate moment
- to change the drama strategy in order to move the drama time-wise or in a different direction

Moving the Drama On

Teachers will need to judge how long each section of the drama should last. Some drama strategies have a clear start and finish, for example, a Conscience Alley lasts for as long as it takes a character to walk through it. Other strategies can carry on until the teacher decides to halt them, for example, Passing Thoughts could continue until no one speaks any more thoughts or the teacher decide to halt the activity if they think that enough thoughts have been shared. Teachers will also need to judge when to halt whole class improvisations. They will be guided hopefully, not by the clock but by how deeply the students are still engaged and whether the improvisation is still developing or not.

Teachers can halt improvisations by freezing them and then using the "Teacher as Storyteller" strategy, gathering and narrating back to the participants what has just been happening within the improvised scene, for example,

> The air was filled with thick smoke. Terrified people were rushing from their houses. The fire was spreading fast. People were clambering down ladders. They were carrying children and heavy bags. Carts were piled high with furniture and other belongings. Soon, the streets were so crowded, it was difficult to get move along them.

Recounting a scene back to its participants (as a narrative) is an opportunity for the teacher to

- model the use of familiar and new vocabulary "in context,"
- model talking, "like a writer,"
- acknowledge and recount the students' contributions to the scene,
- demonstrate the shared ownership of the drama,
- focus students' attention and reflection on selected aspects of the scene, and
- "round off" a section of the drama.

Deviating from the Lesson Plan

Teachers may choose to deviate from their lesson plan to make use of a learning opportunity that has unexpectedly arisen during the drama. They can always return to their lesson plan afterward. For example, in a drama about the Great Fire of London, a student might unexpectedly steal something from a passing cart. Seeing this, the teacher might decide to freeze the action (Freeze Frame) and invite the class to voice aloud the thief's thoughts or those of an eyewitness to the incident.

Sharing Ownership and Responsibility

The teacher and class co-create and co-own the unfolding drama and have shared responsibility for sustaining it. Some days, with some classes, a lesson might not be going particularly well. The reason for this might not always be immediately obvious to the teacher. The teacher can always pause the drama at any point and talk about the drama with the students out of role, maybe seeking their comments and feelings about the drama and even trying out one or two of their activity/strategy suggestions, once they are experienced at Process Drama. Even when the drama is going well, the teacher might simply say, "I'd like to hear some of your ideas about where we might go next in this drama. What or who do you want to know more about at the moment?" Students' ideas and their feedback to teachers can be constructive, professionally helpful, and illuminating. It also helps raise the self-esteem and confidence of the students if they sometimes have their status raised in this way.

Working Together in Groups

Process Drama is often referred to as "whole class drama," although at times during lessons the students will be working individually, in pairs, and/or in small or large groups.

If students always select their own working groups, then they tend to keep working with the same people. This can too easily result in the same students taking the lead each time and the others following. Varying the constitution, size and configuration of working groups will shift the group dynamics and help share opportunities and responsibilities more equitably.

There are activities that teachers can use if they want to change the size and constitution of groups.

Get into Groups of …

The students move about the room, changing direction from time to time. After a while, the teacher calls out a number. The students should immediately get into groups of that size with the people who are standing nearest to them. Any students remaining (not in a group) stay present. The activity is repeated several times until the teacher is satisfied with the groupings for the next activity/drama strategy.

Changing groupings in this way is more subtle and usually less problematic than a teacher just instructing some students to leave their groups and join other groups, which can cause feelings of resentment.

Setting Time Limits

It helps if the teacher sets clear time limits for certain activities and then sticks to them. For example, when a class is involved in "Small Group Playmaking" or devising a still image, some groups may spend too long talking about and planning what they might do, instead of moving on and putting their ideas into action. If they know the teacher's deadlines are strict, they are more likely to complete a drama task on time. If a group is not ready to present or perform their scene or image, for example, then the teacher can offer them the option of going ahead with it anyway or "passing," rather than the students expecting to easily get additional time to complete the task.

Closing the Lesson

Sometimes a Drama Unit takes several lessons to complete. It helps if teachers draw each lesson to a reflective close, rather than abruptly halting it just because time has run out. A "summing up" or "rounding off" activity can help make the drama and the learning deeper and more memorable. Drama strategies can be selected that require the students to pause and think back through the lesson to consider what they now know (or think they do) at this point in the drama. They can communicate what they know and think to themselves and/or others in various ways, as listed below.

Thought Walk (Individually): Ask everyone to move around the room, sleepwalking and talking, as their character at this point in the drama.

This was how Shakespeare revealed Lady Macbeth's state of mind and inner thoughts.

Small Group Playmaking and Performance Carousel (Groups of four): Ask them to devise and perform in slow motion, the dream of a given character, at this point in the drama.

Dreams allow what is troubling a character to come to the surface and communicate itself, often vividly, symbolically, and repeatedly. The dream scenes can each be performed twice in a row and seamlessly.

Voice or Thought Collage (Whole Class): Ask everyone to think back through the drama and select just one sentence that they spoke (or thought) during it. Ask them to stand close together and close their eyes. The teacher joins in and starts by speaking aloud their sentence. Then, the students can join in as and when they wish, speaking their sentences (or parts of sentences) aloud. Anyone can speak out whenever and as often as they wish. A collage of voices (and/or thoughts) will start to build up, which should reach a crescendo, then gradually become quieter and end in silence. The students should stay silent and keep their eyes closed until the teacher tells them to open their eyes again.

After the Lesson

If a Process Drama is continuing over a series of lessons, then the teacher may wish to use and develop it in various ways between lessons. Most drama provides good opportunities for "Writing in Role," either during the lesson itself or between lessons, for example, writing characters' diary entries, letters, notes, emails, texts, in role.

The drama often stimulates the students' interest and curiosity about its subject matter and leads then into researching and enquiring further between lessons (often online). For example, they might decide that they want to search for images or accounts of the Great Fire of London or find out more about Samuel Pepys's diaries, and so on. This would involve them in Content Language Integrated Learning (CLIL). They could search out further relevant vocabulary between lessons, which they can then practice using in the next lesson as well as revise some of the vocabulary from the previous lesson/s to use again.

Next Lesson

The final activity of any lesson can sometimes be repeated as the starting activity for the next lesson. This is a quick and effective way of getting students back into the drama, rather than the teacher reminding the students about what happened in the last lesson or asking them what they remember. Repeating an activity from the last lesson brings the drama alive again and the students will be literally "re-membering" it.

Part II

Process Drama Strategies and Conventions for Use in the Second Language Classroom

Chapter Outline

WHAT ARE DRAMA STRATEGIES AND WHAT DO THEY OFFER?	50
HOW SOME DRAMA STRATEGIES STIMULATE AND ENABLE ASPECTS OF SPOKEN LANGUAGE	53
HOW SOME DRAMA STRATEGIES CAN PREPARE STUDENTS FOR WRITING	54
DRAMA STRATEGIES	55
TEACHER IN ROLE	55
MANTLE OF THE EXPERT	57
STILL IMAGE, FREEZE FRAME, TABLEAU	59
SMALL GROUP PLAYMAKING	60
PERFORMANCE CAROUSEL	61
CONSCIENCE ALLEY	62
THOUGHT-TRACKING	63
PASSING THOUGHTS	64
VOICE AND THOUGHT COLLAGES	64
THOUGHT WALK	64
RUMORS	64
EAVESDROPPING	65
HOT-SEATING	66
ROLE ON THE WALL	68
TALKING OBJECTS	69
ACTIVE STORYTELLING	70
WHOOSH!	71
ESSENCE MACHINE	71
SOUNDSCAPE	72
SOUND COLLAGE AND VOICE COLLAGE	72
FORUM THEATER	73

What Are Drama Strategies?

Drama strategies are well-established techniques used when making drama and theater. Many drama strategies can easily be learned and used by second language teachers to focus the students' attention and stimulate and scaffold their thinking, inter-thinking, talk, and action within linguistically engaging contexts.

Groupings and Configurations

Some drama strategies involve the whole class working as one group (e.g., Conscience Alley), whereas others require students to work individually in pairs or in groups of various sizes and configurations. Some drama strategies use a "whole class circle" configuration in different ways, maybe with the students entering and using the space in the circle (e.g., Whoosh!) or sometimes crossing the circle and speaking (e.g., Passing Thoughts) or interacting with the people standing either side of them in the circle. Some drama strategies require the class to stand in two straight lines facing each other (e.g., Conscience Alley). Others require the students to cluster together in one or two large groups (sometimes with eyes closed, e.g., Voice Collage). The various configurations and different ground rules that apply to each strategy will have an impact on the frequency and type of interactions that each enables and requires.

In a language classroom, some students might feel inhibited about speaking a second language in front of their teachers and peers. In drama, they are often working in supportive groups with their attention on the drama. This can help students to feel less linguistically exposed. Process Drama and the drama strategies it uses help give students a sense of belonging to a group and give opportunities for them to work supportively and collaboratively together. Some drama strategies provide opportunities for students to focus on verbal and nonverbal communication, to practice using the target language with different accompanying gestures, movements, and postures.

Multisensory Stimulation, Response, and Recall

There has been a strong focus on second language teaching, on providing students with multisensory input and experience. Some drama strategies require students to focus and use their senses, individually and in various combinations. Some are visually focused (e.g., still image), others are auditorily focused (e.g., Voice Collage), and others are kinesthetically focused (e.g., mime). When actively participating in drama strategies, the students' thoughts, words, and emotions are being tagged across their memories in multisensory, embodied ways, which make the associated learning and language more memorable and retrievable. Students will remember an acquired language more easily if it is also associated with physical actions and emotions and is learned within meaningful contexts. Students will have different learning preferences and will receive and generate messages in various ways. The more senses that are stimulated, the greater the likelihood that students will remember the associated linguistic structures and vocabulary.

Freedom and Constraint

Some drama strategies enable students to move around the space freely, whereas others require them to remain static or move in slow motion. Some require verbal turn-taking and others require spontaneous verbal responses. Some involve improvised or rehearsed speech, whereas others demand silence (and even "blindness" with eyes closed).

In second language education, teaching can be very static, and many students find it difficult to sit still, concentrate, and listen for long periods. Drama strategies can be used individually as "talk frames," which enable students to get up out of their seats, leave their desks, and work more physically and interactively, as well as linguistically during a language lesson. The drama strategies can also be used to build a drama with varying linguistic demands being made of them.

Some language teachers might initially feel nervous or hesitant about using drama as a teaching and learning medium. However, once they have become familiar with even a few drama strategies, they will start to feel more secure about using them as they are great pedagogical tools, which are clear, structured, and rule bound.

Teachers can experiment with drama strategies and take ownership of them, honing them for their own teaching and learning purposes, rather than safely sticking to repeating the same few. Drama strategies in the hands of different teachers can become a support or a constraint depending on how the teacher uses them. For example, a teacher who is worried about class behavior might overuse certain strategies that keep the students physically still (Freeze Frame) and only able to contribute a few words when it is their turn (e.g., Eavesdropping). This may keep the teacher feeling safe but is not very enabling for their students if overused. Teachers need to try out many strategies and sometimes try out using a strategy in a different way to discover what happens when they do. Also, ringing the changes makes it more likely that teachers will get and keep the students' full attention.

Teachers need to keep their attention on what the students are doing and saying during the drama activities to inform and guide the teacher's own response and to help them guide the students toward achieving language learning objectives.

Teachers as Co-participants

When teaching through drama in the second language context, the teacher can join in and support the students linguistically by offering and using appropriate vocabulary in context and by modelling the appropriate grammar and pronunciation, either in or out of role. The teacher in role can model the use of familiar and unfamiliar language and respond in the drama and "in the moment" to whatever the students are doing and saying in role. The teacher may be working in role for parts of the lesson and will simultaneously be thinking both inside and outside the drama, as they are always the language teacher. The teacher will be deciding when to step into role or out of role and when to pause the drama. This could be to ask a provocative question at a particular moment or to offer some relevant vocabulary and/or linguistic structures. The teacher will also be deciding when to pause the drama to introduce the next drama strategy.

By sometimes taking part in various strategies, the teacher can contribute ideas and model language and behaviors (see Table 2.1).

Name the Strategies and Talk about Them

Teachers should use the names of the drama strategies that they are using with the students. They will then not need to explain repeatedly what each strategy requires of them and the students can start to talk about the strategies themselves, both to the teacher and to each other. The students will also become familiar with the different configurations and ground rules for each strategy. Teachers might even discuss with their students sometimes which strategy they would like to use next and why. This can help them to build their knowledge of drama-specific vocabulary and help deepen their understanding of drama. Being invited to suggest drama strategies sometimes can give the students a sense of

Table 2.1 The shifting role and function of the teacher.

Eavesdropping	The teacher is usually the person who is supposedly overhearing the conversations.
Conscience Alley	The teacher is often in role as the character is walking along the alley.
Passing Thoughts	The teacher often stands in the center of the circle to represent the character that the students pass by and talk to (or about).
Voice or Thought Collage	The teacher usually joins in as one of the voices and can contribute some words and phrases that they want the students to hear and remember.
Forum Theater	The teacher usually takes on the role of "the Joker," acting as the intermediary between the actors and the "spect-actors."

co-ownership and shared responsibility for the drama. If a drama strategy in a lesson is not working as well as the teacher had hoped for some reason, then students (if asked) can often explain to a teacher where the problem lies for them. Such a discussion can of course happen using the target language in a relevant and purposeful way.

Selecting Strategies

When teachers start using drama strategies, they tend to stick closely to the ground rules. It is a little like learning to cook and initially sticking to a recipe. As time goes on and we grow in experience and confidence (as cooks and as teachers), we might start to get a little more adventurous and confident about adjusting the ingredients in various ways and comparing the outcomes.

Teachers can select whichever drama strategy they think will be most helpful to the students for practicing and developing their language skills as well as for developing the drama. They can adapt and experiment with any drama strategy to make it fit well with their learning and language intentions and their own students' needs.

Drama strategies can be used to help the students build and get to know characters, create settings, explore situations, and develop narratives. They can also enable students to delve into and contribute to a character's thinking and speech to immerse themselves in imagined situations and moments of tension, to problem solve and decision-make together within the fiction, to pause and reflect, to explore various ideas and possibilities, and to consider situations and outcomes from different viewpoints.

Drama Strategies as Thinking Frames

Any drama strategy can each be considered as a type of "thought organizer." They can work as thinking frames, stimulating, scaffolding, and enabling students' thinking and enabling it to be shared and communicated in different ways. The actual names of some drama strategies are clearly connected with thinking, for example, Thought-tracking, Conscience Alley, Passing Thoughts, Thought Walks, and Thought Collages. Teachers can tailor their instructions with the intention of stimulating and scaffolding specific types of thinking and/or inter-thinking skills and changing students' thinking patterns. Changing instructions and adapting strategies can also help to stimulate deeper thinking and inter-thinking between students and their teacher.

We are used to organizing our thoughts on paper in various ways, for example, lists, columns, notes, mind maps, jottings. These are all graphic organizers. In drama we can also organize and communicate our thinking in physical, vocal, aural, visual, and aesthetic ways. Students can be given opportunities to use and/or combine both approaches. What is said by participants during a drama strategy can then be recorded in some way. For example, a Conscience Alley consists of two columns of voices (which are often speaking a single character's thoughts). Whatever the voices say can be written down in two columns afterward. Whatever is learned about a character by hot-seating them can be recorded afterward using a Role on the Wall. The configurations used during the various drama strategies can be replicated afterward on paper (see Resource Sheets, pages 132–141).

Various drama strategies can be used to build up, slow down, hold still and/or dismantle significant moments in a drama, giving opportunity and time for deeper thinking, inter-thinking, and talk (in and/or out of role). Different strategies also offer students varying lengths of time for thinking and talking.

Drama Strategies as Talk Frames

Talking provides a way of exploring, communicating, and developing thoughts and ideas. It also is a way of giving information, offering viewpoints and opinions, persuading, reasoning, negotiating, arguing and explaining, questioning and challenging, speculating and predicting, evaluating, synthesizing, and concluding.

The names of some drama strategies directly link to speaking and listening, for example, Rumors, Voice Collage, Eavesdropping, and Talking Objects. Teachers can select strategies and tailor their instructions to enable the students to practice different types of talk for different purposes and different types of audiences.

Strategies can be adjusted to intentionally stimulate and require different types of talk. For example, a character could be walking through a Conscience Alley and the teacher might ask the students to

- speak that character's thoughts aloud as he/she passes by, or
- speak about the character as he/she passes by, or
- speak directly to the character as he/she passes by.

When the students devise a short scene (using Small Group Playmaking), they might be asked to

- play it naturalistically with characters speaking to each other, or
- recount (in either the first or third person) what is happening in the scene as it is being presented, or
- speak the character's inner thoughts during the scene.

The talk protocols will vary for drama strategies, for example, Eavesdropping and Conscience Alley allow students to speak only when the listener passes by, whereas Improvisation and Voice Collage allow students to decide whether and when to speak.

Different drama strategies require and enable students to talk in groups of differing sizes, configurations, and constitutions. Some strategies only invite spontaneous speech. Small Group Playmaking gives opportunity for first improvising and then rehearsing speech before performing to others. Mime removes any verbal expectations.

How Some Drama Strategies Stimulate and Enable Aspects of Spoken Language

Hot-Seating	Enables relevant questions to be asked of characters
Conscience Alley	Enables opposing viewpoints and opinions to be voiced and heard, giving practice at arguing, explaining, and justifying the pros and cons of a particular course of action to a character
Small Group Playmaking	This involves talking together out of role first to plan the scene collaboratively. Then, rehearsing and presenting speaking in role and in turn, using appropriate language registers for different characters within various situations and contexts, as well as communicating information and various character's thoughts and emotions, audibly and fluently, using appropriate tone and volume.
Improvisation	This gives opportunities for practicing speaking and responding "in role" spontaneously to each other in linguistically appropriate ways within shared, imagined contexts and situations.
Collective Role	This requires students to listen carefully to each other and compose sentences orally, which fit seamlessly with each other's verbal contributions to sound as if it is the same person speaking. To ensure continuity this requires everyone to listen carefully to the content, register, and tone of what is being said.
Thought Walks	This strategy can be used to enable a student's "in role" speech to flow without interruption and with no one listening.

Drama Strategies and Listening

Drama strategies also set various expectations and protocols for listeners. The names of some drama strategies directly link to listening, for example, Eavesdropping. Most drama strategies require the students to actively listen and will not proceed successfully if they don't. Voice Collages, Sound Collages, and Soundscapes are often carried out with eyes closed. Speaking and making sounds "blind" helps the students to focus on listening attentively as it removes visual distractions.

Using Drama Strategies as Writing Frames

During a drama, the teacher can set up various reasons for writing in role and can work as a writer, alongside the students. As a co-writer in role, the teacher can model, guide, structure, and contribute to the writing. The teacher in role as a writer can model "talking like a writer" and can invite the students to help with various writing tasks for different purposes and audiences. For example, the teacher could be in role as their fellow journalist or as their newspaper editor. As their newspaper editor, the teacher would have a higher status role in the drama and can set clear and high expectations of the students, who are in role as writers. The teacher as editor has the professional knowledge and authority and can question and inform them about their writing style and linguistic choices, maybe directly teaching and improving their journalistic writing in role. Alternatively, the teacher might decide to have the same role status as the students and be in role as a fellow journalist of equal status. Or, the teacher could give themselves a lower status role than the students', for example, as a novice journalist who needs their help. The students could be the experienced journalists (adopting the "Mantle of the Expert") and they may need to explain to the novice journalist what is expected of them and how they can improve their writing. This provides a temporary, interesting, and productive role reversal of the usual teacher/student hierarchy of the language classroom.

The teacher can also model "talking like a writer" of other types of writing. For example, when the teacher narrates the drama back to the students "as if" they are a storyteller (Teacher as Storyteller), they are modelling a narrative form that will be helpful for the students to hear, especially if they will be writing up the drama as a story afterward.

All drama strategies can be used as preparation for students as writers. The drama and the strategies can get students thinking of themselves as writers and talking like writers before they actually start to write. The drama generates ideas and content for the writing and the drama strategies can be used to help shape the thinking and talk toward writing. They can be used to introduce and share appropriate vocabulary, phrases, sentences, dialogue, questions, in context and through the drama process itself.

How Some Drama Strategies Can Prepare Students for Writing

Small Group Playmaking	This creates episodic scenes which can be written up as paragraphs or chapters. The scenes usually contain dialogue which can then be written with prose or as a short play script. Newsworthy scenes can provide subject matter for newspaper reports, eyewitness reports, and diary entries. The students watching the scenes can do so as "eyewitnesses" and can then write an eyewitness recount of the scene.
Performance Carousel	A series of scenes that are performed in sequence can be used like a storyboard. The scenes can each be turned into paragraphs or short chapters. Together they can form an extended narrative.
Hot-Seating	What a character says can then be scripted. Questions can be listed for the character and answers noted and then notes about the character put onto a Role on the Wall. What a character says when questioned can be used to inform a character study.
Talking Objects	Talking Objects involves the students talking as, to, and with objects and this can lead directly into writing with personification. Objects in scenes are eyewitnesses so can talk and write about scenes they are in. They can also talk and write about characters (who might see, touch, own, steal, carry, or discard them).
Conscience Alley	The two lines in a Conscience Alley can speak to, with, or about the character passing between the lines. The different lines can voice opposing viewpoints to persuade the character to take (or not take) a particular course of action. This yields the pros and cons, which can be written in columns and used as the basis for then writing a reasoned argument.
Rumors	This activity generates many plot possibilities and generates much dialogue that can be selected from, if/when writing the drama as a narrative later.
Improvisation	This generates many ideas and much dialogue, which can be used if/when writing the drama later as a narrative. It also enables characters and situations to be developed, prior to writing then within narratives and play scripts.
Voice Collage	This can be used to focus attention on generating and listening to keywords and phrases that everyone offers. The words that each person repeatedly said during the Voice Collage can be jotted down afterward and then written within a class poem (for example).
Collective Role	This can be used to create together a character's thoughts and speech, which can then be used for composing a written monologue.

Thought-tracking	This strategy is used to give voice to a character's thoughts, which can then be used when writing about a character. The thoughts can be jotted down and visually organized first (in thought bubbles or around a Role on the Wall).
Thought Walk	This strategy requires a student to walk around talking to themselves in role. They are improvising and giving voice to their character's internal thoughts. This generates a monologue that can then be written up.
Still Image	A chronological series of images is like a storyboard. Each image can have a paragraph written to go with it. The combined paragraphs together are a written version of the story and the still images are now illustrating it. The images can be formed as the accompanying paragraphs are read aloud.

DRAMA STRATEGIES

Teacher in Role

Teacher in Role is potentially the most powerful and effective of all drama strategies. It places the teacher and the students alongside each other in role within the unfolding drama and can enable the teacher to model appropriate ways of talking and responding and can help raise the levels of linguistic expectation and challenge.

The teacher might decide to take on various roles at different times during the same lesson, enter and leave the same role several times during a lesson or change roles from time to time. Whenever a teacher decides to work in role, they should have a clear purpose for doing so and know what they want the role to achieve, both for the students' language learning and for the drama. Teachers should also be ready to step out of role once their role has achieved its aims or when the teacher thinks that a different drama strategy would now be more beneficial.

Introducing "Teacher in Role" to a Class

A teacher should never just slip into role without any warning with the students puzzled about what on earth is going on. Before a teacher goes into role they need to tell their students they are about to do so.

A teacher in role is not expected to be a great actor but must work in role with seriousness, commitment, and purpose. It can be helpful if the teacher practices a short Teacher in Role with the class first, especially if it is the first time that the class has worked with their teacher in role. The teacher can tell the class that he/she will just be in role for a minute or two first, as a sort of "warm up." The teacher can then step out of role after just a minute or two to check briefly with the students what their feelings and responses to this way of working were before then stepping back into role and sustaining it for longer.

Make It Clear, Whether You Are In or Out of Role

There are various ways in which the teacher can make it clear to the students when they are entering or leaving a role. For example, the teacher could simply say, "I am going to walk to the edge of the room and when I turn around and come back, I will then be in role as a policeman." Alternatively, the teacher might use an object or simple piece of costume to signal that they are in role, for example, "Whenever I am holding this pen, I am Samuel Pepys, and whenever I put the pen down again, I will have come out of role." Or, "Whenever I put this shawl around my shoulders, I am Martha and whenever I take it off again, I will have stopped being Martha." Or, "Whenever I am sitting in this chair, I am the Mayor of London."

Using objects or simple pieces of costume can not only signal when the teacher is in role. It can be used as a way of letting others take over a role for a while, for example, "Whoever sits in this chair will become the Mayor of London for a while." Or, "We will pass this pen around and whoever is holding the pen will now be speaking as Samuel Pepys." Or, "I am going to pass Martha's shawl around and as you hold it, you become Martha and can speak aloud what she is thinking."

Know the Purpose and Function of the Role?

Teachers must be clear about what they want to achieve through the role. For example, the teacher might use a role to:

- get and hold the students' attention;
- model language register, vocabulary, structures, grammar, and tone, appropriate to the character, situation, and context;
- model role appropriate gestures and behaviors with and/or without speech;
- stimulate and provoke thinking, inter-thinking, talk, and action;
- give knowledge, information, and messages in role to move the drama on;
- gather information from the students in role;
- introduce problems and dilemmas that raise the stakes and build tension levels;
- seek the advice and help of the students in role, altering the usual teacher/pupil relative status for a while;
- commission the students in role, to use their enquiry skills, to gather information, complete tasks, make presentations, and deliver projects for imaginary external clients.

A single Teacher in Role might serve several of these purposes. For example, if the teacher is in role as a people smuggler's agent, then they are functioning as an intermediary between the students in role as refugees and the people smuggler. The teacher in role can offer some information and raise the tension level by getting impatient and avoiding answering some of their questions. In role, the teacher can gather information from the refugees and build the tension further by stressing the payment deadline and hurriedly trying to close the secret meeting for fear of being discovered.

Use Roles of Differing Status

Changing the type and status of the teacher's roles during a drama allows the usual teacher/pupil dynamics to apparently shift for a while and this can be revealing and enabling for students and informative for teachers. The reality is always that the teacher remains in control of course, as they can step out of any role at any time and can pause or stop the drama whenever they wish.

High Status Roles: There will be times when a high-status role will be the most helpful. This might be for the teacher to give information and to organize and direct actions and tasks from within the drama. If the students are interacting with a teacher playing a high-status role, it can give them opportunities to practice speaking formally and precisely to people in various high-status positions. For example, the teacher could be in role as the king and the students could be talking to him as Pepys (in a Collective Role). As Pepys they will be respectfully trying to persuade the king to order the Mayor of London to knock down people's houses and create a firebreak.

Teachers should avoid consistently giving themselves a series of high-status roles. This sometimes happens because a teacher feels insecure about handing over more responsibility for the drama to the students and the teacher wants to remain overtly "in control." This does however reduce the linguistic and dramatic opportunities for the students, which imagined status shifts can provide.

Low Status Roles: When teachers are willing to take on a low-status role in the drama, then the teacher is giving the students more responsibility and a sense of empowerment. For example, if the teacher in role is trapped inside a burning building during the Great Fire of London, then the students in role as other Londoners escaping will need to decide whether to try to rescue the trapped person or put their own lives at risk. The decision lies with the students but whatever they decide to do, the teacher can ensure that they are given an opportunity in the drama to consider and reflect on the consequences of their action or inaction.

Equal Status Roles: Sometimes the teacher and students will be in roles of equal status. For example, the teachers and students might all be Londoners who live in the same street, responding to the news that their homes are going to be demolished to create a firebreak. The teacher can feed in information, comments, thoughts, and provocations as "one of them."

Intermediary Roles: If the teacher decides to go into role as a messenger, then they can introduce problems that create tension without taking any responsibility for the information that they bring. The messenger is often an intermediary between authority and the community in a drama. As a messenger, the teacher can carry welcome or unwelcome, expected or surprising, calming or provocative information to and from the authorities. As a messenger, the teacher can insist that the students in role speak and/or write clearly as their messages will need to be accurately relayed. The messenger can listen carefully to their grievances and opinions, either in a neutral way or in a biased way, taking either the side of the people or the authorities. The teacher needs to decide which way of playing the role will be most helpful to the drama and to the students linguistically.

Coming out of Role

A teacher should only stay in role for as long as it takes to achieve the role's objectives. If it seems like the role is not achieving what is intended for some reason, then the teacher should come out of role and perhaps try a different role or else a different drama strategy.

Linked Writing Activities

1. Using a high-status role, the teacher can commission writing tasks to be completed by the students in role, for example, a newspaper editor asking reporters (the students) to write a report about a newsworthy incident in the drama.
2. When the teacher is in role with the same role status as their students, they can write with and alongside them as equals. The teacher and students can discuss and add content as "one of them," sometimes guiding the process, for example, the teacher and students might write one significant letter together to a character in the drama.
3. The teacher can take on a low-status role as someone who is unable to write and so needs something written for them by the students in role. It could be that the teacher in role has written something in their first language but needs it translated into a different language and the students in role are able to do this.

Mantle of the Expert

Dorothy Heathcote started to use the term "Mantle of the Expert" within her drama practice during the 1970s. The book she wrote with Gavin Bolton about Mantle of the Expert (1994) is entitled "Drama for Learning." Its subtitle is "Dorothy Heathcote's Mantle of the Expert Approach to Education." In the foreword to this book, Cecily O'Neill writes, "Although mantle of the expert does not emphasise its dramatic roots, its purpose is the same as any effective theatre event. It engages the students both cognitively and affectively and requires them not merely to replay and repeat their existing understanding but to see the world afresh."

What is distinctive about Mantle of the Expert is that the students are working in role as "experts" and have usually got work-related tasks to do. Often they are being commissioned to do a piece of work by an imaginary client, and this is usually the teacher in role. The client often commissions work tasks that the students "as experts" may need to enquire about further and research in order to complete. The students will usually find that they need to access and acquire relevant information to be able to present their knowledge, ideas, and outcomes to the client.

Mantle of the Expert is often described and promoted as a form of "inquiry-based learning." The students will be deciding what they need to know and gathering real information to complete their work tasks successfully. Often the client gives the commission and then withdraws for a while. The teacher might decide to take on an additional role such as being the experts' secretary. This means the teacher can stay present and involved in a lower-status role that helps elevate and maintain the students' higher role status and supports them in their "expert" work.

Heathcote intentionally did not actually tell students directly that they were "experts." She spoke to and responded to them "as if" they were experts and the students treated each other as such. The "mantle" of the expert was bestowed upon them and raised her expectations of them. Being treated as experts raises their self-esteem, confidence, and competence. They are being places in a position that requires them to listen well, have and share ideas, talk respectfully, plan and work collaboratively together as/with a team. They need to do all this to be able to complete the commission.

Feeling "expert" can be highly motivational for students and lead to them making a greater effort, which in turn can result in higher-quality outputs. The students know they are not truly experts and that they are working within a dramatic fiction but the sense they have of raised status and responsibility is real. They will often be working with others on tasks that experts do work on in real life, for example, planning a Holiday Centre and writing to a planning officer (see Drama Unit 4).

Heathcote kept students in their expert roles over several lessons and often many weeks. The tension in a Mantle of the Expert–based drama lies mainly in completing the task and meeting the client's needs, for example, "Is this proposed layout going to satisfy my client?" "Will the council agree to this plan?" In contrast, most Process Drama lessons have the dramatic tension lying outside work-related tasks and in more emotionally rooted contexts and situations, for example, "Will the border guard catch us?" "Will the bully pick on me next?"

Heathcote practiced and promoted Mantle of the Expert as an immersive, cross-curricular approach to learning, years before online learning started happening and being expected, in classrooms. Nowadays, online learning and Mantle of the Expert link well as a form of inquiry-based learning. For example, if the students are commissioned to design a holiday park (see Drama Unit 4) then they might need to go online and visit the Websites of some real holiday parks, read about what they offer customers, study and compare their design layouts, look at photographs and maps, read real reviews and advertisements, and so on. If they are asked by the client to draw a plan and also draft a letter for him to send to the planning officer, then the students might need to find and read some real examples of planning letters and applications to make their letter seem authentic in terms of language, form, and layout.

Dorothy Heathcote kept the students in the role of experts when she used Mantle of the Expert. She explained the difference between Process Drama and Mantle of the Expert as an approach.

"If you do Process Drama, you can say to children, "Let's all compose photographs of homeless people." But you can't do that in Mantle of the Expert, because you can't become the homeless [people] you're studying. What you can do is identify with the homeless you are studying. You identify by drawing what you think the photographs looked like. And then, you can "stand up" the photographs you took, in order to decide if they go in the magazine. Am I talking sense? It's very subtle, and it comes from the state of mind. We deal with looking at the homeless. We deal with trying to understand. And we deal with publishing a magazine that enables us first to consider as many aspects of being without a home as we can. And they will publish after half-term their first edition of their magazine."

(Speaking at an NATD event at the University of Warwick, February 9, 2007, Unpublished)

By staying as experts throughout a drama, the students can be placed at, and maintain, a more objective, "cool," and safe distance from dramatic situations and events and it may be that they are engaging more cognitively than affectively and dramatically.

Process Drama practitioners sometimes use Mantle of the Expert more as one drama strategy, rather than as the whole "approach." They might ask their students to work in role as experts for part of the time but to also take on other roles in the drama too. In Drama Unit 4, for example, the students are in role as design experts for some of the time but at other times, they are in role as the villagers who are going to be affected by the experts' plans if they get approved by the council. In Drama Unit 2, the students will gain some knowledge about the Great Fire of London. Having been in role as Londoners in 1666, they could then be asked to change role and become museum curators, i.e., museum experts. The teacher could become the head of museum services and commission them to design and plan an exhibition about the Great Fire of London. This would give them the opportunity to use and apply the knowledge that they have gained already during the drama. They might need to carry out further online research, as museum curators, perhaps finding out about some real objects that survived the fire and which museums currently house them. As museum curators they might wish to draft emails and to borrow artifacts for the (imaginary) exhibition that they are planning. They could also be commissioned to make a short film about "The Great Fire of London," which visitors to the museum can watch. They might be asked to design an information sheet or exhibition booklet for visitors to their exhibition, and this may need to be translated into more than one language.

Mantle of the Expert, used either as a drama strategy or an "approach," works well with CLIL for language teaching. It can provide employment-related contexts, content, and tasks with reasons for using language for specific purposes. It helps if students acquire some of the relevant, work-specific language in advance of the drama lessons. They can then practice using the specific language during the drama.

Still Image, Freeze Frame, and Tableau

In drama there are different ways of arriving at a "still image" (a static picture). "Freeze framing" is the simplest and most immediate way of acquiring a still image. Strictly speaking a "Freeze Frame" results when the movement in a scene is suddenly halted and held still. The teacher can simply call out "Freeze" and the still image that results is referred to as a Freeze Frame. This can be likened to pressing the pause button when watching a film. Strictly speaking, it is not correct to ask students to "make" or "devise" a Freeze Frame, as it does not involve a "making" or "devising" process. A Freeze Frame just requires a quick, compliant reaction from the participants and physical control. It does not involve the participants in any planning process.

Students can on the other hand be asked to make or devise a still image that involves some planning. If they are devising a still image in pairs or groups, they might need to discuss and decide what they want to convey in their still image and how to do so. They might then try out some ideas and decide which to keep. Devising a still image involves them in speaking, listening, negotiating, planning, experimenting, evaluating, and making judgments together. This process is far more challenging than simply halting movement to get a Freeze Frame.

Still images can also be gradually built without discussion. Teachers can ask the students to enter the drama space one at a time and add themselves to a developing tableau. The tableau will be complete when the final person enters and holds their position. The image will keep changing slightly whenever anyone adds themselves to it. Those waiting their turn will be looking carefully and continuously reinterpreting the image, deciding when to enter and where and how they might place themselves within it.

Still images can be devised that are symbolic, for example, "Create a class tableau that conveys, 'Secrecy'" or "Create a tableau that communicates this character's conflicting thoughts and emotions."

Recreating Real Images

Students can be asked to replicate existing images, using actual paintings, etchings, photographs, film frames, statues, tapestries, stained glass windows, and so on, as the stimulus. Having studied the image first, the students can be invited to enter the drama space one at a time and recreate the image with everyone becoming some part of it. They might become the people in the image or else an inanimate object in it or part of the natural or man-made landscape. The teacher can ask the students to speak one of two sentences as they get into position, perhaps just saying who or what they are and giving one piece of additional information, for example, "I am the tall, church tower. From here, I can see crowds of people on the riverbank, trying to escape the fire." This activity requires language students to place themselves within a fictional setting and/or situation and to contribute just a few sentences verbally.

Adding to and Extending a Real Image

The students can be asked to study and then add to an existing image, for example, by entering and becoming additional people or objects in it. Again, they would say who or what they are as they get into position and just speak a sentence or two in role.

The teacher can also ask the students to extend an existing image. The actual image could be projected and the students in turn could place themselves just outside it, to the left or right. It is "as if" the artist had painted more, using a wider canvas.

Fast Forwarding, Rewinding, and Slow Motion

A still image often represents a moment in time. A series of still images can be created and sequenced to represent several moments over time. A sequence of still images results in a type of living storyboard. At the end of a drama, recreating and presenting key moments from the drama as still images can be a way of helping the students to revisit moments and reflect on them. The images can also be presented in sequence with the students asked to provide an accompanying narrative recount of the drama.

A series of still images can also be used as a way of finding out about key moments in a character's past. For example, the photograph album of a character could be created with each group making themselves into one photograph that has the character within it. The photographs can then be presented/performed in a chronological sequence (see Performance Carousel).

Adding Thoughts, Speech, and Captions

The characters within a still image can be invited to speak a sentence. They might be asked to speak to another character in the scene or speak an inner thought aloud as the character (see Thought-tracking). If the image was in a comic or a graphic novel, it would be rather like adding speech bubbles or thought bubbles to the image. The groups could be asked to say out loud an appropriate caption for their image.

Inviting Interaction with the Image

The participants within a still image can be asked questions by students who are not in the scene, that is, "hot-seated" in situ. Anyone who is questioned will answer in role from within the image (see Hot-Seating).

Sculpting Images

A further way of creating a still image is by sculpting or molding another person, "as if" they are a statue. One person is the sculptor and their partner is their compliant lump of clay. The clay can be physically and silently molded through the sculptor's touch or the sculpting can be done with the sculptor only allowed to give verbal instructions to their partner (and not use gestures). This activity demands more of the sculptor than the clay, so it is a good idea to let both students take a turn at being the sculptor and the clay.

Dramas often provide characters and events, which could warrant the creation of a commemorative statue, sculpture, stained glass window, or painting. For example, at the end of the drama, an expert sculptor (or group of sculptors) could be commissioned to design (and become) a commemorative statue of an important character or moment in the drama. This will require them to reflect on the drama and select what they most want to convey and create it in an embodied way.

Making Contrasting Images

Students can be asked to devise two contrasting images, one depicting "the moment before" and the other depicting "the moment after" a key incident or event in the drama.

Contrasting images can also be created and used in drama to show "the reality" and "the ideal" in relation to a character's situation. This is a technique used in "Image Theater" and is based on the work of Augusto Boal (1995) and is sometimes used by drama therapists when helping people unpick situations and overcome some form of oppression (such as bullying).

Some Teaching Points

- Moving around the room at the start of a lesson and "freezing" whenever the teacher calls "Freeze" can be a useful warm-up activity to get everyone's attention before starting the drama.
- The teacher needs to emphasize that a still image must be held very still. They should not accept "still-ish." It helps if the teacher demonstrates "very still" by getting into a still image, holding it very still and then melting it.
- It can help if the teacher makes links with types of still image, for example, "I want you to be as still as a photograph."
- Discourage students from getting themselves into physical positions that cannot be easily held still. If they do, then tell them they should relax and reposition themselves (rather than wobble about or topple).

Small Group Playmaking

There are times when the teacher will ask the class to divide into groups and devise a short scene during the lesson. The groups will usually perform their scenes to the rest of their class. They should be told whether the scenes will be performed before they devise them.

In a Process Drama, the main purpose of groups making and performing short scenes will be to help to deepen and communicate the students' learning. The students need to be able to self-manage the devising and performing process to a deadline. Small Group Playmaking is usually just one part of the overall lesson.

Groups of 3–5 students usually work well with time hopefully for each group member to contribute to the planning and performance process. The teacher will decide whether the groups can self-select their members (sometimes) or whether the teacher will get involved in deciding. Students benefit from working in groups of various sizes and constitutions, as the group dynamics will then be altered each time. There may be times when the teacher invites the group to appoint a scene director from within their group or the teacher can choose one (to equitably share such opportunities).

A teacher might ask the groups to all work on the same or similar scenes, for example, "Create a short scene that ends with the moment that you decide to escape and leave your home." Each group will inevitably devise a different scene, although the drama task is the same for all groups. The students will then watch each other's performances from the perspective of people who have been involved in the same devising task and are co-participants in the same whole class drama, that is, not an external audience.

The teacher will sometimes give each group slightly different tasks. For example, each group could be asked to devise and perform a scene from different parts of the story at different points in time. The scenes can then be performed in chronological order and together they become like a dramatic, episodic storyboard. For example, one group might create a scene that shows Beowulf setting sail to help the Danes; the second group might create and perform the scene of Beowulf's arrival. The third scene might be feasting in the great hall of Heorot, and the fourth scene could be when Grendel is killed, and so on. When students are asked to recreate key scenes from the whole drama, it requires reflective thinking and inter-thinking and is often used toward the end of the lesson.

Another variation of Small Group Playmaking involves the teacher asking the groups to prepare a short scene that a character (the teacher in role) will be walking into. The group scenes are then played in turn and the teacher enters each scene, one after the other, and improvises in each scene with the group before moving on. The opening of the scenes has been prepared but the rest of the scene is improvised once the teacher enters in role. For example, the students may be in role, as villagers within their various homes. The teacher could knock at each of their doors as a fellow villager, who has a petition that they want signed. The petition will be sent to the council and is demanding that the council reject planning permission, for a new holiday center near the village (Drama Unit 4).

The teacher might decide to ask one group to perform their scene and then invite comments and questions to characters in it before moving on to the next group's performance. Alternatively, the teacher might let all the scenes be performed first, one after the other seamlessly, with no comments, questions, or discussion until the end. The teacher could ask for a seamless performance of all the scenes first and then they could all be performed a second time with opportunity then for comments and questions to the performers after each scene.

The scenes that students create will all be contributing to the overall narrative and detail of the drama. Scenes usually consist of moving images and dialogue, which can be recorded in various ways. A devised scene can be written up afterward as a short play script. The scenes could sometimes be filmed and an accompanying narrative (or various, different narratives) can be added later. The accompanying narratives could be spoken by characters who are in the scene and have a particular viewpoint or by an eyewitness or a detached narrator.

Performance Carousel

When groups have created still images or short scenes, they often are asked to perform them for each other. Teachers who are not familiar with Performance Carousel might just ask one group at a time to perform, and the dramatic atmosphere and continuity is easily lost between each group's performance. Performance Carousel however offers a way of bringing the groups images or scenes together sequentially and seamlessly, resulting in one continuous class performance of the images or scenes. This drama strategy is also referred to as Performance Wave (Neelands).

Performance Carousel has some simple ground rules. When a group performs in a lesson, it is important that the rest of the class give the performers their full attention. The teacher can introduce Performance Carousel by asking all groups to imagine that they are all on stage at the same time. They can then be asked to imagine that they have an imaginary audience in front of them. Although only one group at a time will actually be performing, the imaginary audience can see all the groups on stage. The imaginary stage curtain will go back and an imaginary spotlight will shine on one group at a time. The groups left in the shadows must remain still and silent to avoid distracting the imaginary audience's attention from the performing group. There is no real spotlight or stage or audience but when the students are imagining that there is, it will help to keep everyone's attention on the performing group. From the moment the teacher signals that the imaginary curtain is going back, one continuous, collaborative class performance is in progress.

Group 1 will move together in slow motion into their starting position and then freeze (resulting in a Freeze Frame). They hold the Freeze Frame still for a few seconds and then bring the scene to life. At the end of their scene, the performing group freeze again (resulting in a second Freeze Frame). They hold their Freeze Frame still for a few seconds before slowly melting the image and ending up seated and still on the ground. While one group is melting down in slow motion, the next group will be rising up in slow motion. So it continues with each group in turn rising, freezing, performing, freezing again, and melting until the last group finishes and is seated and still on the ground again.

It can help the dramatic atmosphere and continuity to have a piece of music or a soundscape playing during the continuous performance as it helps blend the scenes.

A Performance Carousel can be continued, enabling groups to have several turns at presenting their images or scenes in different ways. For example, the second time round, the students could speak the thoughts of the characters, instead of their direct speech. Or, the second time round, the groups could just silently mime the scenes, while the teacher talks like a storyteller, improvising a narrative commentary about what is happening in each scene. Having heard the teacher model an accompanying narrative, the students could be asked to talk or write a narrative recount of their scene.

Conscience Alley

In various countries, a Conscience Alley is sometimes referred to as a Decision Alley, a Thought Tunnel, or a Corridor of Voices. This drama strategy enables two lines of students to voice the conflicting thoughts of a character at a moment of indecision within the drama.

The whole class stands in two straight lines facing each other (about a meter apart). The character (who is often the teacher in role) walks between the two lines. As the character passes each person, they speak one of the character's inner thoughts. The two lines offer opposing viewpoints. One of the lines may be persuading the character to take a particular course of action and the other line dissuading them from taking it. For example, if the character is a man trying to decide whether to leave his family and go on a dangerous journey as a refugee, then one line of voices could be trying to persuade him to go and the other line trying to persuade him not to. A Conscience Alley provides an opportunity for language students to use antonyms and to practice verbalizing "pros and cons," which could then contribute to a reasoned argument or debate (presented verbally or in writing).

When setting up a Conscience Alley, the teacher's contributions and instructions can be altered with intent to vary the expectations and opportunities for their language learners.

1. The teacher can ask the students to speak *as* the character or *to* the character.
2. The teacher might only allow one sentence from each voice in the line or might linger by some students to allow them to say more.
3. The character can reply to some of the voices if they wish (enabling a comment or short dialogue).
4. A character might go through the Conscience Alley more than once (enabling further contributions from the voices).
5. The teacher might invite some of the students to take a turn at between the lines and listening to the voices (maybe with their eyes closed).
6. If the character passes between the lines more than once, they could do so with different instructions each time, for example, with the character just listening the first time but allowed to respond to the voices the second time. Or, as the character passes through second time, he/she could be asked to rush through, resulting in the voices overlapping chaotically (which can be suggestive of the character's inner turmoil).
7. Once someone has spoken and the character has passed by them, then that person could break away and go to the other end of the line. In this way, the two lines become continuous and the character can keep on walking with everyone getting several opportunities to speak. This works particularly well when the character in the drama is on a journey of some sort.
8. The two lines can be made to represent some part of the drama's setting, for example, the two lines could be an escape tunnel that the character is passing through, rows of trees, riverbanks.

9. There could be something significant at the end of the two lines, for example, a door that the character is approaching and might (or might not) then open or knock on.
10. The character could speak a few sentences at the entrance to the Conscience Alley or maybe at the end after they have passed through it. This allows the person walking through (often the teacher in role) to have the opening and/or final words in order to introduce and/or to round off the activity.
11. The teacher could preface the activity by speaking "like a storyteller" (i.e., demonstrating the use of simple present tense and third person) before and/or after the character walks between the lines. For example, "The man was deeply troubled. He could not decide whether to leave his family now or not. So many conflicting thoughts were echoing in his mind … " (then the character starts walking between the lines). And at the end of the lines the teacher in role could say, "At last, he knew what he was going to do. He had decided that … " Of course, the same activity could be carried out in the first person, "I am deeply troubled. I cannot decide whether to leave my family or not …," and so on.

Linked Writing Activities

1. Afterward, each student can write what they said to/as the character on self-adhesive labels. The labels can then be placed and organized within a large thought bubble. Alternatively, what was said could be jotted around a "Role on the Wall" (see Resource Sheet 17). Alternatively, Resource Sheets 9, 10, 11 or 12 could be used for recording the thoughts and comments voiced during the Conscience Alley. The "Role on the Wall" and the collective thoughts bubble can both be used as writing frames if the students go on to write a monologue for the character or their diary entry.
2. What the two lines of voices say can be jotted down afterward in two separate columns. The columns can be used as a writing frame to inform about writing an argumentative essay or a piece of persuasive writing.

Thought-Tracking

Thought-tracking enables the students to speak aloud their inner thoughts (in role), at a moment in the drama. The teacher can enable thought-tracking by freezing the action during a scene (resulting in a Freeze Frame) and then touching the shoulder of a character (or several characters in turn). When a character's shoulder is touched, the character then speaks their inner thoughts aloud "in role." The teacher can move around any still scene (frozen or devised) and touch the shoulders of several characters, who will each speak their inner thoughts aloud.

If teachers prefer not to touch the students on their shoulders, then the teacher could simply say that they will move around the frozen scene and that when he/she is standing next to any character, they should then speak their "in role" thoughts aloud.

This strategy enables students to practice and develop their metacognitive skills together, supporting inter-thinking in the second language classroom. It gives students time to consider some possible words and formulate possible sentences before it is their turn to speak them aloud.

Some Variations and Extensions

If students are studying a still image, they can be invited to speak the inner thoughts of a particular character in that scene, speaking "as if" they are that character. Alternatively, the teacher might freeze a scene and then invite some of the students who have been watching (as audience) to enter the scene, stand beside a character, and speak the character's thoughts. Several students could be invited to enter the still scene and one character could end up with several people standing alongside them.

Short group scenes can be replayed for a second time (sometimes in slow motion) with the characters now speaking their inner thoughts. Or, a short group scene could be replayed in silent slow motion with observers speaking the character's inner thoughts for them.

Often, a character in a drama (as in real life) has good reasons for concealing what they are truly thinking. Thought-tracking enables characters to reveal their inner thoughts safely before the drama continues. Thought-tracking helps build the students' shared knowledge and understanding of characters and enables them to discuss and analyze them together.

The same character (or characters) might be thought-tracked at several different stages in the drama. This can help to reveal how a character's thinking might have changed and developed over time.

Passing Thoughts

The students in role stand in a circle and a character from the drama stands in the center. The students in random order can cross the circle, each walking past the character. As they pass, they speak one of the characters' thoughts out loud. The teacher can decide whether they can only cross the circle once or may pass by the character more than once.

This activity can be adapted in various ways. For example, as they pass by the character the students could speak their own thoughts about the character, instead of the character's thoughts.

Resource Sheet 13 can be used for recording the thoughts afterward.

Voice and Thought Collages

The students stand close together (usually with their eyes closed). They create an improvised voice performance, based on what has been thought or said by one or more characters during the drama. Each person chooses their own "in role" words, phrases, parts of sentences, and/or whole sentences and repeats them spontaneously at intervals, contributing to the overall performance. Each person can choose to alter and play with the tone and volume of their voices during the activity. The teacher might give instructions that the thought collage should start in silence, build up slowly, reach a crescendo, and then gradually get quieter, ending in silence.

The voice collage could be carried out with eyes open and the teacher (or a designated student) could bring in different voices at various times, conducting the performance, as musical conductors do.

Thought-walk

Thought-walks give students an opportunity to speak an improvised monologue without being listened to. The students are asked to walk around the room, talking to themselves in role. They usually "thought-walk" as the character that they are in the drama but they could be asked to thought-walk as any character in the drama. Thinking aloud as characters helps deepen the students' engagement with and understanding of characters.

Thought-walking provides a low-threat opportunity for students to practice talking in a second language without others listening. They are all talking while on the move and this can provide them with a greater sense of privacy. Everyone walking around and talking in role with no listeners is likely to be less inhibiting for students who are shy and/or lacking in confidence.

The strategy can be adapted and used to help characters think about (and rehearse) what they want to say to someone in the drama, for example, someone who is about to leave their aged mother and become a refugee (Drama Unit 3) might thought-walk to rehearse in advance what they think they will say to her.

Once the students have been on Thought-walk, talking in role, without others listening, the teacher might then ask the students to stand still and speak aloud their character's inner thoughts as the teacher passes by each person in turn (moving on from Thought-walking to Eavesdropping). As the students will have already spoken their "in role" thoughts in their second language, during their thought walk, they will have already prepared themselves for what they might say when others are listening.

Rumors

"Rumors" enable the students in role to quickly generate and spread information, ideas, and opinions. The teacher can join in too. The teacher needs to explain to the students that they can either start a rumor that is true within the drama or can start a false but believable rumor. The students then move around, gathering, spreading, and embellishing various rumors.

The rumors might be about characters or about situations or events that either have already happened, are happening now in the drama, or might be about to happen, for example, "I have heard that our houses are going to be blown up, to stop the fire spreading" (Drama Unit 2), or "Have you heard that the people smuggler is having a meeting tonight? I think it could be a trap" (Drama Unit 3), or "I heard that she lied to the newspapers about her age. She looks at least 60 years old" (Drama Unit 6).

Rumors can be spread openly or furtively depending on the dramatic context. In role, they may not want to be caught talking, for example, spreading information about a secret meeting or escape plan. In this context, "Rumors" can help to build the dramatic tension. The teacher can place themselves in role as someone who must not be allowed to hear the rumors, for example, an official or spy. This adds to the dramatic tension.

The teacher might choose sometimes to use narrative storytelling as a way of leading into "Rumors," for example, "The rumors about Grendel's terrible killings soon spread. He was haunting the people's dreams and filling their daily conversations. Everyone had something to say about Grendel … " (then the teacher signals that "Rumors" can start).

This way into Rumors enables the teacher to model narrative storytelling and build the tension. The teacher can also use narrative storytelling as a way of rounding off the Rumors activity. Having joined in with Rumors the teacher might then ask the students to "Freeze!" The teacher can then recount aloud (as a narrative) what the students in role have been rumoring, for example, "Rumors were spreading fast. The people were terrified. Some people said that Grendel was … and others said that he had ….

If the students in role are not moving around the room enough and not talking to many people, then the teacher can call out, "Move on," or "Change," so that they spread rumors more widely and listen to more. The teacher needs to move around too and listen to the rumors because the teacher needs to know what the rumors are. They might be able to echo or use some of them as the drama develops.

If the teacher joins in, they can add authentic information. This can be particularly helpful during an historically based drama, for example, "Someone has just told me that the king has sent a message to the Mayor of London, ordering him to knock some houses down now to make a fire-break" (Drama Unit 2). Or the teacher could feed in a provocative rumor, for example, "That woman has got no intention of going over the Falls in her barrel. She just wants all the publicity" (Drama Unit 6).

"Rumors" should just last for a few minutes. It does not take long for many rumors to be created and spread. The teacher can stop the activity and then gather the students around to bring the rumors together. The teacher can stop the activity and then gather all the students together to continue talking in role about the rumors. The teacher in role can join in.

When teaching history through drama (e.g., Drama Units 2 and 6), the teacher may need to spend some time afterward out of role, ensuring that the students are clear about which rumors are true (or partly true) and which are false. A respect for historical evidence must be maintained. This differentiation of rumors can be carried out by a simple teacher-led discussion. Alternatively, the teacher can divide the room into three areas (like columns) and designate the three different areas as follows:

1. True rumors
2. False rumors
3. Partly true rumors

The students in turn then enter one of the areas and speak a rumor, which they think belongs in that area. This differentiation could also be done collaboratively in writing with each person writing a rumor on a self-adhesive label and then placing it into one of three headed columns on a whole class chart, headed "Rumors." The columns can be headed as "True," "False," and "Partly True."

Eavesdropping

Eavesdropping is a strategy that is sometimes referred to as "Overheard Conversations." It enables everyone to listen to a conversation in the drama, which is revealing something of interest or importance.

Often small groups will each prepare a scene. When the class groups present their scenes to each other, the teacher can move from scene to scene in turn as if they are eavesdropping. When the teacher is near any group, the conversation in the scene can of course be heard by everyone. When the teacher moves on, the group they leave behind falls silent. This enables everyone to hear what is being said in each other's scenes. Often the scenes are supposedly happening behind closed doors, for example, confidential conversations taking place inside people's homes after having met with the people smuggler's agent (Unit 3).

Eavesdropping can also take place with improvised scenes and with the whole class within a single scene. The teacher might freeze an improvised scene during the drama and tell the students that he/she will now be eavesdropping. Everyone must remain frozen (Freeze Frame) until the teacher walks near them. When the teacher is near, they carry on with what they were saying to each other until the teacher moves away and approaches others in role.

Eavesdropping can be a useful strategy to use in conjunction with Rumors. When "Rumors" has been underway for a minute or two, the teacher can freeze the scene and explain that he/she will now pass among them all in turn, listening to all the various rumors that are being spread.

Hot-Seating

Hot-seating is a popular and well-established drama strategy. It involves a character stepping out of the drama for a while to answer questions in role. Traditionally, the character being hot-seated sits in a chair (the hot seat). While they are in the chair, they are available for questioning. When the character leaves the chair, the hot-seating stops. The questioners are co-participants in the drama but during hot-seating, they are just questioners, who are asking their questions, out of role. This enables the character to answer the questions honestly and in confidence. Detached questioners who are not in role should have no reason or motive for trying to manipulate or steer the character's answers.

Hot-seating can happen at any point in a drama. It enables the whole class to focus on just one character for a while and can help them to get to know and maybe understand a character's thoughts, feelings, motives, opinions, and viewpoints. Characters being questioned can reveal information about themselves, their thoughts, and feelings. They can give information and offer their viewpoints about past events, situations, other characters, and relationships. Hot-seating the same character at different points in a drama can also highlight how that character has changed and developed during the drama. Answers arrived at through hot-seating a character are being listened to by everyone and can then be discussed, analyzed, and maybe recorded, for example, using a "Role on the Wall" (Resource Sheet 17).

Hot-seating does not always have to happen in a chair. The teacher could just freeze the scene and invite the class to ask questions of a character (or characters) in situ. A wide range of vocabulary and grammar structures can be practiced by language learners during hot-seating. The second language teacher can give instructions to the questioners that will help them to meet their linguistic learning goals. Several characters in a scene could all be asked questions in turn and this gives more learners the opportunity to practice responding in their second language. Alternatively, a character could be asked to step out of the scene and might ask for some linguistic support to answer questions. The character then can reenter the frozen scene after they have been questioned.

When a chair is being used as "the hot seat," then the teacher could say that anyone who sits in that chair will become the character for a while and can answer questions as the character. This means that everyone needs to listen carefully to each other because anyone who takes a turn as the character in the hot seat will need to ensure that the character's answers are consistent. Taking turns to answer as a single character provides L2 students with an engaging opportunity to practice listening for information.

It is also possible to hot-seat several people, who are all in role together simultaneously, as a single character; i.e., they are in Collective Role. The questions can be answered by anyone who is in the collective role but with no one allowed to answer two questions in a row.

A group of different characters in the same scene or situation can be hot-seated together, for example, a group of Londoners escaping the Great Fire by boat could be questioned as a group (Unit 2).

It can be helpful to hot-seat someone who knows another character well. For example, if the students want to find out more about Samuel Pepys, they could hot-seat his maid and/or his friend, rather than (or as well as) just questioning Pepys.

Language students are likely to be most motivated to use the target language when they are questioning a character that is of particular interest to them. The students can sometimes be asked who they would most likely to hot-seat and why. The teacher can then enable the desired hot-seating to happen.

As well as asking questions of characters in the drama, questions can also be asked of objects and settings as they can talk in a drama! A Talking Object in the drama might know its owner well, might have heard secrets and significant conversations, and might have been an eyewitness to various situations and events in the drama, for example, an object carried by a refugee on their journey could tell much if asked. Also, the wall can tell us what it saw and heard the bullies do to their victim (Drama Unit 1).

Often the teacher is in role as the character being questioned. If not, then the teacher will be facilitating the questioning and could join in and ask questions too. The teacher might enable a free flow of questions or might choose to restrict or guide the questioning in some way, maybe to avoid an ongoing dialogue happening between one or two dominant questioners and the character. The teacher might say beforehand, "No one is allowed to ask two questions in a row." Or, "No one is allowed to ask more than two questions." Or, "No one can ask their second question, until everyone has asked their first question." Teachers might ask students to ask a prepared question first and then move on to spontaneous questioning. It is important that all the students have an equal opportunity to ask the questions and not just those who are most linguistically confident and/or proficient at questioning in the second language.

The teacher might decide to pause the hot-seating for a short time to give the language students time to consider something that a character has just said. The teacher may also want to pause the activity to help the learners structure the questions they are asking and/or to suggest some more appropriate vocabulary.

The teacher decides when to stop the hot-seating or the character can be empowered to leave. It is generally better to finish, while the students are still highly engaged and still have more questions they want to ask, rather than keep going until there are no more questions being asked. Knowing there is a time limit or a limit on the number of questions they will be able to ask can get students to become more skillful at questioning and better at using the available time.

Improving the Questioning

Teachers may want to give the students time to formulate their questions before the hot-seating starts. They might come up with questions individually, in pairs, or in groups. Giving time and support to formulating questions in the second language will help improve the students' questioning and language skills.

The teacher is often in role as the character being questioned, so it can also be helpful for the teacher to know in advance, at least some of the questions they are going to be asked. The teacher could say, "Before I bring the character in, tell me some of the questions that you might want to ask him/her?" This also gives the teacher an opportunity to (if necessary) correct the language, grammar, and structures of the questions that the students are intending to ask.

Teachers might decide to restrict the number of questions that pairs or groups can ask. This means that they will need to consider their relative value. The teacher could say, "If you and your partner can only ask two of your questions to the character, which two will you choose?" The language learners will then need to use and apply critical thinking skills to decide together which questions to ask and how to best phrase them.

Language students can jot down questions, write the character's answers, and write their observations and thoughts about the person being hot-seated, before, during, and/or after the questioning. Reading, writing, speaking, and listening can easily be integrated during hot-seating. The language students might also take turns at being hot-seated and this will give them a reason for active listening and the opportunity to respond appropriately using the second language.

Teachers can ask their students to formulate specific types of questions for the character, as given in Table 2.2.

It is worth limiting the number of closed questions that can be asked, that is, those which just lead to simple "yes" or "no" answers. Deeper, extended answers are usually going to be more informative and revealing. Also, different types of questions give opportunities for the students to practice different question patterns using the target language.

Linked Writing Activities for Second Language Learners

1. Write the questions down in advance (Resource Sheet 8).
2. After hot-seating, complete a "Role on the Wall" for the character (Resource Sheet 17). This could be done in pairs or groups to stimulate discussion.

Table 2.2 Purposeful questioning.

Type of question	What it's used for	Example
Open	Inviting deeper thought and elaboration	What are you hoping will happen next?
Probing	Gaining more information and clarity	If the king is willing to see you, then what exactly will you say to him?
Recall	Gaining information that the character remembers	What did you notice in the streets that day?
Process	Gaining the character's opinion or viewpoint (as the character has processed information)	What do you think and feel about refugees?

3. Notes of the character's answers can be made and then referred to during a follow-up discussion. The notes can also be used if the students write a character description and/or character study later.
4. They can write a private diary entry as the character, following the hot-seating.

Role on the Wall

A Role on the Wall is a type of graphic organizer (Resource Sheet 17). The teacher can draw the outline of a character onto a large sheet of paper with the name of the character written at the top. The students can then be invited to freely write comments and notes about the character around the outline. This gets the students thinking and inter-thinking about a character and provides a useful record, which can be referred to and used in various ways. It gives an opportunity for recalling and sharing vocabulary that relates to the character and offers a focus for practicing the use of adjectives.

The teacher could place the Role on the Wall, on the floor, in the center of a class circle. The students can then enter the circle one at a time in random order and say aloud what they have written on their self-adhesive label and will now be placing around the character's outline. They can be asked to explain and justify what they are adding. The teacher could simply say that whatever they add must include the word "because," for example, "He is terrified because …." Or, the teacher might simply ask the students to simply place a single word each around the Role on the Wall, for example, "terrified."

The students' notes and comments can be written straight onto the big sheet of paper but self-adhesive labels give more flexibility and enable them to write their comments in advance of placing them. An advantage of writing their comments about the character on self-adhesive labels is that the comments and observations can be meaningfully moved around or even discarded as the drama progresses and more information about the character is revealed. A series of Roles on the Wall can be compiled for the same character at different points during the drama. They can then be analyzed in sequence and used to stimulate comments and discussion about the character's development over time. This can be helpful if the students are going to be writing about a character as the Roles on the Wall can then function as a type of writing frame.

Roles on the Wall can be drawn with just empty space around them for writing in, or the space around the character's outline can be divided into sections with a series of headings as shown below:

What the character thinks	What the character says	What the character does
What I know about this character	What I think I know about this character	What I want to know about this character
Positive characteristics	Negative characteristics	Interesting characteristics
What I have noticed about this character	What I feel about this character	What I wonder about this character

If a full body outline of a character has been drawn (rather than just an outline of the character's head), then the written comments and notes can each be placed in the most appropriate position on or around the body, for example, if the outline is of a refugee who is leaving behind him, someone that he loves, then a comment about this could be placed in the position of his heart or his feet.

Talking Objects

"Talking Objects" is a drama strategy that enables inanimate objects to talk in role. Objects in a drama can talk to themselves and to each other. They can also talk with characters in the drama and can be questioned by the students (out of role, as in hot-seating). Talking Objects has much potential for language teaching. The teacher can differentiate their instructions in relation to the required structuring, depending on the learner's level of linguistic proficiency, for example, " I am a mirror. I am looking at you." Or "I am a mirror that is looking down at you."

Objects in a drama

- can talk to (and about) themselves and each other;
- might be unobtrusive or else prominent and important at times;
- have a past and can reveal their personal narratives and those of their owner;
- belong to someone and can provide information about characters and have opinions about them;
- belong somewhere (maybe with a person or in a particular place);
- may have changed ownership over time;
- may have been on journeys;
- may have eye-witnessed situations and events and/or overheard conversations;
- may be symbolic, functional, treasured, dangerous, valuable, neglected, ignored, worthless, discarded, hidden, coveted, forgotten, stolen, damaged, inherited, have magical powers, and so on.

Students can physically become the objects within real images, such as actual photographs, paintings, sculptures, tapestries, and so on, or they can collectively create scenes and objects using only their own imaginations.

The teacher can show the students an image and tell them that every object within it has significance. For example, during a drama about Beowulf (Drama Unit 5), a painting of a Mead Hall can easily be found on the internet and displayed for the students. They can then be asked to one at a time, enter the drama space (which has now become the Mead Hall), and each place themselves as an object within it. They could be asked to enter as an object they have seen in the actual painting and/or could become another object that could plausibly have been there. As they get into position as the object, they can say just a couple of sentences in role. They need to say which object they are and give one piece of information about themselves, for example, "I am a long table. I am dented by knives."

Once a few students have entered the scene, the teacher can ask those who have not entered yet to stay at the edge and ask questions of the individual objects in the scene. They should address the individual object directly by name, for example, "Chair, tell me about the last person who sat on you?" The teacher might only allow one question per student (to encourage thoughtful questioning) or might say that every object needs to be asked at least one question and no object can be asked two questions in a row (thus giving all objects the opportunity to answer a question).

Objects within a setting are also able to talk directly with (or about) any characters whom they have seen enter or leave. So, when Beowulf is waiting in the hall to murder the monster Grendel, the objects there can talk among themselves (or to Beowulf) as he passes by them in turn, for example, "Grendel will kill you easily, Beowulf. Leave now!" The same objects, for example, candles, benches, shield, and table, can also answer questions later after Beowulf mortally wounds Grendel. They could give eyewitness recounts either verbally and/or in writing.

The Talking Objects strategy will work with any images and can be used in any drama. Images relevant to any drama can easily be found online, for example, the photograph of Annie Edson Taylor walking across a plank to safety (Drama Unit 6), photographs of refugees on journeys (Drama Unit 3), paintings of Grendel and Beowulf (Drama Unit 5).

Becoming Landscapes and Settings

The Talking Objects strategy can be extended to enable the students animate landscapes or settings. For example, they could become the houses in a London street (Drama Unit 2) or physically come together as the sea that Beowulf sails on or the marshes that the mortally wounded Grendel crosses (Drama Unit 5). Man-made and natural landscapes in a drama can be asked to talk to and among themselves and hot-seated by questioners about what they have seen, heard, experienced, and known.

The teacher can ask each person to enter the drama space as a feature of the landscape, say what they are and describe themselves, for example, "I am a heavy gray rock at the edge of this dangerous river. Strong currents swirl past me incessantly." Listening to various parts of the setting speak descriptively can be a helpful step toward asking language students to write descriptively as or about the setting. The teacher can vary the instructions they give to require different types of speech, knowing that they are preparing the students for a particular, linked writing task.

Personification

Talking as an object is a helpful step toward students writing as objects (personification). An object can give information and have a viewpoint. It can listen to characters and verbally recount conversations overheard. What an object says can be written up in the first person. This could be as an eyewitness account or a script. An object can also tell you its life story, which can then be written in the form of an autobiography.

Active Storytelling

Active Storytelling engages the whole class and is an enjoyable and fun way of practicing listening and physically responding to the language of narrative storytelling. It involves the students miming the story, usually as the teacher tells it.

The students will usually be standing in a circle or else each will be in their own space, somewhere in the room. The teacher reads or tells the whole story slowly, pausing from time to time for all the students to listen, comprehend, and then mime appropriately in response. This requires attentive listening as the language students need to respond promptly in a nonverbal way to the words and phrases in the story that they are listening to. They can spontaneously and freely, individually mime and physicalize any aspect of the story, for example, they might become objects, characters, landscapes.

Physically re-enacting the story of the drama through mime helps make the associated language and the story more memorable. The students might try retelling the story out loud again afterward, literally "re-membering" it again, as they speak. Just miming it again can help them to recall the associated words and phrases (and vice versa). Verbalizing the story can help lead them into writing the story. This fits with the approach known in SLA as Total Physical Response (TPR), which is often used when teaching young language learners. It is also similar in some ways to "Talk for Writing," a verbal and physical re-enactment approach, which has been promoted widely in the UK, first officially through the National Strategies and then developed and promoted further by Pie Corbett.

Active Storytelling is usually carried out individually but it can also be carried out in pairs (or even small groups) with the teacher telling the story. Miming collaboratively is more demanding, as response to the story needs to be quite spontaneous and no talking is allowed between pairs or groups of students who are miming collaboratively together.

During a Process Drama, the story is gradually developing. The students are helping to co-create the story of the drama as it progresses. They are often able to influence the direction of the drama and its outcomes. Therefore, if Active Storytelling is used with Process Drama, it is usually done at the end of the drama, rather than at the beginning. Active Storytelling is then being used to retell the story of the drama back to its participants in a sustained narrative form usually with the teacher as storyteller.

There may be times when the teacher wants the students to know the story of the drama in advance. For example, a drama lesson that is based on a Shakespeare play might use Active Storytelling at the start to help the students become familiar with the plots and subplots of the play first before moving on to using other drama strategies to help them explore the characters and situations within the play. Or, when teaching history through drama, the teacher might want the students to know the actual historical story (or parts of it) in advance of exploring it through drama.

Even when a drama is based on a play script or a true story, the teacher can still choose to only reveal the story gradually, rather than tell it all to the students at the outset. When the students don't know what will happen next in the drama they are engaged in, it helps keep their attention and helps build and sustain the dramatic tension. For example, if the students don't know whether or not Annie Edson Taylor will actually end up going over Niagara Falls in her barrel, then the tension will be more easily sustained.

Although Active Storytelling is usually led by the teacher, students can also become storytellers of the drama. They can tell the story of the drama (or parts of it) to each other in pairs and groups. One person can start to tell the story and the others can mime it. When the student who is the storyteller claps their hands, this signals that they are now passing the storytelling role on to someone else, who will continue telling the story. The storytelling can be passed on several times around the group until the story is finished. When storytelling, the students can be specifically asked to "talk like a writer."

Whoosh!

A "Whoosh" is a specific way of carrying out active storytelling with the whole class. The students all stand in a circle. The teacher tells the story. From time to time, the teacher signals to a few students that it is now their turn to enter the space and mime that part of the story. When it is their turn, the students need to respond spontaneously and collaboratively. Once they have mimed their part of the story, they remain inside the circle. The center of the circle will become increasingly crowded and the teacher then pauses then says, "Whoosh! Whoosh! Whoosh!" and gestures that they should all go back to stand at the edge of the circle again. Then the storytelling immediately continues with the next few students being invited back into the circle to mime. The teacher might need to clear the circle by saying and signaling "Whoosh!" several times. The activity continues until the story is over.

Essence Machine

The students stand in a circle. The teacher asks them to enter the space in turn (either in order or randomly) and repeatedly carry out an action with an accompanying sound. The teacher will ask for the sound and action to be connected to the drama in some way, for example, to a character, setting, or a moment in the drama.

Entering and becoming one moving part of an Essence Machine is often used as a warm-up activity, as a way back into an ongoing drama, from the previous lesson. For example, in a drama about the Great Fire of London, linked sounds and gestures might include someone repeatedly throwing of an imaginary bucket of water and making a "whooshing" sound each time they throw. Another student might mime repeatedly slamming and then locking the door of their house with a bang and a click each time.

The students waiting to enter will be looking at the sounds and actions already happening and deciding what to add, as well as when and where. They can decide whether to link their sound and action to someone else's or not. Words and/or sentences can sometimes be allowed in addition to (or instead of) sounds. So if someone is already repeatedly shutting and locking a door, another person might decide to enter and repeatedly touch that person on the shoulder every time the lock clicks and every time says, "Hurry up!"

When everyone has entered the space and is rhythmically making and repeating various sounds and actions, the teacher might start to control the speed of the machine, maybe using an imaginary lever. The sounds and actions can be speeded up, slowed down, and eventually brought to a halt.

An Essence Machine can also be gradually dismantled, one student at a time. There are various ways that the teacher might approach this:

1. The teacher signals to individual students that they should now grind to a halt (or freeze) and gradually all the students will end up still and silent. This can be done by the teacher pointing to students or touching their shoulders in turn.
2. The teacher silently signals to individual students that they should now remove themselves from the machine and return to the edge of the circle.

3. The students can dismantle the machine themselves in reverse order. Whoever entered last now leaves first and returns to the edge of the circle.
4. The students can dismantle the machine in the order that they entered. Whoever entered first now leaves first and returns to the edge of the circle.
5. The students can each leave the machine in any order they wish but only one at a time.

Soundscape

A soundscape is a series of sounds that are created by the students. They can be improvised or prepared and rehearsed. The teacher can ask for the sounds to connect with a drama that the students are engaged in.

Usually, the class is split into two groups. One half of the class will sit on the floor together with their eyes closed, and the other half of the class will stand around them to perform their soundscape. The seated groups are the "blind" audience and those standing on the outside are the performers who will be surrounding the listeners with sounds. The audience will keep their eyes closed until the performers signal that their performance has finished, for example, the performers can applaud themselves at the end so that the listeners know the soundscape has finished and they can open their eyes and applaud too. Then the groups swop positions and the audience become the performers (and vice versa).

Soundscapes can be created for various scenes and settings, for example, a busy street, on board a ship, a feast, a school playground. The sounds can be simply made using only the voice and body, or the students can be given the opportunity to gather and use items from around the room to also make sounds with.

A scene can be introduced and suggested through a soundscape of carefully sequenced sounds, for example, the door opening, then slow footsteps, the sound of something heavy falling on the floor, a gasp, hurried footsteps, the door closing. The students can discuss the sound sequence, suggesting and/or creating different possible opening scenes in groups, based on the sound sequence they have listened to. Sound sequences might sometimes be devised and performed by the teacher.

Sound sequences can be linked to any scene in an ongoing drama, for example, in a drama about refugees, the students could be asked to devise in groups a sequence of sounds that the refugees in the lorry can hear, when the lorry they are hiding in stops and the engine is turned off. The groups can then each present their soundscapes to each other. Those listening can be in role as refugees who are inside the lorry in darkness (eyes closed).

Sound Collage and Voice Collage

A sound collage often uses sound in a more experimental, abstract, and almost "musical" way. It can consist of (or include) words too but is then more likely referred to as a Voice Collage.

Sound and Voice Collages can be carried out with the students' eyes closed. This helps them to concentrate on the sounds and words and helps their imaginations. Everyone may contribute sounds and/or words spontaneously and experimentally, maybe changing the tone, volume, pace, or pitch of the sounds and words for overall effect. The students usually are asked to repeat the same sounds and/or words during this activity. They might also choose to remain silent at times. When students are performing a collage with their eyes closed, then the teacher can instruct them to "build the collage up gradually, let it slowly become louder until it reaches a crescendo, then let it gradually get quieter and slower and end in silence."

Alternatively, the students can be asked to keep their eyes open and a designated conductor can control the sounds and voices, signaling when various students should start and stop making sounds and/or speaking words, as well as conducting the pace and volume of their contributions. Students can take turns at being the conductor.

The language teacher can offer some relevant words, phrases, and sentences for the students to experiment with during the collage and might ask the students to speak phrases or sentences during the Voice Collage and not just use single words.

Forum Theater

Forum Theater is an inter-active form of applied drama, which is attributed to Augusto Boal (a Brazilian theater director and playwright). It is used to support and enable those present to see and consider how they might change real-life social and political situations that are oppressive to them.

Forum Theater starts with a scene or short performance, portraying oppression. The audience watch the performance once through and then it is played again but this time they can stop the performance and ask a character to make a change to their words and/or actions. It is intended that any suggested changes will lead to an improved outcome for the oppressed character in the scene when it is replayed.

The audience who may intervene are referred to as "spectactors" (a combination of spectators and actors). Someone who is known as "The Joker" acts as the intermediary between the performers and the spectactors. With language students, this is likely to be their teacher.

In a piece of Forum Theater that contains a scene about bullying (Drama Unit 1), a spectactor might tell the victim to walk more confidently and keep looking the bully in the eye next time, rather than quickly look away. The scene can then be replayed with the victim following the new directions to see whether this leads to any positive outcomes or not. The other actors in the scene will accommodate the change, improvising their response to it. The scene can be reworked repeatedly with the victim (and others in the scene) being directed in a range of ways, by different spectactors, leading to a variety of outcomes. Everyone will be seeing and hearing "in the moment" the difference that various changes in speech and behavior can make when dealing with oppressors. This reflective activity might lead to changes in the students' own behaviors in real life next time they are being oppressed, witnessing oppression, or being oppressive themselves to others. Forum Theater can provide good opportunities for students as spectactors, to talk together about the possible impact of linguistic content and style, various actions, and outcomes. They are doing so within a fictional context that stimulates them metacognitively and can affect them personally. Forum Theater provides an interactive forum within which the students can safely experiment with different ideas, actions, viewpoints, opinions, and language.

The power to stop and change the performance lies with the audience but in classroom situations some teachers might prefer to stop the action themselves at certain moments and then invite audience suggestions. The power of "Stop!" could be handed over sometimes to empower the students and enable them to practice and develop assertiveness.

The Joker can decide to invite a spectactor to come on stage and demonstrate what they are asking the actor to do and say. The Joker might even suggest that the spectactor could substitute themselves for the actor when the scene is replayed or stay with the actor, directing and prompting them, during the replay.

Part III

The Drama Units

Chapter Outline

INTRODUCTION	75
UNIT 1—BULLYING	77
UNIT 2—THE GREAT FIRE OF LONDON	84
UNIT 3— REFUGEES	91
UNIT 4—CONSERVATION OR CHANGE?	100
UNIT 5—BEOWULF	108
UNIT 6—OVER THE TOP—The True Story of Annie Edson Taylor, the "Queen of the Mist"	116

Introduction

The following section of this book contains six Process Drama units, which can be used by language teachers in various ways. Ideally teachers will progress through entire drama units with their students. Each unit is developmentally planned and can be divided into a series of lessons if the timetable requires this or if the teacher prefers this. If a teacher decides to only select certain activities from the drama units rather than use them all, then this is likely to hamper the gradual build-up of the dramatic tension, which Process Drama generates and uses.

Teachers will know how much preparation and support their own students need and knows their levels of linguistic competence. They will also know what their timetable allows in terms of the time available for drama. Although each drama unit is made up of carefully sequenced activities, designed to be followed in order, the teacher will need to decide how much of the drama unit they want to cover during any lesson. The plans can be adapted to give more time for certain activities, for example, introducing additional vocabulary or giving more time and emphasis to certain drama activities, skills, and tasks that are particularly appropriate and necessary for their own students at the time.

Teachers are encouraged to adapt the drama strategies in each unit if they wish to help ensure they match their own students' language skills, competencies, and needs.

Each drama unit contains some suggested writing activities that are linked to the drama, and teachers will probably have their own ideas for other writing too. The drama units are designed to meet relevant learning objectives and develop the twenty-first-century skills of the language learners. Each drama will stimulate language within different contexts, in a range of ways, for different imagined purposes and audiences, and this will help develop the linguistic competencies of the learners. Each drama unit provides many opportunities for speaking and writing with reading and listening embedded and there are also suggestions as to which grammar structures can be practiced during various activities.

The drama units are intended mainly for use with teenagers and adults, but teachers may decide to adapt the activities and use them with younger students.

The drama units will be useful to teachers of any second language and particularly for teachers of English. Some of the drama units are based on British history and culture and will contribute to the students' cultural and historical learning and understanding of English.

Each drama unit has some suggested vocabulary that is expected to be pre-taught. When historical or cultural information is going to be relevant and helpful to the drama, then this can also be discussed with the students before the drama lesson and possibly researched online by them too. This can help the students to participate more confidently and authentically during the drama.

The Drama Units include both verbal and nonverbal activities and strategies, sometimes in combination and sometimes separately. This can be particularly helpful for students with lower levels of linguistic confidence and proficiency. The students will be using gesture, body, voice, and sound to communicate, symbolize, and literally "re-member" facts, events, moments, and the associated language.

Drama is a social, collaborative activity that stimulates and provides affective and cognitive challenge. Each individual student will hopefully be motivated by the dramas to contribute to the limit of their linguistic competencies. Teachers will be able to support and challenge their students linguistically during the drama by being alongside them in role, speaking with them in the shared, imagined contexts and modeling the use of appropriate vocabulary. Teachers may wish to pause the drama at times to teach and talk about the drama and about the language.

UNIT 1 Bullying

Bullying among students at school is a universal problem, of increasing concern. Language teachers are expected to deal with discipline issues that arise, as well as teach a language. This drama unit is intended to help teachers to do this.

This lesson is based on the poem "Only the Wall" by Matthew Sweeney. In drama, objects can come alive and talk, and as Sweeney has personified the wall, this poem lends itself to being approached through drama. The wall witnesses and recounts daily incidents of bullying. The drama strategies used will help the students to enter and literally "make sense" of the poem and to engage with imagined incidents of bullying. They will explore and reflect on these incidents together and consider the ways in which they might be able to help and support the victim in the drama. Hopefully, the drama process will help the students whenever they experience or witness bullying in the future.

The lesson is intended to help develop the students' empathetic and social skills and enable them to explore together the issue of bullying in schools. They can use the target language to talk about interpersonal relationships, fears, and anxieties connected with bullying and can consider ways in which they might be able to take the initiative and actively support a victim, rather than remain inactive as a bystander The drama gives them ample opportunity to empathize with the victim and practice moving together against bullying.

Resources Required

Resource Sheets 1 and 2 (see pages 125 and 126)

There are six objects that the new boy could have been carrying, for example, a school bag, a pencil case, a sandwich box, a house key, a wallet, a mobile phone. Real objects would be best but photographs of objects or the names of the objects written on strips of paper could be used.

Useful Vocabulary (to be pre-taught)

Ordinal numbers: First, second, third, fourth, fifth, sixth, seventh

Words used in the poem: Bully, trip, stick, toffee, fight, around, cheers, lean, ambush, thumps, blood, missed, picked, instead, savage

Additional vocabulary (optional): victim, danger, frightened, vulnerable, nickname, injured, pain, witness, gang, onlooker, hiding, seeking, unsafe, safe

	Drama Strategy or activity	Grouping	Teacher guidance	Comments and suggestions	Language links and opportunities
1.	Still Image	Individual	Ask the students to walk around the room. When you call out a word or phrase, each person should quickly make a still image that portrays it. Then ask them to walk on again until you call out the next word or phrase, e.g., 1. The new boy 2. The bully 3. Hiding 4. Seeking 5. An onlooker cheering 6. Hurt 7. Safe	The images should be held as still as possible. **Pairs:** This activity can be changed by asking the students to turn to the nearest person (when you call out a word or phrase). They should quickly make the still image together (without discussion). These activities engage the students with key words and themes in an embodied way at the start.	This is an opportunity for students to practice some relevant vocabulary. They are being asked to represent various words physically (nonverbal representation). This helps make the words more memorable and can aid recall later. The teacher could add or substitute other words with similar meanings and/or ask the students to suggest some (which can also be physicalized).
2.	Tableau	Whole class	Now, ask them to stand in a circle with you. Explain that one at a time, anyone can enter the circle and recreate one of the still images they made during Activity 1. They can position themselves in relation to someone else or separately.	You could ask them to speak their word or phrase as they get into position. Alternatively, you could ask them to extend the word or phrase as they get into position, e.g., by adding an adverb or adjective, or putting the word or phrase into a sentence.	
3.	Visualization	Individually	Ask your class to close their eyes while you read the poem aloud. Ask them to keep their eyes closed at the end until you ask them to open them again. Ask them to try and visualize the scenes in the poem (as pictures in their "mind's eye").	The students are being asked to listen and to visualize the images that are in the poem. Keeping their eyes closed for a while afterward will help them to visualize the images for longer.	This "blind" activity relies on them using their listening skills. You may wish to discuss the imagery within the poem with the students and ask which images were/are most vivid for them and why this might be.
4.		Pairs	Give copies of the poem to everyone (Resource Sheet 1). Now ask them to read the poem with a partner, underlining any words that link to the senses, i.e., sight, hearing, smell, taste, touch.	Different colors could be used for the different senses. This activity gets them reading the poem and draws their attention to the way the poet is engaging our senses.	**Vocabulary:** They could make lists together of alternative or additional sensory words that the poet might have considered using.

	Drama Strategy or activity	Grouping	Teacher guidance	Comments and suggestions	Language links and opportunities
	Choral Speaking	Whole class	Now read the poem aloud again. Whenever you say a word that they have underlined, they should join in and say that word aloud with you.	This activity requires them to read at your pace. It amplifies the sensory words, making them more memorable.	
5.	**Talking Objects**	Whole class	Ask them to stand in a long line, facing forwards. Together, they are now the wall. Everyone needs to think of one new sentence that the wall can speak out loud about the scenes it has witnessed. As you walk slowly along the line, each person speaks their sentence aloud as you pass by. The sentences could start in any way or you could ask them to start them with a sensory sentence stem: I saw … I heard … I felt … (touch) I smelt … I tasted … You could replay this drama activity differently, passing the wall as the bully or the new boy. What might the wall say to each of them?	You could ask them to accompany their sentence with an exaggerated mime, e.g., cupping or blocking their ears as they say, "I hear …" and staring or covering their eyes as they say, "I see …," etc. Linking speech with movement makes it more memorable.	**Writing opportunity (Poetry)** After the lesson, they could try removing a line (or lines) of the poem and substituting others of their own. Their additional sentences (spoken by the wall) could be written onto individual paper "bricks" afterward, which could be fitted together to make a wall. Alternatively, bricks could be moved around and positioned in different, meaningful ways. The different outcomes can be evaluated and compared. Additional verses can be created, based on what the wall could say to the bully and/or the new boy.
6.	**Still Image**	Small groups	Divide the class into six groups. Each group needs either a copy of the poem and/or a copy of the sentences below (Resource Sheet 2, page 126). Allocate one of the days to each of the groups: 1. **First day:** The bully made the new boy trip up and called him a name. 2. **Second day:** Some boys stood around and watched the new boy being bullied. They were cheering. 3. **Third day:** Three boys were leaning against the wall, waiting for the new boy. When he arrived, they started hitting him and he started bleeding. 4. **Fourth day:** Five bullies were looking for the new boy. They could not find him today, so they hurt another boy instead. 5. **Fifth day:** The five bullies found the new boy again today. His face hit the wall again.	The teacher may need to model "stillness" and the "slow motion" pace that is required. **Possible alternatives** The groups could be asked to bring the scene to life for a few seconds, in slow motion, and then freeze it again and melt it. They could be asked to bring the scene to life for a few seconds with everyone then speaking just one sentence or thought in turn before freezing and melting the scene.	The students are practicing reading and speaking. The teacher decides whether the poem and/or the simple sentences are most appropriate for his/her cohort of students. **Writing opportunities (Eyewitness recounts)** Having taken part in the scenes, the students can give verbal accounts of the scenes and then write eyewitness reports or recounts.

	Drama Strategy or activity	Grouping	Teacher guidance	Comments and suggestions	Language links and opportunities
			6. **Sixth day**: The new boy did not come back today, so the bullies hurt the other boy again, instead. Give each group an object that the new boy could have been carrying, e.g., a school bag, pencil case, sandwich box, house key, wallet, mobile phone, etc. The object will represent the victim in the scene. No student will be in role as the victim. Ask them to devise a group still image for their allocated day. Extras can become objects and/or more than one person can be the same character in the scene. The groups need to rehearse moving into their still image in slow motion, holding it still for a few seconds and then melting the image (in slow motion).	They could give the scene a title and say it as they freeze the image. As the image or slow-motion scene is being performed, someone in the scene could speak an accompanying narrative (in the first or third person).	
7.	Performance Carousel	Whole class	The groups will now present their still images in time sequence (from days 1 to 6). As each scene is being performed, you read the corresponding verse aloud (or the simple prose version on Resource Sheet 2). Remember that verse 4 of the poem covers both days 4 and 5.	The scenes could be replayed with appropriate music as a background, instead of the poem. The music could be replayed later, during associated writing activities to aid recall and re-evoke associated, emotional responses.	**Writing opportunity (Personification)** The object that represents the new boy is an eyewitness to the bullying and knows the boy. The students could afterward write about the scene as the object. The writing could be in prose or poetic form.
8.	Improvisation	Pairs	Ask them to improvise a difficult conversation between the new boy and someone else, e.g., a parent, teacher, friend, brother, sister, etc. The conversation should start with the person saying to the new boy, "Are you alright?" The students in role as the new boy will each need to decide during the improvisation whether to admit that they are being bullied.	Before this activity, the teacher could ask the students why people who are being bullied might find it difficult to confide in others about bullying incidents.	**Writing opportunity (Script-writing)** The first few lines of the improvisation could later be redrafted and scripted. The script will start with the opening line, "Are you alright?" The short scripts could then be passed between groups for script-reading and maybe performance.
9.	Eavesdropping	Whole class	Pause the improvisations after a few minutes. Explain that you will now pass by each pair in turn. When you are nearest to any pair, they will carry on improvising. When you move on, they should freeze and be silent again. Every pair will be heard for just a few seconds.	You may need to remind the students that their voices will need to be loud enough to be heard by everyone during this activity.	**Writing opportunity (Writing in Role)** 1. The boy could write in his secret diary, revealing that he is being bullied (or alluding to it). 2. The boy could start to write a letter to tell someone (but not finish it). 3. The boy could complete a letter to tell someone.

	Drama Strategy or activity	Grouping	Teacher guidance	Comments and suggestions	Language links and opportunities
					In a class circle, each person can read their letter aloud and then ritualistically put it in one of three centrally placed piles: 1. Delivered letters 2. Hidden letters 3. Destroyed letters
10.	Teacher in Role	Whole class	Tell them you will now be going into role as the new boy. Remind them that the boy did not go to school on Day 6. It is now dawn on Day 7. You can improvise and/or use the script provided at the end of this unit (see page 83). Admit that you stayed off school and hid yesterday and say you can't go back to school. Ask for their advice. What do they think you should do today (and in the future)?	Play the role as if you really don't know what to do next. Try to get the students to elaborate, explain, and justify their suggestions to you.	**Writing opportunity (Role on the Wall)** This activity can be done individually or in pairs (see Resource Sheet 17, page 141). Give them an outline of the boy (or they could draw one) and ask them to write information about him around his outline in note form. Self-adhesive notes can easily be moved around and reorganized into various categories, e.g., "What we know about him" (referential) and "What we *think* we know about him" (inferential).
11.	Small Group Playmaking	Small groups (of up to four)	Ask them to imagine that the new boy does go back to school. In groups, they will now devise a scene that must end with "a moment of hope." The students should suggest some moments of hope, which might, for example, include the following: • A bystander goes and gets a teacher. • A passer-by intervenes. • A gang member (or members) walks away. • The victim stands up to the bully. • A friend comes to help the boy. Tell them that the scenes will be performed and should include some dialogue.		**Writing opportunity (Playscript)** The playmaking has already generated a scene with characters, action, and dialogue. This could be written up afterward in the form of a playscript. The short scripts could later be given to other groups to read, rehearse, and perform (and maybe evaluate).

	Drama Strategy or activity	Grouping	Teacher guidance	Comments and suggestions	Language links and opportunities
12.	Performance Carousel	Whole class	The scenes will now be presented in turn one after the other (with no breaks). The results will be a whole class performance of "Moments of Hope." You could finish the lesson here or decide to go on to Activity 12 now (or in the next lesson).		
13.	Forum Theater	Whole class	You could choose one of the scenes from Activity 12 to explore and develop, using "Forum Theater" (see page 73). The audience (the spectactors) will try to positively influence the outcomes of the scene for the new boy, using "direction" and/or "substitution." The teacher becomes a neutral facilitator (The Joker), an intermediary, between the audience and the actors. The scene is replayed and then the teacher invites willing audience members in turn to direct an actor to play the scene (or part of it) differently in order to help the new boy. The "Joker" can also invite audience members to take over from an actor or come and play the role with them during a replay.	Forum Theater should not be rushed, so might be best done in a separate lesson. Forum Theater enables a class to work together to influence the words and actions of the characters in scenes in ways that might help someone who is being oppressed.	

Activity 10

Teacher in Role—A Possible Script for the New Boy on Day 7

"I feel sick. I just can't go to school today. I didn't go yesterday. I went to the kids' playground and hid there all day, until home time. If I go to school today, I know they'll beat me up again and there's nothing I can do about it. The trouble is, I can't stay off school every day but I don't know how to stop them. I just don't know what to do. If I tell anyone, it's just going to make it worse. What do you think I should do? Help me, please!"

UNIT 2 The Great Fire of London

This Drama Unit is a good opportunity for language teachers (especially teachers of English), to explore part of British history and culture. It enables the students to learn about the Great Fire of London and English city life in the seventeenth century. Often, students just read a short text about this event in their course books but this drama offers them a way of actively and emotionally engaging with this tragic event. The students will be acquiring vocabulary and phrases that are connected with seventeenth-century life and occupations and may empathize with what the Londoners at that time experienced.

Disasters and tragedies are universal. They have happened (and are happening now) across the world and will continue to happen in the future. Teachers can help the students to make meaningful links between what happened to people and communities during and after the Great Fire of London and what is still happening across the world to people, families, and communities now. This drama provides an opportunity for deepening empathy, understanding, and a stronger personal connection with what others are experiencing in their lives.

This drama unit can also provide a platform for discussing both individual and group resilience and how people can "bounce back" from situations in which they lose their homes, possessions, and maybe even the people they love. They might consider ways of being supported and supporting others practically, mentally, and emotionally. During the drama, the students will be making decisions, analyzing situations, and problem-solving together. They will be practicing critical and creative thinking, leadership, and collaboration. This drama unit also gives many opportunities for language teachers to practice grammatical structures, vocabulary, and a range of skills in a highly integrated way.

London Streets in the Seventeenth Century

Before starting the lesson, it is helpful to have some images and information about seventeenth-century London streets available. These can be easily found online. The streets were narrow and cobbled. The houses were mostly timber (wood) framed with tiled rooves that contained tar. The houses were often three of four stories high with workshops and shops on ground floors and living quarters that often leaned forward over the streets. The houses often had rushes on the floor. These were highly flammable and harbored mud, rubbish, and smells. The streets were crowded and dirty with streams of litter and sewage flowing along them. There were many carts, often resulting in slow-moving crowds and traffic jams. Cattle and sheep were taken through the streets to market. The houses and streets were infested with rats. On foggy days, the air quality was very poor with coal and wood smoke hanging in the air (creating smog). From dawn until dusk, the streets were very busy and noisy with stinking, slippery slime, mud, and excrement underfoot. The sounds of barking dogs, horses, cartwheels, church bells, and street cries filled the air. Many people had small shops inside their houses or stalls set up outside their houses. There were also many ale houses and taverns. By the riverside, there were warehouses, many of which stored flammable materials, such as tallow and oil.

The Great Fire

The fire started in the early hours of Sunday, September 2, 1666, with a stray spark from a baker's oven in Pudding Lane. The oven was in the shop of Thomas Farynor, the king's baker. It had been a hot, dry summer, so the fire spread quickly with a strong easterly wind. On Tuesday, September 4, St. Paul's Cathedral was destroyed. The fire spread quickly to warehouses on the banks of the River Thames (some of which contained oil). The fire did not spread over London Bridge to south London, as there was a section of the bridge missing. By the time the fire ended on September 6, 1987, churches and more than 13,000 houses had been destroyed. Only six people died but 70,000 people were left homeless. Lines of people with leather buckets formed human chains to get the water from the Thames to the fire but this was ineffective. There was no organized fire brigade.

Useful Vocabulary (to be pre-taught)

Timber, overcrowded, infested, cobbled, flammable, stinking, firebreak, leather, flammable, stinking, sewage, warehouses, arson, extinguished, eyewitness, diarist.

Some occupations: Carrying and selling water (water-bearer), spinning, weaving, sewing, working leather, making shoes (cobbler), making and selling herbal remedies (herbalist), blacksmith, wheelwright, carpenter, butcher, fishmonger, baker, washerwoman, builder.

Optional Script (for Activity 2)

It is early in the morning on Sunday, September 2, 1666, and the streets are stinking and already crowded. It has been a long, hot, dry summer and we are longing for rain but there is none. Today, there is a strong wind blowing from the east, so with luck, it will not get too hot today. Dogs are running around and barking at the carts, as they rattle along our cobbled street. And there are plenty of rats, of course, running across the rooves and along the streets. It seems like an ordinary Sunday here in London … but is it?

Samuel Pepys's diary extracts (for Activities 10 and 11)

Diary Extract 1:

Everybody endeavouring to remove their goods, and flinging into the river or bringing them into lighters that layoff; poor people staying in their houses as long as till the very fire touched them, and then running into boats, or clambering from one pair of stairs by the water-side to another. And among other things, the poor pigeons, I perceive, were loathe to leave their houses, but hovered about the windows and balconies till they were, some of them burned, their wings, and fell down.

Diary Extract 2:

I did tell the King and Duke of Yorke what I saw, and that unless his Majesty did command houses to be pulled down nothing could stop the fire. They seemed much troubled, and the King commanded me to go to my Lord Mayor from him, and command him to spare no houses, but to pull down before the fire every way.

London's Burning—A Song about the Great Fire (for Activity 8)

London's burning, London's burning
Fetch the engine, fetch the engine
Fire, fire! Fire, fire! Pour on water, pour on water

Selected Online Resources

Wikipedia's "Great Fire of London" page has historical information about the fire, set out by the day. https://en.wikipedia.org/wiki/Great_Fire_of_London

An animation that recreates the seventeenth-century streets of London, using maps from the British Library: https://www.youtube.com/watch?v=UFRrDKaa8EY&feature=youtu.be and https://www.historyextra.com/period/gamers-explore-streets-of-17th-century-london/

A painting of "The Great Fire of London" (1675—artist unknown): https://en.wikipedia.org/wiki/Great_Fire_of_London and https://commons.wikimedia.org/wiki/File:Great_Fire_London.jpg

Famous diary entries about the fire by Samuel Pepys: http://www.pepys.info/fire.html and http://www.bbc.co.uk/culture/story/20160902-retrace-samuel-pepys-steps-in-the-great-fire-of-london

An online, interactive animation that teaches about the Fire of London: http://www.fireoflondon.org.uk/game

	Drama Strategy or activity	Grouping	Teacher guidance	Comments and suggestions	Language links and opportunities
1.	**Occupational Mime (as a game)**	Individually	Explain that they will move around the room and you will call out a seventeenth-century occupational activity. Explain that when you call one of these activities, they need to stop walking and mime the activity until you call out, "Move on …." They keep moving around until you call out another activity. Go through the activity list with them first briefly explaining/demonstrating each. • Carry two leather buckets full of water. • Wash your clothes in the Thames. • Sew clothes. • Carve wood. • Weave at a loom. • Hammer nails into horseshoes. • Mix a herbal remedy. • Knead a loaf of bread.	There are many paintings and etchings of London in the seventeenth century, available on the internet. You could display and discuss some of these images and list a few activities shown within them. Looking at historical images can help the students to engage with the setting of the drama.	This is an opportunity for the students to practice the present continuous tense and to learn and use the vocabulary that relates to some traditional occupations and professions of seventeenth-century England. The teacher could ask them to make a response in the first person, present tense, as they carry out the action, e.g., say aloud, "I am carrying two buckets of water," or, "I am washing my clothes in the Thames," etc. The teacher could also offer the past tense of each verb as they "move on", e.g., the teacher could say, "They carried heavy buckets of water" and "They washed their clothes in the Thames," etc.
2.	**Tableau** **Freeze Frame** **Occupational Mime**	Individually	Tell them that it is the morning of Sunday September 2, 1666. Sunday is not a work day but the streets are busy. They are Londoners in the same street, who don't know about the fire yet. Explain that they should enter the space, one at a time and position themselves somewhere within the street. As each person gets into a still position, they should say their name and add one piece of information about themselves and/or what they are doing, before "freezing," e.g., "My name is Martha and I am taking food to my friend Elizabeth, who is sick." "My name is William and I am going to feed my master's horses."	You could project online images of seventeenth-century London streets to help set the scene. This is a way of getting everyone into a role and helping them find out everyone else's roles. It is a way of getting them to own and engage with their role and the shared, imagined scene.	The students need to adopt traditional names that would have been common in the seventeenth century, e.g., biblical and royal names. Deciding on and using appropriate Christian names provides a cultural learning opportunity for language students. The language demands could be amended and/or developed, e.g., "Now as I pass by you, say your name again and what your character is thinking."

	Drama Strategy or activity	Grouping	Teacher guidance	Comments and suggestions	Language links and opportunities
	Teacher as Narrator		Once everyone is in the scene, you recount what is in the scene. You can use the script provided, page 85 and/or you can draw on the additional information that they have given. For example, It is early on a windy Sunday. People are already out and about in the street. Martha is looking forward to meeting her friend Elizabeth today and William is going to feed his master's horses ….		
	Improvisation	Whole class	Now explain that when you give a signal, they should bring the scene alive and improvise. You will join in. After a few minutes of improvisation, ask them to "Freeze" the scene again and say, "It was September 2, 1666, and the day started much like any other day …. but things were about to change …."		
3.	**Teacher in Role** **Rumors**	Whole class	Explain that the scene will come alive again and this time, you will join them in role and start a rumor. They should spread the rumors they hear. The teacher can spread some historically accurate information "in role," i.e., "Have you heard? A baker's shop in Pudding Lane is on fire!" "Someone told me that it started at Thomas Faynor's bakery." "They say that his maid's been burned alive, poor girl." "I think that it is Thomas's own fault. He did not put his oven fire out properly last night." "The fire is going to spread fast in this wind." "Some are saying say that the foreigners started the fire!"	The purposes of the teacher being in role at this point is to • give important information (about the fire) • provoke in role responses, action, and interaction. Try to get a scene of growing concern with people chatting together, rather than panicking.	The various rumors could be gathered and written inside speech bubbles, using Resource Sheet 15.
4.	**Voice Collage**	Whole class	Gather the class together. Ask them to all choose one sentence or phrase that they heard spoken during Activity 3.	This activity requires them to reflect on what has been said, to make a linguistic selection, to work playfully and creatively with words and phrases, and to listen to and cooperate spontaneously with others.	The words and phrases could be jotted down on self-adhesive labels, and an actual collage of words and phrases could be arranged by negotiation. When the various words and phrases are placed, their placement should be able to be explained and justified.

	Drama Strategy or activity	Grouping	Teacher guidance	Comments and suggestions	Language links and opportunities
			Now, ask them to close their eyes and use the phrase or sentence repeatedly, improvising with it and building up together to a crescendo of voices that gradually gets quieter until they end still and silent. Once silent, they should keep their eyes closed until you ask them to open them again.		
5.	Improvisation	Pairs	Ask them to get into pairs inside their homes. The fire is getting closer and one of the pair thinks they should pack some belongings and leave now. Their partner does not want to leave yet. Ask them to improvise their conversation.	This activity should not last more than two or three minutes.	The dialogue could later be written up as short play script. The play script could subsequently be handed to others to read aloud and/or perform.
6.	Improvisation	Groups of four (two pairs)	Ask them to bring pairs together to make groups of four. Explain that they are now pairs of neighbors, standing out in the street together and talking about whether to leave yet or not.	They have already discussed what they should do with their partner and are now bringing their practiced opinions and viewpoints, to a small group discussion. They are likely to speak quite confidently, having already discussed/rehearsed this in pairs.	
7.	Eavesdropping	Groups of four	Ask the groups to "freeze." Explain that you will now pass by each group in turn. As you pass by each group of neighbors, they come to life and everyone will listen in on their conversation. Only the group you are near can move and speak. The others should be still, silent, and listening until you reach them.	All the groups have been involved in the same verbal task. The similarities and differences will now become evident with regard to what the various groups are saying.	**Writing activity:** The arguments they have given, "for and against" leaving their homes, could be written down in columns.
8.	Mime Thought-tracking	Whole class in a line	No fire brigades existed. Some people stood in long lines, passing leather buckets of water to each other, from the river to the fire. Ask the class to get into a line and pass imaginary buckets along the line to the fire. Ask them to all sing the English nursery rhyme, "London's Burning," (page 85), as they pass the buckets along the line.	This enables a well-known English nursery rhyme to be sung within its dramatic context. The tune can easily be found online.	**Writing activity:** You could invite the class to make up additional verses for the song that fit with its rhyme and meter. Then, all sing it with the additional verses.

	Drama Strategy or activity	Grouping	Teacher guidance	Comments and suggestions	Language links and opportunities
9.	Talking Objects	Class circle (standing)	The time has come to take some possessions and leave. Some people have hand carts but others are only taking what they can carry in sacks and/or bags. Ask them to imagine that they are an object and that their character will take with them. Everyone in turn enters the circle and becomes the object, saying what they are and why they have been chosen, e.g., "I am a wooden cross that was carved by her father. She thinks if she takes it, God will keep her safe."		**Writing opportunity:** Speaking as an object can help students to then move into writing as if they are the object (personification). Also, the objects can become eyewitnesses, and if they survive, they can later provide recounts of the journey and events (which could be spoken and then written).
10.	Eyewitness	Whole class	Most people made their way to the banks of the River Thames, hoping to escape the fire by boat. Ask them to look carefully at paintings of the fire, including *The Great Fire of London* (1675—artist unknown). Samuel Pepys looked across at the fire from his boat and wrote about it in his diary (see Extract 1, page 85). Ask them to look at the painting and to imagine that they are with Pepys, looking at the scene from a boat. Tell them that any of them can speak aloud in role, about what they can see. They should start their sentences with "I can see …," e.g., "I can see many carts on the riverbank. They are overloaded with people's belongings." Now ask them to imagine they are experiencing the scene with their other senses, e.g., "I can hear the sound of people shouting to boatmen." "I can smell smoke and tar." Bring this activity to a close by reading aloud Pepys's Diary Extract 1, page 85.	It is easy to find paintings, etchings, and animations of the Great Fire of London online.	

	Drama Strategy or activity	Grouping	Teacher guidance	Comments and suggestions	Language links and opportunities
11.	**Teacher in Role** **Collective Role**	Whole class	Pepys went to the king and the Duke of York and told them what was happening in the streets of the city and what he had seen from his boat. You become King Charles II and the students collectively become Pepys. You then gather information from Pepys about what he has seen and heard. The Lord Mayor of London won't demolish houses in the path of the fire. They need to report to you what is happening and persuade you to order the mayor to get houses pulled down to create a firebreak. As Pepys, they may only speak one at a time to you and should not speak twice in a row. As king, ask questions and end up telling Pepys to go to the Lord Mayor with a message from you, commanding him to pull some houses down and create a firebreak immediately. Afterward, you can tell the students what Pepys wrote about his meeting with the king and Duke of York. (see Diary Extract 2, page 85).	As the king, you can ask Pepys for more information. Get them to work hard at getting you to insist that the mayor takes action.	**Writing opportunity:** You could ask the students to create an additional diary entry, which can be written as if they are Pepys'. They could start a new entry or add to one of Pepys's diary entries. **Writing opportunity:** Ask them to write the letter from the king to the Lord Mayor of London, commanding him to create a firewall.
12.	**Improvisation**	Pairs	The firebreak ordered by the king, coupled with less wind, resulted in the fire gradually being put out. Ask them to get into pairs. They should now imagine that it is fifteen years after the Great Fire. One of them escaped the fire and the other is about thirteen years old so was not born until after the fire. The older person is telling the younger person about their experience of the fire. The young person will listen and ask questions.	This activity requires one person to give a verbal recount and the other to listen well and ask relevant questions. They could swap roles afterward and both have a turn as the older and younger person.	**Writing opportunity:** A verbal recount can be good preparation and rehearsal for then doing a written recount.
	Hot-Seating	Whole class	Alternatively, a few of the students can together become a group of Londoners who lived through the Great Fire and the rest of the class are questioners who are in "shadowy role," i.e., they are just questioners.		

UNIT 3 Refugees

This drama unit provides an opportunity for language students to cognitively and affectively engage with some of the tragic situations that many people find themselves and their families in due to, for example, civil wars and oppressive regimes. Refugees have fled their homes and countries throughout history and there are ever-increasing numbers of refugees nowadays. This drama unit will hopefully deepen levels of human understanding and care about the dangerous, difficult choices and gambles that refugees need to make and the terrifying, inhumane situations that they can find themselves in.

During the drama, the students will be considering some of the reasons why people might be driven to leave their homes and become refugees. It explores some of the thoughts and feelings they might have, while deciding who they can or cannot trust to take them on a perilous, journey to another country where they may (or may not) find safety and help.

The drama provides opportunities for practicing the language of mediation and negotiation. It also will stimulate and scaffold students' critical and creative thinking skills and give opportunities for showing initiative and collaborative problem-solving.

Useful Vocabulary (to be pre-taught)

Home, danger, safety, fear, escape, trust, distrust, secret, payment, deposit, luggage, smuggler, refugee, hiding, homesick, separation, hope.

Before the Lesson

Display the following words around the room (on a wall or on a floor space): Home, danger, hope, frightened, secret, hiding, separation, homesick.

Ask the students in pairs to move around and visit each word in turn. Ask them to explain the meaning of the word to each other. You could also ask them to agree on an associated movement or gesture to go with each of these words.

	Drama Strategy or activity	Grouping	Teacher guidance	Comments and suggestions	Language links and opportunities
1.	Still Image	Individual	Ask the class to walk around without getting close to each other. When you call out a word from the vocabulary list, they should all stop walking and instantly make themselves into a still image that portrays that word: home, dangerous, hope, frightened, secret, hiding, separation, homesick **and/or**	This is an individual yet inclusive activity that focuses their attention on the forthcoming themes. It involves expressing and communicating the meaning of relevant vocabulary through the body.	Before the lesson you can display the "useful vocabulary" around the room. Ask the students to go around in pairs, taking it in turns to explain the meaning of the words to each other.
		Pairs	They could do this activity in pairs (spontaneously creating a still image with the person nearest to them without talking).	The activity in pairs is more challenging and requires non-verbal collaboration.	In pairs, each person can choose one of the words, put it into a sentence, and speak the sentence aloud to their partner. As they speak the sentence, they also make a still image to go with it, e.g., "Home makes me feel warm and safe" (while hugging themselves). They take it in turns with different words.
2.	Move If …	Whole class circle	Stand in a circle with the students. Ask them to move across the circle when a sentence that you call out applies to them. You join in this activity too. Say the following statements in turn. Move if: • You are living in the country that you were born in • You have lived in more than one country • You can speak a second language (at any level) • You have been in a country where you could not understand the language at all • You have ever felt that your life was in danger (for any reason) • You have ever experienced exclusion	The students are being asked to personally connect with the theme and respond physically. This activity stimulates metacognition, self-awareness, and also connectivity with other people.	Applying the conditional clause, "if." Practicing present perfect and present perfect continuous
3.	Discussion	Whole class	Ask them why people might leave their homes and risk dangerous journeys to other countries, e.g., war, hunger, oppression, etc.	This encourages shared, reflective thinking about a range of situations that may prompt people to become refugees.	
	Poem		Read aloud the poem provided, "Changing Home (see page 98)." Home gradually changes from being a place of safety to a place of danger. The poem does not tell us why. This is left to our imagination. Ask the students what incidents might make people feel increasingly unsure about staying in their homes?	This poem uses simple words but is deep in inference. Home is personified. Each verse indicates a gradually worsening situation in terms of personal safety. They are practicing their listening skills and analysis and evaluation.	**Follow-up writing opportunity:** In pairs, the students could try to change some words or a line in the poem, substituting a different word or line, while trying to keep to the same pattern and rhythm.

	Drama Strategy or activity	Grouping	Teacher guidance	Comments and suggestions	Language links and opportunities
4.			Ask them to imagine that they all live in the same town. Tell them that incidents are happening in their town most days that are making them feel increasingly unsafe.		
	Still Image	Groups of three or four	Ask them to create a group still image of a recent incident in their town that makes them consider becoming a refugee. Explain that it is not a major incident but it is "the Final Straw" in a series of incidents.	This collaborative activity gives a sense of belonging and does not expose individual student's levels of linguistic competence.	**Idioms:** "The Final Straw" is an idiom. **Writing opportunities:** The still images could be photographed and their titles could be added to the photographs. The photographs can be used later as a stimulus for recalling and recounting the incident (in role) to someone.
			Ask them to give their still image a title.		
5.	Performance Carousel	Whole class	Explain that they need to practice getting into their group still images in slow motion, holding them still for a few seconds and then melting them. Once the image is still, someone in the group should say aloud the title of the scene. As one group finishes and "melts" slowly downward, the next group will start to move slowly upward into position. A seamless presentation of the scenes will result in a whole class performance.	It helps if the teacher demonstrates the speed at which they should move into and back out of their still image and how long to hold it for.	**Follow-up writing opportunities:** The titles of the scenes can later be used to prompt a narrative recount. The students could write about the incident in a letter to a friend or relative. They could write a recount of it in a personal diary. Newsworthy incidents might also be written up by the students (individually or in pairs) as newspaper reports.
	Thought-Tracking		When the image is frozen, you could ask them to each speak the inner thoughts of their characters in turn.	This invites deeper engagement with their characters.	Their own (or other group's scenes) could be written up as eyewitness reports. The teacher could suggest that the students use particular "sentence stems as they speak," e.g., " I think …," " I feel …," I wonder …," " I know …," " I suspect …," " etc.
	Improvisation		Ask the groups to bring their still images to life and improvise for a short time.	This helps develop and extend the dialogue and narrative.	
	Hot-Seating		Replay the sequence of images and invite questioning of the characters, who will answer from within the image. Answers should be given in role.	This activity enables deeper engagement with the role.	Improvised scenes generate spontaneous dialogue that can be scripted later. Hot-seating enables students to practice questioning. They could be asked to decide on just one question (maybe with a partner). The teacher could define the types of questions, tenses, and structures they should use or could allow any.

	Drama Strategy or activity	Grouping	Teacher guidance	Comments and suggestions	Language links and opportunities
6.	Rumors	Whole class	As townsfolk they will now cautiously gather and spread rumors about what has been happening (based on the incidents from Activity 5). Keep the activity going for around two minutes.	This helps build a sense of belonging to the community under threat.	The spreading of rumors gives a reason for listening, repeating what has been heard, and maybe elaborating on it. This repetition aids fluency.
	Teacher in Role (optional)		**Possible addition** The teacher could join in this activity in role too as one of them and/or as a spy for the authorities. Let them know first what your role is. If they know you are a spy, they need to swiftly change the subject of their conversations when you are near them, listening.	A spy in their midst helps build dramatic tension and requires the students to quickly change the content and style of their speech. This is a skill needed in real life.	This activity enables appropriate vocabulary and phrases to be generated and repeated within a specific context, e.g., "Have you heard …?" "Can you keep a secret?" "My lips are sealed …," etc. The spy (eavesdropping) is a change of audience, requiring a change of speech register and content.
7.			Tell them (out of role) that there will be a chance soon to escape in a lorry. The smuggler's "go-between" will meet them tonight in a disused garage to answer their questions and maybe take payments. They need to get to the meeting without being seen by guards. Place two chairs about a meter apart to represent the entrance.		
	Teacher in Role Improvisation	Whole class	Tell them that you will be in role as the guard. They are still the townsfolk and should chat to each other and try to sneak through the entrance unseen (when you are not looking). Once inside, they need to wait silently for the "go-between" to arrive. Enable them to all sneak through unnoticed but create tension, asking questions of some, as you walk around suspiciously, "Where are you going?" "Do I recognize you?" etc.	The purpose of the teacher in role here is to build the dramatic tension. The activity is reminiscent of some children's games but the aim of it here is to increase the tension, so it must be carried out seriously.	**Writing opportunity:** The same activity could be carried out but with a handwritten, anonymous note being passed secretly between townsfolk. If they had written the short anonymous note, what might they have written in it?
8.	Improvisation	Whole class	Ask them to talk quietly to those nearest to them as they wait for the arrival of the smuggler's go-between. Explain that when you re-enter, you will be the go-between. To meet like this is dangerous. The meeting will need to be short. Ask them to talk to those nearest to them and come up	This is an opportunity for deciding on and formulating key questions before the go-between arrives. It is also an opportunity to share and listen to each other's concerns and build the dramatic tension before the meeting starts.	This is an opportunity to teach some question starters and then enable students to use them within the dramatic context, e.g., "How much …?" "What if …?" "Will you …?" "When will …?" "Why does …?" "Who will …?"

	Drama Strategy or activity	Grouping	Teacher guidance	Comments and suggestions	Language links and opportunities
	Teacher in Role		with a list of questions that they most want answered, e.g., How much will it cost and when do we have to decide by? Have they done this journey often? What are the dangers? Where will we finally get left? etc. Enter as the go-between. You can use the script provided (see page 98) and/or improvise. Provide information, answer questions (improvising), and avoid being too friendly or confrontational. They need to feel able to question you about the journey. You might not answer all their questions and that is OK. You can make up answers that sound plausible or you could just say in role, "I can't answer that" or "I don't know."	This is an opportunity for students to practice the language of enquiry, negotiation, and mediation.	**Writing opportunity:** Before the go-between arrives, they could write (in pairs or small groups) a list of the questions that they most want answered. They could prioritize them, giving opportunity for explaining and justifying choices to each other.
	Improvisation		They cannot risk guards finding the meeting, so it will be a short meeting and the go-between will leave, once the main questions have been answered.		
9.	**Freeze Frame**	Whole class	Freeze the scene.	This holds a key moment still, i.e., "the moment just before the go-between arrives."	
	Thought-Tracking	Individual	Now ask what each person might be thinking at the moment that the go-between leaves. Invite them to speak their "in role" thoughts aloud as you pass by each of them in turn. You could suggest some sentence stems for this activity, e.g., "I wonder if/whether ….," "I am thinking that/about ….," "I am worried about/that ….," "I am concerned that ….," etc.	You will need to decide whether to allow them to speak just one or more thoughts. The "sentence stems" provide an opportunity to focus on teaching and practicing present continuous verbs and vocabulary that expresses doubt, fear, and uncertainty. Different sentence stems can stimulate and scaffold different types of thinking.	**Writing opportunity** Ask them to write their thoughts on self-adhesive labels and place them all into one central, collective thought bubble. When completed, this could be used as a visual writing frame. The thoughts recorded in the bubble could be revisited later in the drama when more is known.

	Drama Strategy or activity	Grouping	Teacher guidance	Comments and suggestions	Language links and opportunities
10.	Improvisation	Pairs or small groups	Ask the class to get into pairs or small groups. They are with people they know and trust from the meeting so can speak safely. Ask them to talk together in role about whether they have decided to go on the lorry yet (or not) and why. You could ask them to see if they can reach a joint decision to both go or both stay. You could offer some sentence stems, e.g., "Why don't we … ?" "How about … ?" and "What would you say if we … ?" "Shall we … ?" etc.	Improvisation provides an opportunity for thought and talk to flow and to engage with their own and other characters' viewpoints more deeply. Trying to reach a joint decision adds a goal and increases the level of challenge.	**Writing opportunities** Sometimes we write down the pros and cons of a course of action before reaching decisions. Ask the students to write a list of the pros and cons of going or staying. The improvisation will have generated dialogue. A few sentences of it could be selected and written up in different ways, e.g., verbatim (as a short play script) or as a personal narrative (in a diary).
11.	Conscience Alley	Whole class	Ask the class to split into two lines, facing each other (about a meter apart). One line will represent a mother who wants her son Nizar to stay home. The other line represents his father, who wants him to take this chance to leave. Explain that you will now pass between the lines as Nizar, their undecided son. You might use the script (see page 98). As you pass each person, they should speak a persuasive sentence or two to you and try to justify what they are saying, e.g., "Nizar, please don't leave me. I may never see you again and it will break my heart" and "You must go, son, because if you stay here, you will have no future," etc. Afterward as Nazir, thank them and tell them that you have decided to leave on the lorry. You could also explain why.	Ensure you stand by each person long enough for them to have their turn and be heard. They should only speak when you are near them. You could decide to just listen as you pass by each person or you might choose to reply or comment sometimes. Ask the students to speak loudly and clearly as everyone needs to hear what is being said.	This is an opportunity to teach and practice conditionals, e.g., "If you stay then the outcome might be that …," "If you leave, the outcome might be that …," etc. **Writing opportunities:** This activity enables some of the "pros and cons" of staying or leaving, to be considered and shared. The pros and cons could afterward be written on self-adhesive notes and placed in two columns. Nazir's parents could write in a personal diary their differing thoughts about the possibility of Nazir leaving. When Nazir has made his decision, his parents could each write their next diary instalment in response to his decision.

	Drama Strategy or activity	Grouping	Teacher guidance	Comments and suggestions	Language links and opportunities
12.	Writing in Role	Pairs	Nizar has decided to leave on the lorry. Tell them that he will write a letter to his parents, which they will find once he has left. Ask them to work in pairs to write just one sentence that could appear in Nazir's letter. Each pair should agree and write one sentence on a strip of paper. They then place it anywhere within a class circle, where everyone can see and read all the finished sentences.	They are drawn into the process of shared writing because they want to help the character with his deeply personal writing task.	**Alternative writing opportunity:** The teacher could become Nazir with a large blank piece of paper and a pen. In role as Nazir, the teacher can ask them to help him write this letter. The teacher in role (and the students) can ask for clarification, explanation, and justification when sentence additions and amendments are suggested.
	Shared and Guided Writing	Whole class	After they have read all the sentences, ask them to collect their own sentences and stand in a circle with them. Whoever thinks they are holding a good opening sentence can step forward first and place it down on the floor, as the start of the letter. Then whoever thinks they have a sentence that could come next can step forward and place it. Continue until the sentences have been placed. They will now have together assembled some of Nazir's letter. It can be read through, reviewed, and sentences moved. If someone wants to reposition a sentence, then they need to explain why.	The drama provides the motivation, purpose, and context for practicing writing an important informal letter with empathy and sensitivity. The students have met Nazir and are familiar with his parents (through Activity 11). The teacher can encourage them to try the different sentences out in various places and encourage discussion about which sentence works best in which position and why.	This engages the students in the process of shared writing. They are using and combining information and collaboration skills, as well as writing skills.
	Teacher in Role		Finally, the teacher reads the sequence of sentences aloud in role as Nazir.		
13.	Proxemics	Large whole class circle	Explain that some people will have decided to go and others to stay. Some may still be undecided or have no money for the fare. Within the class circle, you need to indicate where the back door of the lorry is. Explain that you will stand next to it in role now as the lorry driver. They will enter the circle one at a time and either position themselves near the lorry driver (indicating that they are going with him) or position themselves in a way that signals that they are not going with him. As each person enters and positions themselves, they speak a sentence that explains why they are positioned where they are. The sentences will start with the sentence stem, "I am standing here because ….," e.g., "I am standing here because I want to join my brother in England" or "I am standing here because I do not trust this man. I think he will take our money and then dump us somewhere." Once everyone has entered, the lorry driver (in slow motion) bolts the imaginary door.	The way and place in which people position themselves will communicate meaning. This activity makes links between physical positioning and what is being said, i.e., spacing and physical positioning hold meaning	**Writing opportunity:** Ask them to imagine that they are carrying a pen and paper with them on the journey. At some point in the future, they will write something on the paper. What will they write? For example, an address, a note they leave for someone, a note to themselves, a letter they hope can be sent, a personal poem, an annotated drawing, etc.

Poem for Activity 3

Changing Home

> My home was a safe place.
> It held me close, like a warm hug.
> I felt peaceful.
>
> My home became less safe.
> Its hug loosened a little.
> I felt nervous.
>
> My home became unsafe.
> It pushed me slowly away.
> I felt frightened.
>
> My home became dangerous.
> It threw me into the unknown.
> I felt terrified.

Patrice Baldwin

Activity 8

Teacher in Role—A Possible Script for the People Smuggler's Agent

"OK. Listen to me very carefully and then I'll answer your questions. This meeting's got to be short. We can't be found here by guards. If you decide to come on this journey, you will be taken to Turkey by lorry. I won't be coming with you. I am just selling the places for the driver. The lorry leaves on Wednesday night. That's in three nights time. The journey costs 7,500 dollars for each person. The deposit is 3,000 dollars. There aren't any discounts, so don't ask for one. The driver will take 20 people on his lorry. He's got 10 places left. When you pay me 3,000 dollars deposit, then I'll tell you when and where to find the lorry. You won't know where you are going to be left in Turkey, until you are in the lorry. You can pay me the deposit now or you can pay me the full amount now. I'll be here tomorrow evening at the same time and that will be your last chance to pay. The first 10 people to pay will get the places. After that, you are too late. Don't ask me when the next lorry will be. I don't know. You can only bring one small bag each. You may need to move fast with it. Bring your own food for a three-day journey. The driver has water for you. No babies. No old people. No disabled. Any questions?"

Activity 11

Teacher in Role—A Possible Script for the Undecided Person before They Pass through the Conscience Alley

"My name is Nizar and I live in a town in Syria. I don't know what to do. This is a chance to escape to another country and I hope to make a new life. But if I go, I would have to leave my elderly parents. They are too old to come on the journey. My father says I should go and he will give me some money for the journey. My mother says it is my duty to stay and that they cannot afford to give me their money. I don't know what to do."

Some Additional Language Opportunities

Students can search online for refugees' personal recounts of their journeys, read them and then recount them to each other. This gives them practice at reading comprehension and verbal recounting. They could be asked to recount either in the first or third person.

Some Additional Writing Opportunities

- Use the poem below as a writing frame and ask the students to add a fifth verse, starting with either, "My home became a lorry" or "My home is now a lorry."
- Imagine that one of the refugees kept a secret diary during the journey and that it was found somewhere in the future. Write the last diary entry.
- A refugee's diary could talk and then write about how it ended up being parted from its owner, The students can talk to themselves as the diary first (monologue), before writing, or could recount the event to a partner first and then write about it, as the diary (personification).

Recommended Additional Resources

An interactive online learning activity. You become a refugee on a journey and discover the consequences of any decisions you make. https://www.bbc.co.uk/news/world-middle-east-32057601?fbclid=IwAR0GAknUtnWxH9ni0w0TWRQt205Ogel-nDDFlMydlWUMkEj9Q_9HWBewJZE

"Home"—a poem by Warsan Shire that is full of powerful images and metaphors, explaining why people leave their homes. It also powerfully presents some of the shocking situations that refugees find themselves in.

UNIT 4 Conservation or Change?

The theme of this drama clearly links with issues around sustainable development and the ecological implications of changing land use. Although the drama is set in an English village, the issues it focuses on are of universal relevance to people living in many other small villages across the world. The drama will help raise the student's cultural awareness and hopefully connect them with and deepen their respect for nature.

Language teachers can use this drama with students at different levels of proficiency by shaping and adapting it to meet their students' needs and competencies. The linked vocabulary provided should be pre-taught and can then be recalled, used, and practiced during the drama itself. The drama gives many opportunities for practicing a range of language skills in an integrated way. It gives opportunities for active listening and thoughtful speaking. Additional activity suggestions for both speaking and writing are offered.

The drama conventions and strategies used are intended to stimulate and scaffold the student's critical and creative thinking and inter-thinking skills. During the lesson, the students will be formulating arguments, actively listening, analyzing arguments, defending various viewpoints and opinions, and negotiating and persuading others to change their thinking. As in all Process Drama, this lesson will help to develop the students' social, communication, and collaboration skills as well as their linguistic proficiency.

The drama is set in the imaginary, quiet, and traditional English village of Hopham. Matthew Trunch, the owner of Forest Larks Holiday Company, intends to build a residential holiday center in nearby Hopham Forest. He is hiring professional planners to help him (the students). The students will at times change roles and become the villagers, considering the implications of this proposed development on villagers' lives and livelihoods.

Background Information for Students

Hopham is a pretty, rural village that tourists often visit during the holiday season. Hopham is situated next to the River Core, which flows into Hopham Lake. The lakeside walk and nearby forest walks are popular with bird-watchers. The lake is used by fishermen and sometimes by canoeists. About half the forest is nationally protected land and the other half is privately owned by a local farmer (Bill Trunch).

Most of the residents of Hopham have never lived anywhere else. Hopham has one small village shop, a small school, a church, a small village hall, and a run-down pub that is only busy in the summer. Local houses are increasingly being bought as second homes and some are being rented out to holidaymakers. There are very few local jobs. Most people need to travel by car to work in the city of Corchester, which is 20 miles away, and there are two buses a day that go to and from the city.

Information for the Teacher

The owner of Forest Larks Holiday Company (Matthew Trunch) intends to build a residential family holiday park in Hopham Forest. The farmer has agreed to sell him the land. Initially, Mr. Trunch wants to get planning permission to build thirty log cabins, outdoor adventure structures, and an indoor activity center with swimming pool. The center will stay open all year round and the pool and outdoor activities will also be open to day visitors. Phase 1 of the holiday center (if approved) will not be visible from the village. Visitors arriving will not have to go into the village, to enter and leave the holiday park but it is an attractive village that they may well visit too. Forest Lark Holiday Company expects the holiday park to provide local jobs (building, maintenance, and cleaning). The park will be built by Mr. Trunch's own building company but some local builders will also be employed for the construction work.

Resources Required: Thick felt tips. Before the lesson, make a large copy of the map of Hopham (see Resource Sheet 3, page 127). Alternatively (before the drama lesson), the students could jointly create their own map of Hopham village (using the information provided above for the teacher).

Useful Vocabulary (to be pre-taught)

Wildlife, conservation, opportunity, benefit, threat, residents, employment, tourism, tourists, support, oppose, private, public, business, leisure.

Some Possible Villager Occupations (Optional Vocabulary Practice): shopkeeper, pub landlord, cook, gardener, tree surgeon, carpenter, builder, painter and decorator, plumber, cleaner, game-keeper, tractor driver, vicar or priest, second home owner, unemployed man, unemployed woman, accountant, author, artist, photographer, musician, computer technician, teacher, headteacher, retired banker, handyman.

Before the Lesson: Make sure that the students are familiar with the map of Hopham and the first two paragraphs of the background information. *Don't share the information in paragraph three at the start.* When the drama starts, the villagers don't know that the forest is likely to be used for a holiday development.

	Drama Strategy or activity	Grouping	Teacher guidance	Comments and suggestions	Language links and opportunities
1.	Occupational Mime	Whole class	The students should have studied the map of Hopham and been given some background information. Ask the class to stand in a big circle. In turn, each student will enter in role as a villager who lives in Hopham (or has a second home there). They can decide on a role for themselves or maybe choose an occupational role from those above. Don't let anyone become the local farmer.	You could gather some suggestions for villager occupations first, e.g., shopkeeper, school teacher, cleaner, vicar, housewife, gardener, game-keeper, tractor driver, etc. The occupational mime is being used to help get the students into role at the start of the drama and to get them physically engaging with the fiction.	You could start with a warm-up activity that uses and reinforces the occupational vocabulary linked to the lesson (see above). The students move around, and when you call out an occupation, they stop and mime it until you call out, "Move on."
	Tableau		As each villager enters, they should get into a still position as if they are carrying out an occupational task or other everyday job. As they get into position, they should say • their name • what they are doing • one additional piece of information e.g., "I am Susan. I am stacking shelves in my shop. I was born in this village." "I am John. I am unemployed. I used to work on the farm." "I am Peter. I am a children's author. I have a second home in Hopham. I let it out in the summer and come here to write in the winter."	They are now starting to verbally engage with the role in a simple way and getting to know who else is in the village.	They could draw and label their homes on the class map and write a sentence or two alongside, giving additional information. You could ask them to get into pairs. One person is in role as a villager, talking about themselves. The other listens and asks questions. This will help build and deepen engagement with their role. It also is an opportunity for practicing descriptive language, associated with self-presentation. They could be asked to use different linguistic structures and tenses. **Writing opportunity** Information about the villager could be recorded on a "Role on the Wall" (see pages 68–69 and Resource Sheet 17, page 141). This could form the basis of a short biography or autobiography.

	Drama Strategy or activity	Grouping	Teacher guidance	Comments and suggestions	Language links and opportunities
2.	**Teacher as Storyteller** Mime	Whole class	Bring the still scene silently to life for a few seconds. As they mime, you can narrate what is happening in the scene, as if you are a storyteller, e.g., "It was an ordinary day in the village of Hopham. Susan was filling the shelves in the village shop, Peter was writing and John was walking his dog and looking for someone to chat to. No one in Hopham knew that at that moment, hundreds of miles away, the owner of Forest Larks Holiday Company was meeting with his team. He was planning to build a residential holiday park in nearby Hopham Forest."	The teacher is modelling a third-person narrative. They are retelling what is going on in the tableau by "talking like a storyteller" and/or "talking like a writer." Having modeled this, the teacher could ask the students to narrate what they are doing. As the teacher passes by each villager, they retell it as a third-person narrative, e.g., the student in role as Susan would say, "Susan was stacking shelves …" instead of "I am stacking shelves …"	**Speaking and writing opportunity** The students hear their tableau scene being retold as a spoken narrative by the teacher. They could try retelling the whole scene aloud to themselves as a narrative (with no one listening). This could be a step toward them writing the scene as a narrative. They could be asked to speak and write the narratives in the first or third person (or both).
3.	**Teacher in Role** Mantle of the Expert	Whole class	Tell the students that they are now changing roles and will become professional planners and designers of holiday parks. You will be in role as Matthew Trunch, the owner of Forest Larks Holiday Company Ltd. You are hiring them to design your next park, near Hopham.	This is an opportunity for students to practice business language (ESP—English for specific purposes). They will be using a more formal language register, practicing business-focused conversations, and using language to explain, justify, persuade, and negotiate.	Working together as planners and designers, sharing ideas, negotiating, compromising, agreeing a plan, and presenting it (according to the client's criteria) opens up many opportunities for the students to use technology, e.g., creating a PowerPoint or short film. Or, they can make hand drawings, maps, and models of their plans and designs.
		Groups of four	In role as Mr. Trunch, you need to formally welcome them to the meeting and display or give them a map of Hopham (See Resource Sheet 3, page 178). Tell them that you have arranged to buy part of Hopham Forest and will be applying for planning permission to build thirty log cabins, outdoor adventure structures, and an indoor activity center with swimming pool. Their job now is to come up with some great design ideas and layouts for you. They should discuss and list their ideas and perhaps start to sketch them. Nothing can be constructed that would be visible above the tree line.	You could just give ten minutes for this task or much longer if you want them to do a more detailed and annotated plan before the groups present their ideas in turn.	This is an opportunity to work on a team project together and practice presentation skills. They need to get and keep the attention of those they will present to and can practice this together and give feedback to each other. Preparing a plan for presentation requires good time management, cooperation, collaboration, and sometimes leadership skills.

	Drama Strategy or activity	Grouping	Teacher guidance	Comments and suggestions	Language links and opportunities
			Answer any questions and then ask them to work in groups of four. Explain that each group in turn will be formally presenting their initial ideas for the development content and layout. Set a time limit for the task. You may decide to nominate a group leader, or let the group do so, or not have a nominated group leader.		
4.	Mantle of the Expert	Whole class	Each group now will formally present their ideas for the park (as professionals) to Mr. Trunch, answering anyone's questions, at the end of their presentation. Once all the groups have presented, Mr. Trunch can say that the final plan will probably use some ideas from each of their plans.	This provides an opportunity for practicing presentational skills. The teacher can decide the level of formality required for this activity. This activity could be set up as competitive "pitching" or as a collaborative activity but the next activity (5) will pool and use everyone's ideas.	**Writing opportunities** The owner of Forest Larks Holiday Company Ltd. could require his planners and designers to write • a key information sheet (bullet points) to accompany their group plans, • a labeled plan • a PowerPoint presentation.
5.	Mapping	Whole class	Put a large sheet of paper and felt pens in the center. In turn, the students now enter and write (or draw) one thing they want to place in the final layout/plan. They should say what it is and briefly justify and explain why they want it included, e.g., "I want to include a seating area here for outdoor puppet shows and storytelling, **because** ...," "I want to put a rope bridge here between two tree houses that are reached by ladders, **because** ...," etc.	This produces a collective plan that everyone will have contributed to and will have shared knowledge and ownership of.	**Writing opportunities** Once a joint plan has been created, they could be asked later to draft and write an accompanying letter or email that could be sent to the planning officer with the plan.
6.	Rumors (and Opinions)	Whole class	The villagers have now heard rumors that there is a plan to build a holiday park in the forest. Different villagers might have different viewpoints. Some may have seen the plan. Rumors are spreading fast (some true, some false). Ask them to move around as villagers, gathering and spreading information and rumors about the plan. They might also share their different opinions about whether the development should be allowed or not.	Because they were developers in Activity 5, they know what is planned for the park but in Activity 6, they are playfully pretending that they don't know. Students can create rumors themselves or repeat what they have heard others say or elaborate and add to what they have been told.	During this activity, they will be using language to give and gather information, comment and express opinions, agree, and disagree. They will be practicing present perfect tense.

	Drama Strategy or activity	Grouping	Teacher guidance	Comments and suggestions	Language links and opportunities
7.	Eavesdropping	Whole class	Freeze Activity 6 once it is well underway. Explain that as you pass by each "frozen" villager in turn, they should continue speaking a rumor or opinion aloud until you move away (when they should freeze again).	This enables everyone in role to select and share a rumor or opinion that everyone will hear. This provides everyone with information that will help them during Activity 8, when they are going to be interviewed by a newspaper reporter.	The activity requires them to listen purposefully for information. They can select some of the information later when they are being interviewed by a newspaper reporter.
8.	Teacher in Role Working in Role	Whole class	Tell them that you will now be in role as a local newspaper reporter, interviewing the villagers about the proposed park near Hopham village. You could invite a couple of students to join you as newspaper reporters (from other newspapers). Invite villagers who are willing to be interviewed to step forward. Others stay nearby as villagers and listen in. You might decide to be coaxing or provocative at times, e.g., "What are your main concerns about the plan?" "What differences do you think it will make to life in your lovely village?" "Do you think the council should refuse this development? Why?" "Can you think of one good thing about having a big holiday park in the forest?" "What do you feel about the farmer, selling this land to developers?" "What would you like to say now to the owner of holiday company?"	This is a way of telling what they know (or have heard rumored) to a different audience (newspaper reporters). They have already talked about the plan as planners and designers, then as villagers gossiping with each other and they now are talking as villagers still but to an external audience (the media). The language students will need to change speech register and adjust the content of what they say for each different type of conversation.	**Writing opportunity** The students not being interviewed by the reporter (teacher in role) could be asked to take notes for the newspaper report (including carefully recording quotes from various villagers). They can then use the notes as the basis of a newspaper report that they write later (and can give it a headline). The students listening, taking notes, and then writing a newspaper report need to listen well and employ critical thinking skills to do the task. They will be analyzing information and considering different villagers' viewpoints and arguments. They will need to write, using the language and style of newspaper reporters. The teacher could ask the students to write in a biased way, i.e., half the reporters writing a report that comes across as positive about the proposed development and the other half writing a newspaper report more negatively. Media bias (and the reasons for it) could be discussed.

	Drama Strategy or activity	Grouping	Teacher guidance	Comments and suggestions	Language links and opportunities
9.	Collective Voice Collective Role	Two large groups	Tell them that the council planning committee have not decided yet whether to allow planning permission or not. Some councilors support the plan and some are against it. Divide the class into two groups. Each group collectively represents the voice of a single councilor. The two councilors are speaking to each other at a formal planning meeting. One voice is speaking for the development and the other voice is speaking against it. Anyone in either group can speak just a single sentence at a time, as the councilor whose group they are in. No one can speak twice in a row but everyone can speak more than once. The whole class is improvising a dialogue between the two opposing councilors with everyone able to contribute sentences as one or other of the councilors.	It helps to have the two groups facing each other in two clusters. They should try to make the dialogue flow, even though they are each contributing only individual sentences to it. It might be that some students do not contribute and that is fine. They will still be standing with a group as one or the other. You could have some students sitting out, taking notes about what both councilors say as if they are newspaper reporters attending the meeting or they could take notes as villagers or representatives of Mr. Trunch.	**Writing opportunities** Following Activity 9, the students could jot down some main points that were made by either or both councilors at the meeting. The students could create some notes that were written by a newspaper reporter at the meeting and could then write a short newspaper report about the meeting (maybe just a paragraph). They could write notes as a member of the public (a villager of Hopham) who attended the meeting. The villager who did not attend) about the meeting. The villager's notes could then be used when writing a letter to the local newspaper (which the villager hopes will get published). Or, they could be writing detailed notes to then accurately report back (verbally or by email) to Mr. Trunch (teacher in role).
10.	Improvisation	Pairs	Ask the students to get into pairs. Tell them they are both villagers and are good friends. One of them wants the holiday development and the other does not. Each will try and persuade their friend to change their viewpoint.	This activity is still between two people with different viewpoints but informal, persuasive speech is now required.	

	Drama Strategy or activity	Grouping	Teacher guidance	Comments and suggestions	Language links and opportunities
11.	Proxemics	Whole class	**"Where do you stand?"** Indicate an imaginary line across the room. Explain that one end of the line represents the viewpoint, "I definitely want the park." The other end of the line represents "I definitely do not want the park." Each villager in turn will enter and place themselves somewhere along the line. They should briefly justify aloud their positioning, beginning with the sentence stem, "I am standing here because …," e.g., if someone stands half way along the line, they might say, "I am standing here in the middle because although I don't want any buildings in the forest but I am unemployed and maybe I can get a job at the holiday center."	Point out that there could be advantages and disadvantages to the development. Some villagers may have more to gain from it than others. This activity is asking for justification and explanation. It is a way of visually and physically representing the range of different viewpoints and "positions" that the villagers hold.	The students are being given the opportunity in role to express their opinion and are expected to explain and justify it to others. This requires them to employ and communicate their critical thinking.
12.	Small Group Playmaking Freeze Frame	Groups of four	Tell them that the holiday park was built and has been open for five years. This has led to some good and bad moments for various villagers. Ask them to get into groups of four and create two short scenes (each no longer than a minute). One short scene should freeze on "a positive moment" that has resulted from the park being built. The other should freeze on "a negative moment" that has resulted from it being built.	Alternatively, the memorable moments could be portrayed as still images, rather than presented as brief, animated scenes. Afterward, they could all be asked to step out of their scenes and start gossiping "in role" with each other about these memorable moments (as in Rumors), e.g., "Do you remember …," "I will never forget the moment when …," etc.	
13.	Performance Carousel	Whole class	You can now either ask to see: • all the groups' scenes seamlessly (as a whole class Performance Carousel); • or one group at a time performing both scenes. After each group, you can invite questioning of the characters (Hot-seating); • or see all the groups' negative scenes first, followed by all the groups' positive scenes.	Following the presentation of the scenes, you could ask them in groups to imagine they are all remembering (recounting) the scene together later.	**Writing opportunity** These contrasting "moments" could be written up as personal diary entries by a villager or could be included in an email or letter that they send to a friend who used to live in the village years ago (before Forest Larks Holiday Center was built).

UNIT 5 Beowulf

This drama lesson provides an opportunity to learn a target language and employ twenty-first-century skills, while exploring a Scandinavian legend set in the sixth century. The story was told in an epic poem, written in Old English, sometime between 975 and 1025. The original manuscript is now in the British Library. The poet is unknown. Advanced language students may be interested in reading the original poem and learning more about "Old English" after the drama. This drama unit, however, uses a simple version of the story.

The legend offers a metaphorical context within which the students can learn about and explore diverse forms of the language, while practicing and developing a range of skills. Before the drama, the teacher could ask students to research the story online. This would give then the opportunity to use and develop some of their media and information literacy skills, as well as learn more about Beowulf. The students could also easily find various paintings of Beowulf online. These could be used before or after the drama to stimulate critical thinking and discussions around their content and the different interpretations of scenes and characters in various paintings. This drama unit provides much opportunity for creative thinking and will help students to develop their understanding of symbolism. The legend of Beowulf is full of strong emotions at various points, for example, pride, terror, bravery, grief, relief. The spectrum of emotions the dramatic legend can stir in the students (both positive and negative) might be used skillfully by some teachers outside the drama to help the students to talk about and manage their own emotions.

The Legend

Beowulf is a prince and a hero, living in Geatland (Sweden). He hears of a monster called Grendel, who has been killing Danes in King Hrothgar's splendid Mead Hall (which is called Heorot). Grendel has been terrorizing the Danes and killing them in the hall relentlessly for twelve years. Beowulf decides to sail to Denmark and is accompanied by fourteen Geat warriors. He is greeted warmly by King Hrothgar. That night, Beowulf waits for the monster. Grendel arrives, kills a Geat, and then turns his attention to Beowulf, who has tightly gripped Grendel's arm and will not let it go. Beowulf keeps twisting Grendel's arm around and eventually rips it off. Grendel is mortally wounded and limps away to die. The drama lesson finishes at this point. However, Beowulf goes on to kill Grendel's revengeful mother, and many years later, he slays a dragon and is mortally wounded himself in the process.

Resources Required

A version of the story has been written in pairs of sentences for use with this lesson (see Resource Sheet 5, page 129). This should be photocopied for the students before the lesson (as it is needed for Activities 12 and 13).

The teacher needs a copy of Resource Sheet 4, page 128 for Activity 2.

There are many paintings and drawings of Grendel, Beowulf, and Anglo-Saxon Mead Halls that can be found online. These could be studied and discussed before or after the lesson. Projecting an image of a Mead Hall for Activity 8 would be helpful (optional).

The full soundtrack for the Beowulf film (Warner Brothers) is available online. Parts of it could be played when the students are entering the hall of Heorot as Talking Objects (during Activity 8). It could also be played in the background as groups are preparing and presenting their still images (during Activities 12 and 13).

Useful Vocabulary (to be pre-taught)

Hero, victim, killing, terrified, feast, celebration, monster, twisted, ripped, fight, winner, loser.

Additional Vocabulary (Optional): Epic, mortally wounded, revenge.

	Drama Strategy or activity	Grouping	Teacher guidance	Comments and suggestions	Language links and opportunities
1.	**Warm-Up Activity**	Whole class	Ask the students to move around the room. Whenever you call out a word, they should respond to it physically as follows: "The king" (or "Hrothgar")—bow down "The monster" (or Grendel)—freeze "The hero" (or Beowulf)—raise your arms in the air.	You can decide whether to call out the common nouns, the proper nouns, or both for this activity. This actively familiarizes the students with the names and roles of the main characters before they hear the story.	You could extend this activity by also adding other vocabulary that is useful and relevant to the drama (see above).
2.	**Active Storytelling** Mime	Whole class	Ask everyone to stand alone in a space. Now slowly read aloud the simple version of the legend of Beowulf (Resource Sheet 4, page 128). Check that the plot and vocabulary have been understood. Explain that you will now read the story a second time. This time they should individually and spontaneously mime the story as you are reading it. They can physically become characters and/or objects. As you read the story, pause between each sentence to give time for the students to listen, comprehend, and physically respond.	This enables the students to act out the story simply and individually. Listening and simultaneously miming the story will help the students to learn and remember the story and vocabulary. The activity could be made more challenging by asking the students to mime the sentences collaboratively and silently with a partner. The story could also be told using the "Whoosh!" storytelling strategy (page 71). The students stand in a circle and as the teacher tells the story, he/she signals for students to enter the circle at various points and silently act out the sentences in turn. The teacher clears the central space by calling "Whoosh!" when necessary.	The students are listening for understanding to be able to mime the story. They are responding non verbally and together, so this is a relatively low threat activity if there are any "drama/ language anxious" students. **Sentence sequencing** Copies of the sentences can be given to individual students or to pairs of students. Ask them to mix the sentences up and then sort and sequence them correctly. **Writing opportunity** They could be asked to make the simple sentences more descriptive and effective by adding more words, e.g., "Beowulf heard about the terrible monster, Grendel" could be changed to "Beowulf heard gruesome tales about the terrible, evil monster, Grendel."

	Drama Strategy or activity	Grouping	Teacher guidance	Comments and suggestions	Language links and opportunities
3.	Tableau Still Image	Whole class	**What might Grendel look like?** Explain that in turn the students will enter the space and get into position, as some part of Grendel's body. As each person adds themselves to the monster, they need to say which part of its body they are and describe it, e.g., "I am Grendel's skin. I am very thick and very rough."	This enables all students to contribute ideas and together to have a shared vision of what Grendel looks like. Everyone is contributing descriptive vocabulary that helps them (and others) to imagine the same monster. They need to listen attentively to each other to be able to add appropriately to what has already been offered.	**Writing opportunities** 1. Each person can write their sentence on a separate sentence strip. 2. The sentences can be added to or rewritten for greater effect. 3. Additional sentences can be added. 4. The sentences can be arranged and rearranged in various ways and read aloud for different effect. 5. Sentences can be written on self-adhesive labels and positioned where it is physically appropriate within or around a drawn outline of Grendel's body (as a large Role on the Wall, see pages 68–69 and Resource Sheet 17, page 141). 6. The sentences could contribute to a shared, guided class description of Grendel, guided and scribed by the teacher.
4.	Rumors	Whole class	**What do the Danes say about Grendel?** Grendel has been killing Danes for twelve years and this has led to much gossip and rumor. Ask the students to each make up a rumor about Grendel and then everyone will spread and gather rumors. Maybe they have seen Grendel (or think they have) or know someone who says they have seen Grendel. Maybe they knew a victim of Grendel. You can join in too if you wish. After a couple of minutes, freeze the scene.	You could offer some sentence stems for this activity, e.g. "I heard that …," "Someone told me that …," "Have you heard about …," etc.	Individual students could write the rumors they have heard inside one big speech bubble. Each person could write one rumor onto an individual speech bubble. The speech bubbles can be gathered and displayed together (maybe within one big speech bubble or around the outline of a big ear). This is an opportunity for the students to practice reported speech, e.g., "They said that …" and the present perfect tense, e.g., "Have you heard that …?"

	Drama Strategy or activity	Grouping	Teacher guidance	Comments and suggestions	Language links and opportunities
5.	Eavesdropping	Whole class	The scene is now frozen. Explain that you will now move around the scene listening into the rumors and gossip. Whoever you are standing nearest to should come alive and carry on talking about Grendel. They should freeze again when you move away and start listening to someone else. You can then gather everyone together to carry on sharing and discussing the rumors within one large group.	Ask the students to speak loudly enough for everyone to hear what is being said. Additionally, the students could sit in a circle. One person starts to tell a story about Grendel and then claps to pass the story on for the next person to continue. Or, the teacher can clap to signal that the story must now move on to the next person. An object could be passed around with the story, e.g., a stick.	**Writing opportunity** The shared gossip and rumors can become a stimulus for more extended storytelling (and this can be used as preparation for story writing). Following Activity 5, ask the students to get into pairs. Ask them to take turns at recounting to each other (in role as Danes), something they experienced first-hand (or have heard about) that relates to Grendel. Afterward, the listener can question further the person telling the story.
6.	Conscience Alley Teacher in Role	Whole class	**Should Beowulf sail to Denmark and try to kill Grendel?** Ask the class to get into two lines and stand facing each other. Explain that you will be in role as Beowulf and will walk between the lines. Only the person you are standing nearest to is allowed to speak to you as you pass by. Those standing in one line will try and persuade you to go and kill Grendel. Those in the opposite line will each try and persuade you not to go. As you reach the end of the line, you can speak to them all (as Beowulf) and say that you have decided to sail to Denmark, kill Grendel, and free the Danes of this monster. You want to be a hero!	You can just stand by each person in turn and listen to them, as Beowulf. Or, you may prefer to respond briefly "in the moment" as Beowulf to what is being said to you as you pass.	**Writing opportunities** What was said to Beowulf by those in the opposing lines can be written down afterward within two separate columns (Resource Sheet 12, page 136, could be used for this). The notes in columns can be used to inform a written monologue consisting of Beowulf's conflicting internal thoughts that might have preceded his decision to go and kill Grendel.
7.	Collective Role Improvisation	Two groups (of 6 to 8 students) and audience in role	**Beowulf arrives in Denmark and goes to meet King Hrothgar.** Ask 6–8 students to get into a group together as Beowulf and another 6–8 students to get into a group as King Hrothgar. The remaining students can position themselves in the scene in role as silent eyewitnesses who are present. Beowulf and King Hrothgar now have their first meeting. Their initial conversation will be improvised by those in the two groups. No student in either group may speak twice in a row.	This enables the whole class to engage in various ways with a dialogue between main characters. It allows about 12–16 people to contribute some of a character's dialogue. Those in collective role need to listen attentively and contribute cohesively to make it sound like one character speaking. No-one can speak twice in a row.	**Writing opportunities** The dialogue between Beowulf and Hrothgar can be written up afterward as a playscript. The eyewitnesses in the scene could talk about the scene to an imaginary friend (or a partner) and then write an eyewitness account of the scene afterward.

	Drama Strategy or activity	Grouping	Teacher guidance	Comments and suggestions	Language links and opportunities
8.	Talking Objects	Whole class	**Inside the great Mead Hall of Heorot** Ideally, project an image of an Anglo-Saxon Mead Hall. Ask the class to stand in a circle. Explain that one at a time, they will enter the space and position themselves as an object in the hall, e.g., sword, table, tapestry, bench, goblet, etc. "In role" they should say which object they are and add one piece of information about themselves, e.g., "I am a heavy shield hanging on the wall. My owner was killed in a battle."	They are physically creating the setting. It helps if the students look carefully at some pictures of Mead Halls. You could project an image of a Mead Hall, ask them to study it silently, and then invite them to say what they notice. Tell them that their sentences must start with "I notice … " e.g., "I notice there are wooden barrels piled up at the side of the room." etc.	**Writing opportunities** Talking as objects can lead into personification in writing. The objects are part of the setting but they are also eyewitnesses. For example, the objects in Heorot could talk (and write) about the fight between Grendel and Beowulf. Students in role as objects in Heorot can answer questions later about the fight (and the moments before it), if asked (see Hot-seating, pages 66–68).
	Teacher in Role	Whole class	**Waiting for Grendel to arrive** Explain that you will now be going into role as Beowulf. As you pass by each object in the hall of Heorot, the object can speak to you, e.g., the shield might say, "You need a shield Beowulf. Take me off this wall and use me."	This is a way of building up dramatic tension and enabling everyone to interact with Beowulf at this key moment. The students are also sharing their ideas "in the moment" and in role.	The students (as objects) can write an eyewitness recount later. They can also be interviewed and provide information later to someone who is going to write a third-person narrative or a commissioned, factual report of the fight.
9.	"Making Sense" of the Moment	Whole class	**Waiting for Grendel** Tell the students they will now be Geats, waiting with Beowulf for Grendel to arrive in the hall. Ask them to spread themselves around the room and imagine they are hiding in the shadows. Ask them to imagine what they might see, hear, smell, and touch, as they wait? Now ask them to use these sentence stems to verbally share their multisensory responses, i.e. "I can see … " or "I can hear … " or "I can smell … " or "I can feel (touch) … " They are all helping each other to imagine what it is like inside the hall, so they need to use language descriptively, e.g., "I can see candle wax, dripping down onto a long, wooden table."	Dramatically tense music could be played in the background. The student's voices must be loud enough to hear above any background music. This activity invites the students' multisensory engagement with the setting, thus making it more vivid and memorable. The sharing of ideas is supportive and helps build the shared, imagined setting collaboratively. The teacher can join in this activity, modeling descriptive language at the start and later, maybe adding more detail to the setting.	**Writing opportunity** The sensory sentences can be jotted down and gathered. They could then be displayed randomly or placed within columns (with a different column heading for each sense). The collection of sentences can be referred to and used by the students later, e.g., when writing in role about as a Geat who was waiting and who then witnessed the fight. The teacher could become the scribe for a piece of shared and guided narrative writing that sets the scene. The students can refer to and redraft the jotted sentences, suggesting (a sentence at a time) what the teacher could write next.

	Drama Strategy or activity	Grouping	Teacher guidance	Comments and suggestions	Language links and opportunities
10.	Voice Collage	Pairs Whole class	**The killing of Grendel** Ask the students to work with a partner and create just *one sentence* together that can be spoken by a Geat, who is at that moment watching Beowulf fight with Grendel. The sentence should be in the present tense, e.g., "Grendel has streams of spit dripping from his mouth … " and "The muscles in Beowulf's arms are sticking up like ropes." Now, let everyone listen to all the sentences in turn. Then explain that they will be closing their eyes and improvising, using just their own sentence. During the improvisation, they can repeatedly speak the whole sentence or sometimes just part of it, e.g., "spit dripping, spit dripping," or individual words from the sentence, e.g., "muscles." Individuals can also remain silent at times during the improvisation. Explain that the volume of their collective voices needs to gradually rise to a crescendo and then the voices should gradually get quieter, and in the end, everyone needs to be silent. They should keep their eyes closed in silence until you ask them to open their eyes again. The teacher could round off this activity by adding a final line or two of narrative, e.g., "And they watched Grendel limp away in pain. He was limping toward his Death."	The students have their eyes closed for this activity, so their attention is being focused on the aural and oral. It is a spontaneous, experimental, collaborative activity. This activity can be set up differently with the class divided into two large groups. One group sits on the floor with their eyes closed and the other group stands in a circle around them. The standing group improvises a voice collage performance for the seated group to experience. They then swap over. Or, each group can be given time to prepare a Voice Collage performance for the other group to experience (with eyes closed).	**Writing opportunities** Each sentences can be written on a sentence strip and then together the sentences can be arranged (and rearranged) in various ways. The impact of the different positioning of various sentences can be discussed. Which sentence positions and combinations work best and why? **"Proxemics" with words** The sentence strips can be cut up into separate words. They are all collected into one class pile and shuffled. The students get into groups of eight. The teacher shares the words out between the groups. The groups are then asked to work together to physically position the words in any meaningful way that they can justify and explain; e.g., the piece of paper with the word "Beowulf" written on it could be positioned above ground level. The justification could be that his status as a hero places him above others. Or, the word "Grendel" could be turned to face down as he is now dead. This activity stimulates discussion about the meaning and relative positioning of words. There is no right or wrong place for any word as its position can be logically explained and justified.

	Drama Strategy or activity	Grouping	Teacher guidance	Comments and suggestions	Language links and opportunities
11.	Improvisation	Pairs	When the Geats returned home, they would have told friends and family about what happened in Heorot.		**Writing opportunity** Telling and retelling a story in role can be good preparation for writing the story in role afterward.
			Ask the students to get into pairs. One was with Beowulf in Heorot and saw what happened. The other was not there and wants to hear about it. The listener can ask questions afterward. The teller and listener then swap over roles and the other person tells the story (as if it was theirs).	When a storyteller is questioned, they will stay in role and improvise, giving plausible answers that fit with the story. The listener needs to concentrate and listen attentively in order to steal the story and be able to then tell it as if it is their story.	Stories that are created and told in pairs can then be written in role by pairs. This enables discussion and negotiation about what to include in the writing and what to omit.
	Storytelling	Pairs and/or groups of four or whole class	Alternatively, a pair of students can be asked to tell one Geat's version of events. One student (in role as a Geat) starts telling the other what happened in Heorot. After a while, either the storyteller or the listener can clap. This is a signal that other will now take over and continue the story (until the next clap ... and so on, until the story is finished).	When students are both improvising to create one story, they have a compelling reason to listen well to each other. Having created one version of the story together, they could split up and each tells someone else the whole story.	
12.	Freeze Frame Still Image	Small groups	The story is told in ten pairs of sentences on Resource Sheet 5, page 129. Divide the class into five (or ten) groups and share out the pairs of sentences between the groups. Explain that each sentence can be represented in a single image. Ask the groups to create one still image for each of their allocated sentences. Explain that the groups will all be		

Drama Strategy or activity	Grouping	Teacher guidance	Comments and suggestions	Language links and opportunities
		asked to present (perform) their still images and sentences to each other in sequence. They need to practice moving into and out of their still images in slow motion. They will also need to hold each image still for a few seconds (see Still Image and Freeze Frame, pages 59–60). You can ask them to speak aloud the sentence that goes with their still image as they present it. Alternatively, you could speak the sentences for each image in turn, i.e., the whole story.		
13. Performance Carousel	Whole class	All the groups' still images can now be presented seamlessly in sequence as a continuous class performance. This creates a human storyboard of the whole story. One group's images should be immediately followed by the next group's images. As one group melts its final image (in slow motion), the next group should be moving into their first image in slow motion (until the last group finishes).	The sequence of still images is rather like a living storyboard. The sentences are acting as captions for the images. Resource Sheet 5 has a version of the story in ten pairs of sentences. These are used for Activities 12 and 13. However, the groups could rewrite and elaborate on the pairs of sentences that they have been allocated, creating their own sentences instead for the performance.	**Writing opportunity** Photographs of the images could be taken and sequenced to produce a storyboard. The accompanying sentences can be added (maybe digitally). Some appropriate speech and thought bubbles could also be added. Each group could work together to produce a paragraph for each of their still image photographs. The teacher needs to decide whether their paragraphs will be written in the first or third person. Once the paragraphs are completed and sequenced with the images, an illustrated version of the whole story will be the outcome.

UNIT 6 OVER THE TOP—The True Story of Annie Edson Taylor, the "Queen of the Mist"

This drama is based on a true story. It is about Annie Edson Taylor, who was the first person to survive going over Niagara Falls in a barrel. As the story is true, it provides language teachers with the opportunity to introduce the students to some authentic photographs, newspaper articles, and historical recounts that can be easily accessed online. During the drama, the language students will be interacting in role with Annie Edson Taylor (teacher in role). A drama based on an historical event may be of particular interest to some students and can motivate them to use a target language. The story can be framed as an example of one person's personal strength, determination, and courage to overcome personal difficulties. Others might say that it is an example of one person's stupidity and desperation. Either way, it is certainly an example of one woman's persistence and resilience.

The Drama Unit provides various opportunities to practice the language of mediation, negotiation, and persuasion, as well as using language creatively and descriptively.

The True Story

Annie Edson Taylor was the first person to go over Niagara Falls in a barrel and survive. She carried out this daredevil feat on October 24, 1901 (her sixty-third birthday).

Annie was born on October 24, 1838, in Auburn, New York. She was one of eight children. Her father died when she was twelve years old and she was then sent away to school. When she was seventeen years old, Annie married David Taylor. Tragically, their baby boy died when he was a few days old and her husband was killed in the American Civil War a year later.

Annie became a teacher and lived and worked in many places across America. Eventually, she opened her own dance school in Bay City, Michigan, but it was not making her much money. She was worried that she might end up living in a poorhouse in her old age, so she came up with a plan to make a lot of money quickly. She decided that she would be the first person to go over Niagara Falls in a barrel. She was desperate and thought that this would either kill her or make her rich. She was also confident that she would survive the trip and that people would pay afterward to listen to her tell her story and see her barrel.

Annie designed the barrel herself and then had to persuade someone to make it for her. At first, barrel makers were reluctant to help, as they did not want to be associated with what could end up looking like a suicide but eventually, Annie persuaded someone to make the barrel for her. It was built from strong Kentucky oak with seven irons rings around it and she selected every plank herself. A heavy weight was attached to the base to make sure that the barrel would end up floating upright. Hand grips were put inside and leather straps to stop her body from rolling around and to try and prevent her head from hitting the top of the barrel. The barrel was padded with many cushions and Annie decided to also take her lucky, heart-shaped cushion with her.

In Bay City, Annie hired a manager called Frank Russell. He usually worked with carnivals and circuses. He went to Niagara Falls ahead of Annie and arranged for newspaper reporters to interview her when she arrived by train from Bay City. Frank also hired a man with a rowing boat called Fred Truesdale with his helper Billy Holleron. They would row Annie and her barrel upstream of the Horseshoe Falls (the largest of the three Niagara Falls). Annie lied to Frank and the press about her age, telling them that she was only forty-two years old. Two days before going over the falls herself, Annie put her cat in her barrel and sent it over. The cat survived with just cuts to its head and she was photographed with it soon afterward.

Thousands of people came to witness Annie Edson Taylor going over the falls in her barrel. Fred and Billy rowed her and the barrel away from the crowds on the shore. They stopped at a small island in the river for her to get into the barrel. She strapped herself down and filled the barrel with cushions. After screwing down the lid tightly, they pumped compressed air into the barrel with a bicycle pump through a small hole, which they then hammered a plug into. The two boatmen towed Annie in the barrel, toward the falls and then untied the barrel, just before 4 p.m. (see Resource Sheet 6, page 130, Quote 1). Strong currents pushed the barrel toward the edge of the falls, where it paused for a few moments (see Resource Sheet 6, Quote 2), before tumbling 158 feet down and disappearing under the churning waters below. The barrel resurfaced and starting drifting turbulently toward the Canadian side of the river where it was held back by some rocks. The rescuers waded out with hooks and poles and pulled the barrel ashore. They sawed it open and helped Annie to get out (see Resource Sheet 6, page 130, Quotes 3 and 4). She was shocked and giddy, and her head and jaw were cut but Annie walked ashore to cheering crowds and the waiting photographers and reporters.

Annie's manager arranged a speaking tour for Annie, and for a while, she earned some money but she was a dull storyteller and her audiences soon lost interest. It was not long before her manager disappeared with her barrel. Annie hired a private detective and got the barrel back. She then hired a different manager who also disappeared with her barrel. He started touring with the barrel and a younger woman, who was pretending to be Annie. Annie never saw her barrel again and ended up poor. She set up a small stall on the river, selling postcards and telling her story to passing tourists (Resource Sheet 6, Quotes 5, 6, and 7). Annie died in poverty on April 29, 1921, in Niagara County Infirmary when she was 82 years old.

The Drama

This drama invites the students to learn about and engage with an incredible, true story. The drama strategies will help the students to engage with and consider Annie's motives, actions, experiences, and emotions, as well as the practical challenges she faced before, during, and after her historic journey over Niagara Falls.

Before the Lesson

It is recommended that before the lesson, you search online for vintage film footage, photographs, and newspaper articles relating to Annie Edson Taylor and her daredevil stunt. Seeing photographs and film footage of the Horseshoe Falls and a photograph of Annie will help the students to imagine the setting and the main character during the drama. The students will probably want to search online themselves after the drama and this will help to use and develop their media skills and deepen their knowledge of this true story.

During the Drama

You could project authentic, vintage photographs of Annie and the event onto a screen during the relevant points in the drama, for example, Annie getting into (or out of) the boat (Activity 11). This is optional but worthwhile.

After the Drama

Second language teaching always involves some elements of cultural and historical learning that is related to the target language. After the lesson the students could be asked to find, select, and share additional information with each other about Annie, her personal history and journey over the Horseshoe Falls, and information about what happened to her and her barrel afterward.

When history is being taught through drama, it is important that a respect for evidence is maintained. The drama unit is evidence based. During the drama, the students will be using what they know, have found out, and have been told by the teacher but will also be elaborating on it, in ways that feel authentic within the drama with respect to the evidence. They might unintentionally say or do something in the drama, which is not congruent with the evidence. If this happens, then the teacher will need (at some point) to remind the students of the evidence. This could be after the lesson, unless the teacher considers it necessary to do this during the lesson.

Resource Sheets

A version of this true story has been provided for use with this lesson (see pages 116–117). It can be used alone or in conjunction with Resource Sheet 6 (see page 130), which contains Annie's actual comments about her experience. Her comments have been cross-referenced.

Resource Sheet 7 (see page 131) contains a list of facts, which are used during drama Activity 6 (Rumors). You can make a paper copy of each fact before the lesson and give a copy of a fact to each student before Activity 6. Alternatively, you could just tell each student a different fact before they start Activity 6.

Useful Vocabulary (to be pre-taught)

Widow, brave, stupid, desperate, barrel, oak, iron, straps, pillows, rowing, pumping, hammering, floating, sinking, drifting, falling, suicide, rescuers, survived, cheering.

Some relevant occupations: Barrel maker, newspaper reporter, events manager (advertising and marketing).

Warm-up activity (optional): The students walk around the room and whenever you call out a verb, they mime the corresponding action before walking on again. You may decide to mime with them, to begin with. The verbs are all relevant to this lesson, for example, rowing, screwing, hammering, pumping, floating, falling, sinking, drifting, pulling, cheering.

Annie's Monologue (for Activity 1)

The monologue below contains the basic information that you need to give to the students at the start of the lesson (when you are in role as Annie, during Activity 1). You can either read the monologue aloud as Annie or use it to improvise from. Either way, make sure the students get some factual background information about Annie at the start.

> I was born near New York almost sixty-three years ago.
> My father died when I was twelve.
> I had eight brothers and sisters.
> We were sent away to school, after my father died.
> I married when I was seventeen years old.
> I became pregnant and lost the baby soon after it was born. It was a boy.
> My husband died about a year later, fighting in the American Civil War.
> I became a teacher.
> I have worked in various places across America.
> I moved to Bay City, Minnesota, a few years ago and started a dance school. It is not making me enough money.
> I am worried that I could end up living in a poorhouse in my old age. They are terrible places.
> I need to find an honest way to make a lot of money quickly.
> I have an idea and I am going to tell you my idea now.
> I am going to become the first person to go over Niagara Falls in a barrel!

After the Lesson

Your language students will learn quite a lot about Annie Edson Taylor through this Drama Unit. After the lesson, the students could tell someone else about her and then maybe write a brief biography.

Recommended resources

1. *Queen of the Falls* by Chris van Allsburg. This is a well-researched picture book version of the story with some evocative illustrative drawings that could be used in the drama.

2. A short film (less than four minutes long), which was produced by Niagara Fall Museum. It contains the main information, illustrated with a series of authentic photographs. https://www.youtube.com/watch?v=gMwg7yu4Dco

3. A detailed, written account of the story with authentic photographs and a press interview. https://web.archive.org/web/20161025032751/http://bay-journal.com/bay/1he/people/fp-taylor-annie.html

4. A short account of the story. https://www.niagarafallsinfo.com/niagara-falls-history/niagara-falls-tourism-history/daredevils-of-niagara-falls/annie-edson-taylor/

	Drama Strategy or activity	Grouping	Teacher guidance	Comments and suggestions	Language links and opportunities
1.	**Teacher in Role** **Hot-Seating**	Whole class	Explain that you will be going into role as Annie Edson Taylor and that they can ask questions to Annie after she has spoken to them. You now either read Annie's monologue (see page 118) or use the information in it to improvise. You need to introduce yourself as Annie and explain what your idea is and why you need to see your idea through.	The main purpose of the teacher in role here is to give information. They also need to ask you questions and reason with you, so avoid being too forceful as Annie. They will hopefully be intrigued by Annie and maybe feel concerned for her and not just dismiss her as mad.	**Writing opportunity** They could create a "Role on the Wall" for Annie. This would involve the students writing notes around an outline (or photograph) of Annie. Each note has something written on it that they know about her. Further notes can be added at different points in (or after) the lesson as they find out more about Annie.
2.	**Passing Thoughts** **Teacher in Role**	Whole class	Ask the students to get into a circle. You stand in role as Annie in the center. Tell them that Annie spent a lot of time thinking about the design of her barrel. You stand silently as Annie and the students pass by you and cross the circle, one at a time (in any order). As each student passes you, they should offer you a piece of design advice with an explanation, e.g., "You need to be tied into the barrel, Annie, so that your body doesn't get thrown around." Students may cross the circle and offer further advice but not twice in a row. Close the activity by saying, "I know what the barrel needs now. I just have to find a good barrel maker who is willing to make it for me."	They are engaging with and supporting Annie within the imagined situation by giving her helpful ideas. They are considering the potential problems and how to possibly solve them.	**Writing opportunities** The ideas offered to Annie as "Passing Thoughts" could each be jotted down on self-adhesive labels and/or gathered in one collective thought bubble. The notes could then be referred to, if the students were later asked to write in role (as Annie) a list of her requirements for the barrel maker. **Drawing and writing opportunity** If they were going across Niagara Falls in a barrel themselves, what would their design for a barrel look like? Individually (or in pairs or small groups) you could ask them to design, draw, and label a barrel. This is what Annie did for the barrel maker.

	Drama Strategy or activity	Grouping	Teacher guidance	Comments and suggestions	Language links and opportunities
3.	Conscience Alley	Whole class	Annie had to persuade a barrel maker to make her a barrel and to her design. Ask the students to get into two straight lines, facing each other. You then walk between the lines as a barrel maker who is undecided as to whether to make the barrel for her or not. One line of students will try to persuade the barrel maker to make it and the other line will try to persuade him not to. Each student speaks only when you (the barrel maker) are standing closest to them. End by saying that you have decided to make it for her.	The students need to reason, justify, and explain to the barrel maker why he should (or should not) make a barrel for Annie. You could pass between the lines more than once. The barrel maker took a lot of persuading!	**Writing opportunity** The students could draft a business letter from the barrel maker to Annie, confirming that he is willing to make the barrel for her but cannot guarantee it will not break in the fall and accepts no responsibility for her life.
4.	Improvisation	Pairs	One person becomes the barrel maker and the other is a close friend. The barrel maker is telling his friend about Annie's visit and her request. Freeze the scenes after a few minutes.	Activity 3 generated many conflicting thoughts, some of which might now emerge within the context of an informal conversation.	**Writing opportunity** Pairs of students could write a playscript of between six and ten lines of dialogue, based on their improvised conversation. They then swap their short playscript with another pair of students' script. Each pair will end up reading (and maybe performing) another pair's script.
5.	Eavesdropping	Pairs	Explain that you will now pass by each pair. Whichever pair you are nearest to will bring their scene alive and continue their conversation until you move away from them. They freeze again as you move away.	Remind the students that everyone needs to be able to hear their conversation, not only the person they are talking to.	

	Drama Strategy or activity	Grouping	Teacher guidance	Comments and suggestions	Language links and opportunities
6.	Rumors	Whole class	Give each student one fact from Resource Sheet 7, page 131. Explain that the barrel has been made. They will now move around, listening to and spreading both facts and rumors about Annie and her barrel. They can make up plausible rumors and/or tell facts accurately or inaccurately. **Separate fact from rumor** The facts must now be separated out from the exaggerated and/or false rumors. This can be done through a teacher-led discussion or using the following activity. Divide the drama space into two areas. Tell them that one area is where the "True" statements will be spoken and the other is where the "False" statements are spoken. In turn, the students enter the appropriate area and say one fact or one rumor. They can have more than one turn and can change areas when necessary.	Resource Sheet 7 lists twenty-five facts. The sheet can be copied with one written fact being given to each student. The students could be asked to spread and gossip about one fact and make up and spread one plausible rumor. This activity highlights the need to critically consider sources of evidence when we read or hear "facts."	**Writing opportunity** The list of basic facts could be gathered and used as notes to inform a piece of information writing.
7.	Working in Role	Groups of three or four	In role, as groups of newspaper reporters, the students in small groups need to decide on some questions that they will ask Annie at a press conference, arranged by Frank Russell (her business manager).	You could ask the groups to agree and then prioritize the questions in case they do not get the opportunity to ask them all.	**Writing activity** As newspaper reporters the groups could write down a list of the questions they want to ask Annie.
8.	Collective Role Teacher in Role Improvisation	Whole class	Invite six students to all become Annie together. The other students will remain as newspaper reporters who are now going to ask her questions. You will be in role as her business manager (Frank Russell) and will manage the press conference.	The group of students who are in role as Annie need to listen to each other carefully to make it sound as if the answers are being spoken by the same person.	**Writing opportunities** As newspaper reporters, they can jot down notes about what Annie says at the press conference. These can be used as the basis of a newspaper report.

	Drama Strategy or activity	Grouping	Teacher guidance	Comments and suggestions	Language links and opportunities
			The students who are collectively Annie will now answer press questions. No one in the "Annie" group is allowed to answer two questions in a row.	It is better to end the activity with them wanting to ask more questions, rather than let the questioning go on too long and become less focused.	Following the press conference, those students who were Annie could write a diary entry about it (either collectively or individually).
9.	Tableau	Whole class	Thousands came to watch Annie going over the falls. Explain that each student should enter in turn and place themselves within a photograph of the waiting crowd. As each person gets into position, they offer one piece of information, such as why they have come and/or what they are expecting to happen, e.g., "I want to be able to say that I saw history being made." "I think she is mad and will end up killing herself today."	This is giving the students the opportunity to engage with and explore an historic moment of excitement and dramatic tension, i.e. "the moment before" she comes over the Falls.	**Writing opportunity** The students are imagining themselves to be present as eyewitnesses to an historic event. This can be helpful to them when writing an eyewitness recount later. They could write a letter in role afterward to an imaginary relative or friend, recounting the event that they attended. They could write a personal diary entry afterward about the day.
	Improvisation Teacher in Role	Whole class	When all the students are in the tableau, bring it alive for a few minutes, enabling them to talk to each other in role. You could move among them and join in as a newspaper reporter or just as an onlooker.		
10.	Active Storytelling Teacher as Storyteller	Whole class	Ask the students to stand in a big circle. Explain that you will be reading (or telling) part of the story to them. As you tell the story, they will need to act it out individually with their bodies in response to what you are saying. They can become the people and/or the objects in the story and carry out the actions, i.e., strapped, pumped, hammered, etc.	This is a simple telling of the main part of the story. By acting it out as you tell it, the students are all actively involved and embodying the story. Acting out verbs helps students to learn them and make them more memorable.	**Writing opportunity** The students could be given a simple version of the story (see pages 116–117) and asked to add more detail to elaborate on the simple version of it and make it more vivid. This could be done individually or in pairs. They could practice telling a partner, a more vivid version of the event before writing it.

	Drama Strategy or activity	Grouping	Teacher guidance	Comments and suggestions	Language links and opportunities
			You can either read the penultimate paragraph of the story provided, starting with the words, "Thousands of people came to witness …." or you can remember the main points and improvise a storytelling of it. You will start from when Annie is being rowed out in the boat and will finish at the point when she walks ashore again, having been rescued. You will need to read or tell the story slowly, pausing from time to time for the students to enact what you are saying.	If they retell the story again themselves actively, verbally and/or in writing, the actions will help them to literally remember the story.	
11.	Still images	Groups of four to five	Photographs of Annie's journey to and from the falls are available online, e.g., sitting in the boat, lying inside the barrel, and being rescued. Ask the groups to create an undiscovered photograph with Annie in it. Ask them to also make up a newspaper headline to go with their photograph. They will be performing their images, so they need to practice getting into the still image together (in slow motion), holding it still for a few seconds and then melting it down again. When the image is still, someone in the group needs to call out the newspaper headline. Alternatively, each group could recreate a real photograph of Annie (available online).	Set a time limit for this activity and keep to it. You could find and play a soundtrack of fast-flowing water during the performance. This would help the continuity of scenes. It could also be played again later to re-evoke the memories during any follow-up writing activities. This gives a reason for studying an authentic photograph carefully together.	**Writing opportunities** The newspaper article (or part of it) that goes with the group's photograph and newspaper headline could be written afterward.
12.	**Small Group Playmaking**	Groups of four or five	The groups could be asked to devise a short scene that leads into the moment that their photograph was taken (at which point they freeze).	This gets the students inter-thinking more deeply about what might have been thought, said, and done, moments before an historic photograph was taken.	

	Drama Strategy or activity	Grouping	Teacher guidance	Comments and suggestions	Language links and opportunities
13.	Performance Carousel	Whole class	Position the scenes around the room in chronological order. Explain that each group will now perform their photographs and/or scenes in order seamlessly.	The scenes should blend into a single, whole class performance. The scenes could be reworked and replayed in various ways, e.g., silently or with speech with only the character's thoughts heard with a narrative accompaniment to music with the sound of turbulent water with some of Annie's own words added or in the background, etc.	**Writing activity:** The scenes can be considered as illustrated episodes. They could each be written up as different paragraphs within a single recount. The short scenes could be written up as playscripts later. They can be kept and given in the future as play scripts to be read or performed by other groups.
14.	Teacher in Role	Whole class	You could close the Performance Carousel with you in role as Annie, speaking some of her actual words, e.g. "If it were my dying breath, I would caution anyone against attempting the feat." "I would sooner walk up to the mouth of a cannon, knowing it was going to blow me to pieces, than make another trip over the Fall."		**Writing opportunity** Some of Annie's actual comments about the experience can be found on Resource Sheet 6, page 130. The students can create and add sentences to her actual words. They could write in role Annie's imagined diary entry or memoir. This could be written individually or by the whole class collectively, using the teacher as a scribe. The teacher writes one of Annie's actual sentences and speaks it aloud and then any student can suggest the next sentence, which the teacher then adds (and so on). No one can offer two sentences in a row. The teacher reads it back from time to time (as Annie).

Resource Sheet 1

Only the Wall

1 That first day only the wall saw the bully trip the new boy behind the shed, and only the wall heard the name he called, a name that would stick like toffee.	2 The second day the wall didn't see the fight because too many boys stood around, but the wall heard their cheers, and no one cheered for the new boy.
3 The third day the wall felt three bullies lean against it ready to ambush the new boy, then the wall heard thumps and cries, and saw blood.	4 The fourth day only the wall missed the new boy though five bullies looked for him, then picked another boy instead.
5 Next day they had him back, his face hit the wall.	6 The sixth day only the wall knew the bullies would need that other boy to savage. The wall remembered the new boy's face going home, saw he'd stay away.

By Matthew Sweeney

Resource Sheet 2

First day

The bully made the new boy trip up and called him a name.

Second day

Some boys stood around and watched the new boy being bullied. They were cheering.

Third day

Three boys were leaning against the wall, waiting for the new boy. When he arrived, they started hitting him and he started bleeding.

Fourth day

Five bullies were looking for the new boy. They could not find him today, so they hurt another boy instead.

Fifth day

The five bullies found the new boy again today. His face hit the wall again.

Sixth day

The new boy did not come back today, so the bullies hurt the other boy again, instead.

Resource Sheet 3 A Map of Hopham

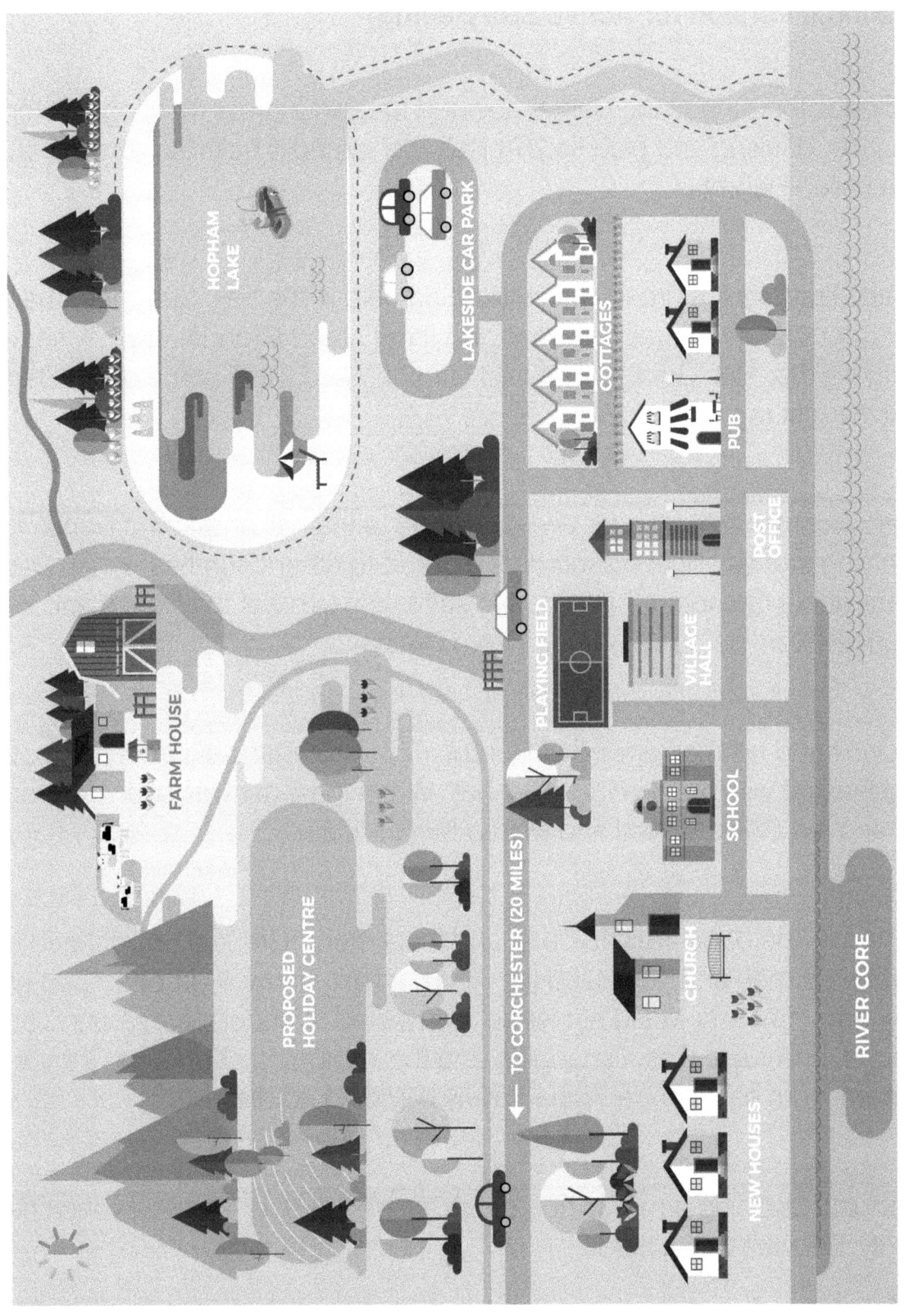

Resource Sheet 4

Beowulf
(a simple version for Active Storytelling)

Hrothgar, the King of the Danes decided to build a great meeting hall for feasting, drinking and planning. At last, the splendid hall was finished and it was called Heorot.

On the first night, a great feast was being held in the hall. Suddenly, the big oak door of the hall crashed open and there stood Grendel, an evil, fierce and terrifying monster. Grendel grabbed, crushed and killed some of the Danes and the rest ran for their lives.

Every night for twelve years Grendel came to the hall and found Danes to kill. Terrifying stories about his murders, spread to other countries. When Beowulf heard about Grendel, he decided to sail to the Land of the Danes and kill him. Fourteen warriors came with him from Geatland.

Beowulf and his men arrived at Heorot. King Hrothgar welcomed them warmly and feasted with them in the great hall. When the feast was over, the Danes left and the Geats stayed and waited for Grendel.

Suddenly, the door crashed open and there stood Grendel. He grinned as he grabbed a man and squeezed the life from him. Beowulf grabbed and gripped Grendel's arm and would not let go. He twisted Grendel's arm around and around, until there was a snapping and then a ripping sound, as Grendel's arm was torn off. Grendel limped away bleeding, to die.

Grendel's dripping arm was hung high above the door and everyone cheered loudly. Beowulf was a hero.

Resource Sheet 5

The Legend of Beowulf (in 20 sentences)

1.	Hrothgar, the King of the Danes, had a great Mead Hall built. He called it Heorot.
2.	A monster called Grendel, came to Heorot every night for twelve years. He killed many Danes in the hall.
3.	In Geatland, Beowulf heard about Grendel's killings. He decided that he would go to Heorot and kill Grendel.
4.	Beowulf sailed to the Land of the Danes. He took fourteen men with him.
5.	He was welcomed by King Hrothgar. A feast was held for Beowulf and his men.
6.	When the feast was over, the Danes left the hall. Beowulf and his men waited for Grendel to arrive.
7.	Suddenly, Grendel crashed through the door. He killed one of the Geats and then turned to kill Beowulf.
8.	Beowulf grabbed Grendel's arm, held it tight and twisted it around and around. He ended up tearing Grendel's arm off his body.
9.	Beowulf had won the fight. Grendel limped away, to die.
10.	Grendel's arm was hung above the door of Heorot. Beowulf was celebrated as a hero.

Resource Sheet 6

Annie Edson Taylor said … (True quotes)

1.	The trip to the rapids was nothing but a pleasant sensation
2.	As I reached the brink, the barrel did exactly what I predicted it would do, paused for a moment and then made the awful plunge of 158 feet to the boiling cauldron below.
3.	When I realised I had been rescued, my senses immediately left me. Like a person falling to sleep, I became unconscious.
4.	**Rescuer:** The woman is alive **Annie:** Yes, she is!
5.	I prayed every second I was in the barrel except for a few seconds after the fall, when I went unconscious.
6.	If it were my dying breath, I would caution anyone against attempting the feat.
7.	I would sooner walk up to the mouth of a cannon, knowing it was going to blow me to pieces, than make another trip over the Fall.

Resource Sheet 7

Facts about Annie Edson Taylor
Her name is Annie Edson Taylor.
She is a widow.
Her husband was killed in the Civil War.
She was born near New York.
She has lived in lots of places across America.
She owns a dance school in Bay City.
She is only doing it to make money.
She says she is only 43 years old. She looks much older.
She designed the barrel herself.
The barrel is made of white Kentucky oak.
She chose every oak plank herself.
The barrel has a heavy anvil at the bottom, to try and keep it floating upright.
The barrel has got ten iron rings around it.
The barrel has grab handles in it for her to hold onto.
The barrel has leather straps in it, to stop her body from moving about.
She is going to fill the barrel with cushions.
She is taking a heart-shaped cushion with her. She thinks it will bring her luck.
She has had 'The Maid of the Mist' painted on it. That is what she is calling herself.
She has hired herself a business manager.
She has already been talking to newspaper reporters. Her manager arranged it.
She says she is 43 years old. No-one believes that.
Her barrel is on display at an hotel. You can go and see it.
Her manager has hired a boatman to row her and her barrel out to the falls.
They are going to pump air into the barrel and then seal it.
She is going on a tour with her manager afterwards. They are going to charge people to look at her barrel and listen to her talking about it all.

APPENDIX
RESOURCE SHEETS

DRAMA STRATEGY RESOURCE SHEETS

Resource sheet 8 / **Hot-seating**

Appendix: Resource Sheets

DRAMA STRATEGY RESOURCE SHEETS

Resource sheet 9 / **Conscience Alley – Thinking as the character**

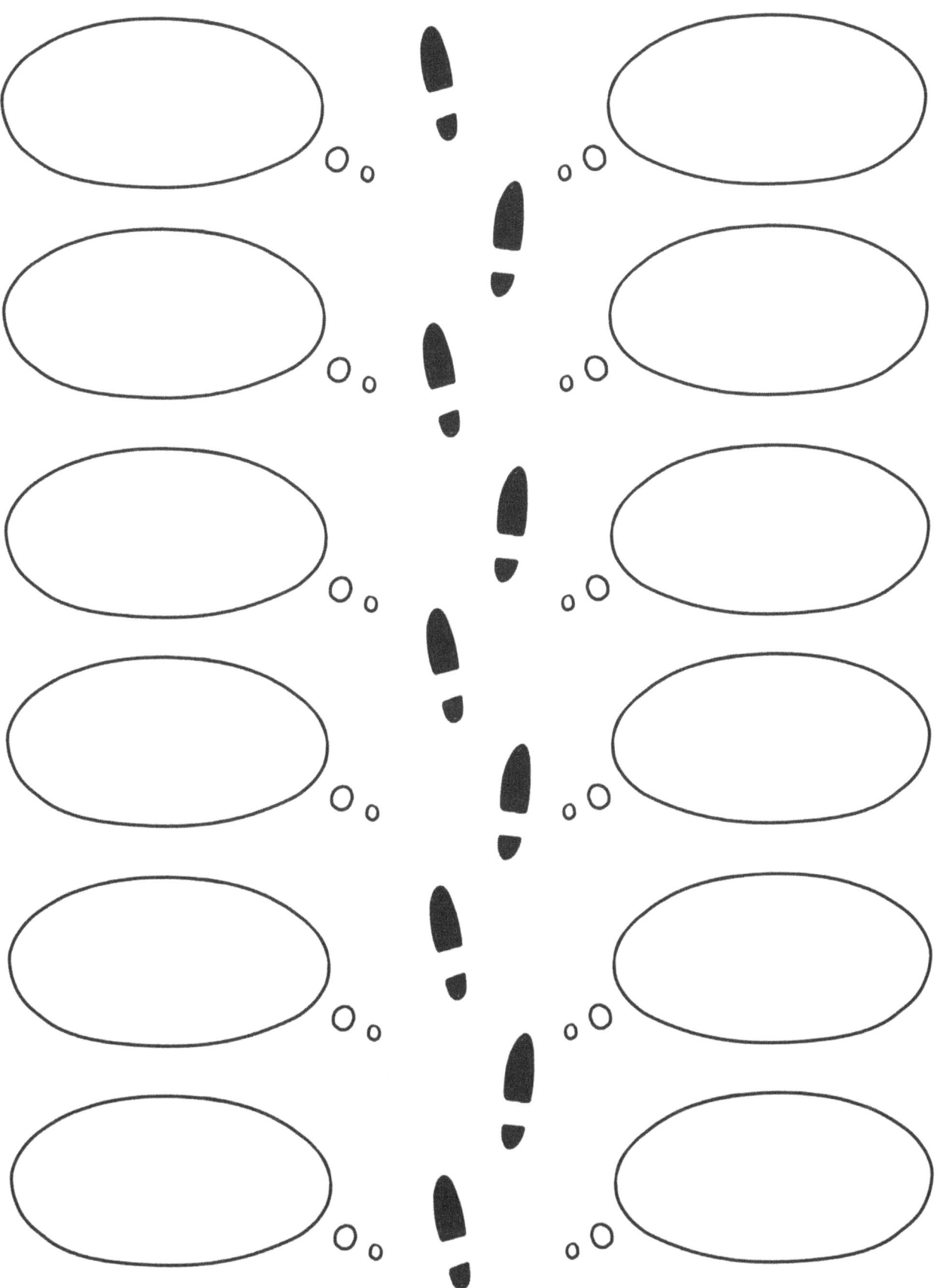

DRAMA STRATEGY RESOURCE SHEETS

Resource sheet 10 / **Thinking about the character**

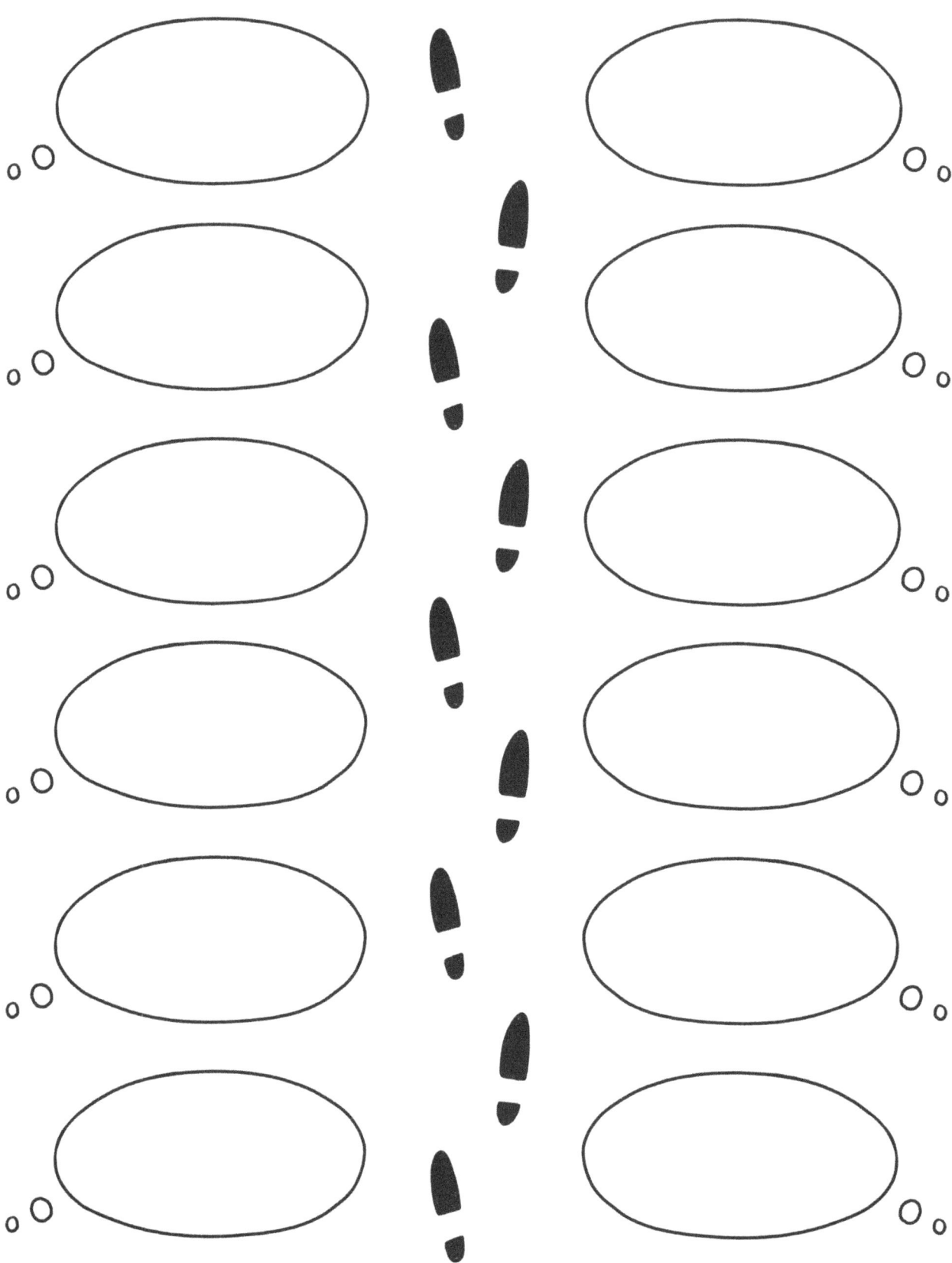

Appendix: Resource Sheets

DRAMA STRATEGY RESOURCE SHEETS

Resource sheet 11 / **Speaking as the character**

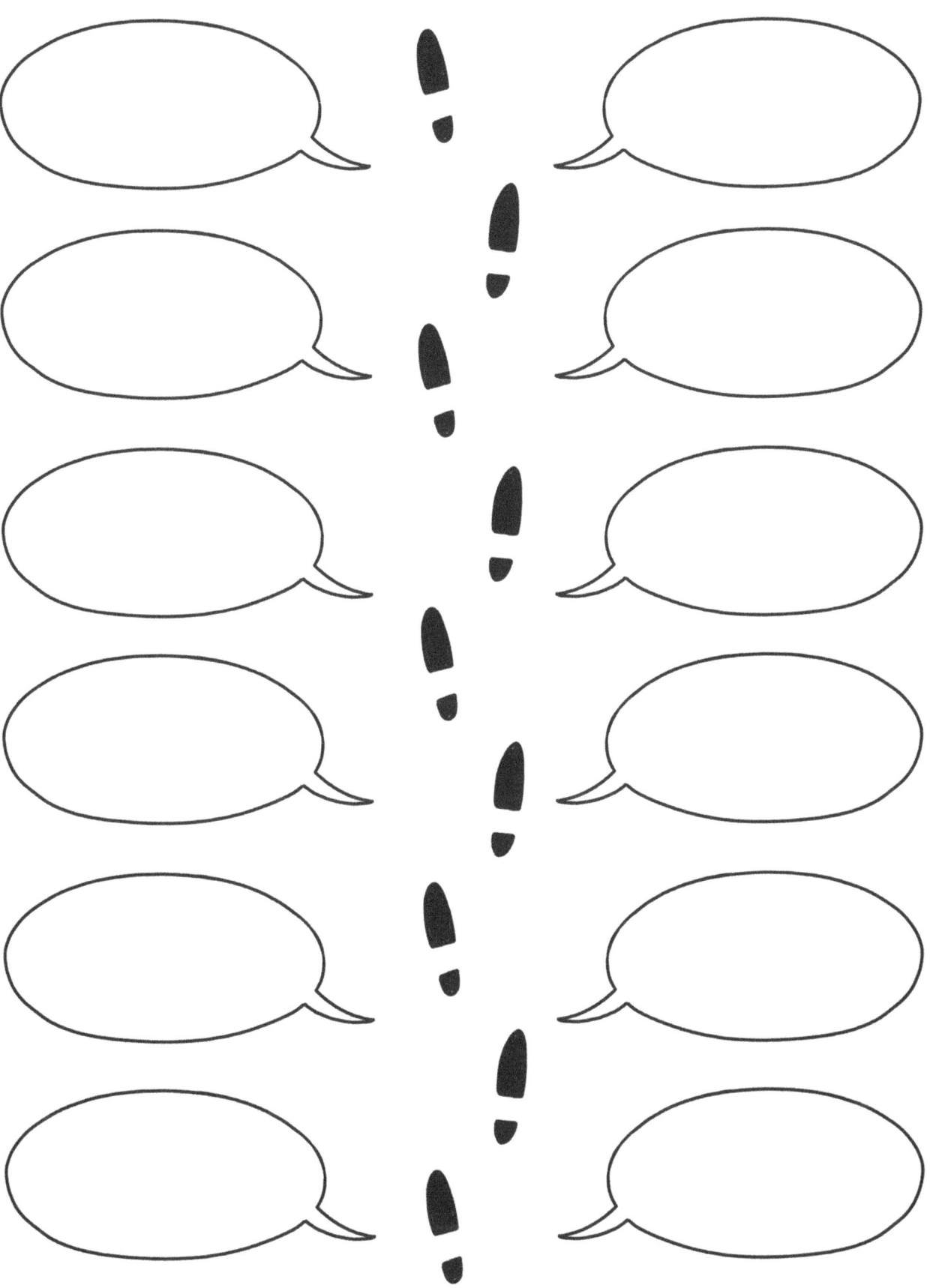

DRAMA STRATEGY RESOURCE SHEETS

Resource sheet 12 / **Speaking about the character**

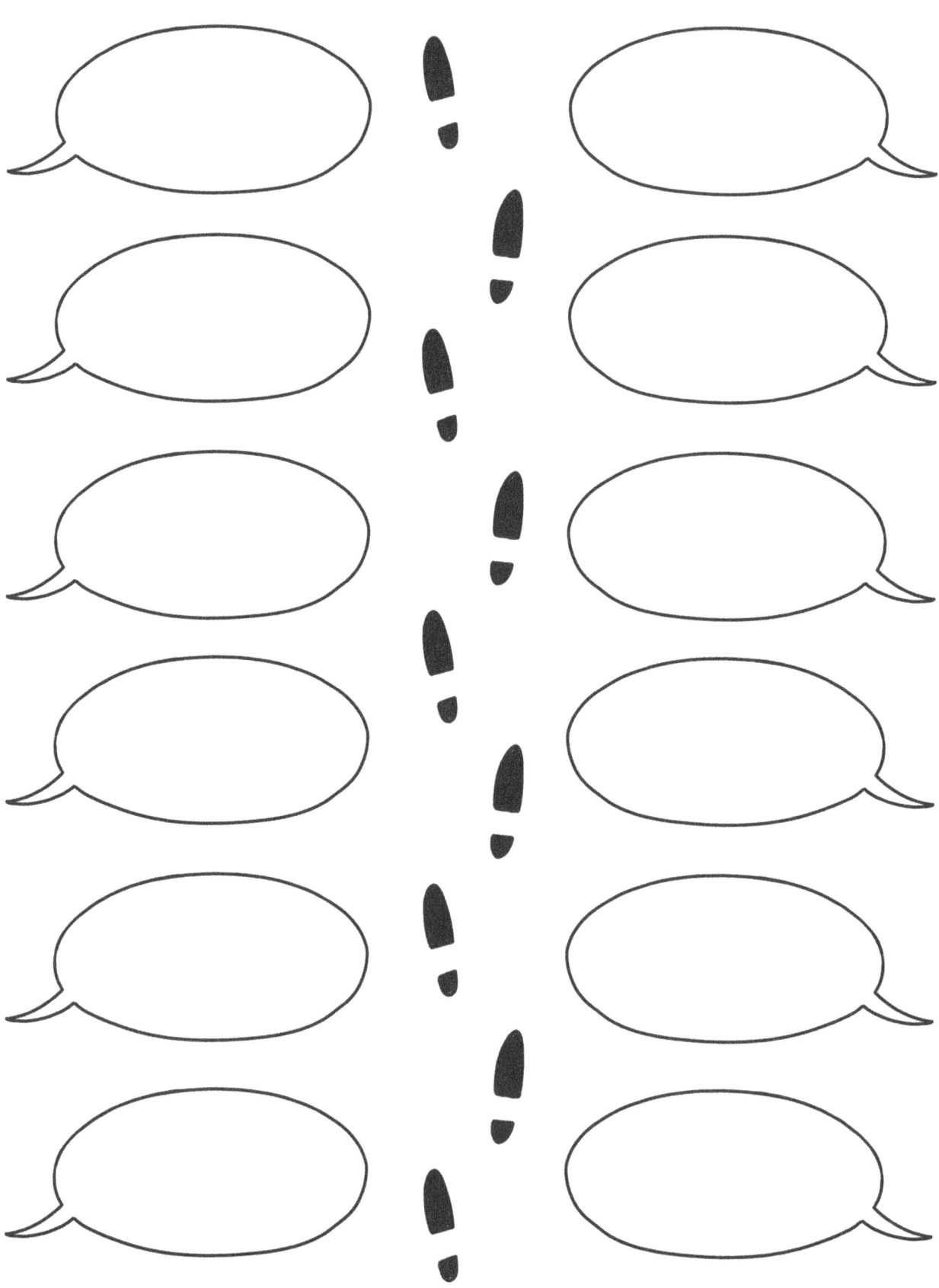

Appendix: Resource Sheets

DRAMA STRATEGY RESOURCE SHEETS

Resource sheet 13 / **Passing Thoughts**

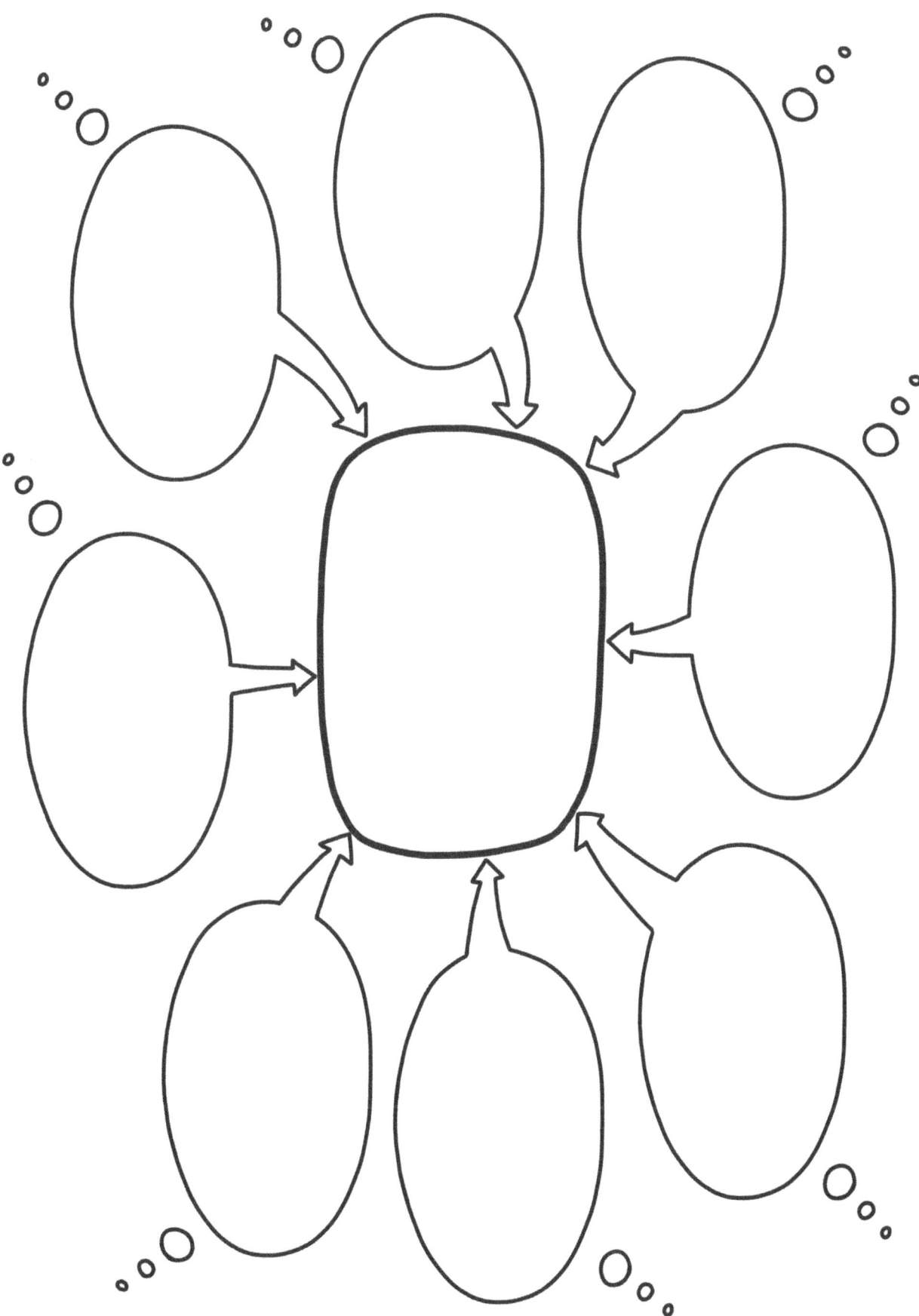

DRAMA STRATEGY RESOURCE SHEETS

Resource sheet 14 / **What the character is saying. What the character is thinking**

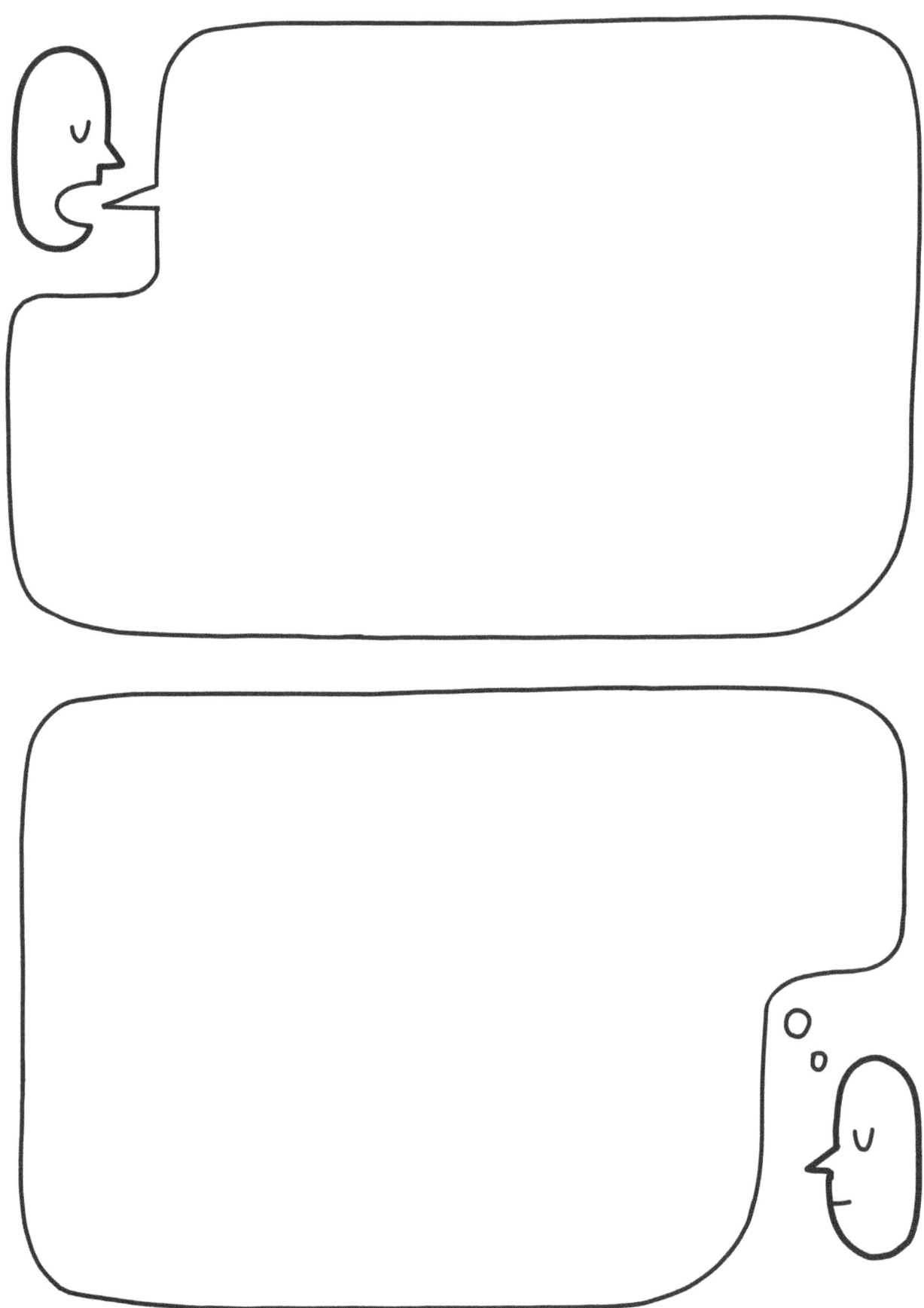

Appendix: Resource Sheets

DRAMA STRATEGY RESOURCE SHEETS

Resource sheet 15 / **Rumors**

DRAMA STRATEGY RESOURCE SHEETS

Resource sheet 16 / **Eavesdropping (Overheard Conversations)**

Appendix: Resource Sheets

141

DRAMA STRATEGY RESOURCE SHEETS

Resource sheet 17 / **Role on the Wall**

DRAMA STRATEGY RESOURCE SHEETS

References

Ackerman, P. L. (1996) A Theory of Adult Intellectual Development: Process, Personality, Interests, and Knowledge. Intelligence, 22 (2), March–April 1996, 227–57.

Ackroyd, J. (2004) *Role Reconsidered: A Re-evaluation of the Relationship between Teacher-in-Role and Acting*. Stoke on Trent, UK: Trentham Books.

Adolphs, R. (2003) Cognitive neuroscience of human social behaviour. Nat Rev Neurosci, 4, 165–178 (2003). https://doi.org/10.1038/nrn1056.

Alexander, R. J. (2008) *Towards Dialogic Teaching: Rethinking Classroom Talk*, 4th edn. York: Dialogos UK.

Alexander, R. J. (2017) The Arts in Schools: Making the Case, Heeding the Evidence', at the Conference on Intercultural Dimensions of Cultural Education. University of Chester.

Alexander, R. J. (2017) *Towards Dialogic Teaching: Rethinking Classroom Talk* (5th edition of text first published in 2004 and from March 2020 superseded by A Dialogic Teaching Companion). Dialogos.

Almond, M. (2005) *Teaching English with Drama*. Pavilion Publishing and Media Ltd, UK.

Applied Educational Systems (2019). What Are the 4C's of 21st Century Skills?

Bacová, Daniela & Phillips, Tim (Eds) (1999) *As If … Drama-Based Lesson Plans for English Language Teaching*. Bratislava: The British Council.

Baldwin, P. (2004, 2012) *With Drama in Mind—Real Learning in Imagined Worlds*, 1st and 2nd edns. London and New York: Continuum.

Baldwin, P. (2008) *The Primary Drama Handbook*. London, California, New Delhi, Singapore: Sage Publications Ltd.

Baldwin, P. & Fleming, K. (2002) *Teaching Literacy Through Drama—Creative Approaches*. London: Routledge Falmer.

Baldwin, P. & John, R. (2012) *Inspiring Writing through Drama: Creative Approaches to Teaching Ages 7–16*. London, New York, Delhi, Sydney: Bloomsbury.

Bar-Tal, D. & Bar-Zohar, Y. (1977) *The Relationship between Perception of Locus of Control and Academic Achievement*. Contemporary Educational Psychology, 2, 181–99. https://www.sciencedirect.com/science/article/abs/pii/0361476X77900200.

Bedyńska, S. & Brzezicka, A. (2007) *Statystyczny drogowskaz*. Warszawa: SWPS Academica.

Block, J., & Kremen, A. M. (1996). IQ and Ego-Resiliency: Conceptual and Empirical Connections and Separateness. *Journal of Personality and Social Psychology*, 70 (2), 349–61.

Bloom, B. S. (1956). *Taxonomy of educational objectives: the classification of educational goals; Handbook: Cognitive domain*. New York: David McKay.

Boal, Augusto. (1995) *The Rainbow of Desire*. London: Routledge.

Boal, Augusto. (1997) *The Rainbow of Desire: The Boal Method of Theatre and Therapy*. New York: Routledge.

Boal, Augusto. (2002) *Games for Actors and Non-Actors*, 2nd edn. New York, NY: Routledge.

Bolton, G. (1979) *Towards a Theory of Drama in Education*. London: Longman.

Bolton G. and Heathcote D. (1995) *Drama for Learning: Dorothy Heathcote's Mantle of the Expert Approach to Education*, Portsmouth, New Hampshire: Heinemann.

Bolton, G. & Heathcote, D. (1999) *So You Want You Use Role Play? A New Approach in How to Plan*. Stoke on Trent, UK: Trentham Books. https://www.amazon.com/You-Want-Use-Role-Play/dp/1858561965

Bowell, P. & Heap, B. (2001) *Planning Process Drama*. London: David Fulton.

Brown R. T. (1989), Creativity—What Are We to Measure. In J. A. Glover, R. R. Ronning, C. R. Reynolds (Eds.), *Handbook of Creativity*, 3–32. New York: Plenum Press.

Bruner (1990), See J. *Acts of Meaning*. Cambridge MA: Harvard University Press.

Bruner See J. S. (1996) Folk Pedagogy. In J. S Bruner (Ed.), *The Culture of Education*, 44–66. Cambridge: London Harvard University Press.

Burke, A. & O'Sullivan. (2002). *Stage by Stage: A Handbook for Using Drama in the Second Language Classroom*. Heinemann Drama. https://www.amazon.com/Stage-Handbook-Second-Language-Classroom/dp/0325003807.

Burn, A. & Durran, J. (2007) *Media Literacy in Schools: Practice, Production and Progression*. London: Paul Chapman Publishing.

References

Byram, M. & M. Fleming (1998) *Language Learning in Intercultural Perspective: Approaches through Drama and Ethnography*. Cambridge: Cambridge University Press.

Byron, K. (1986) *Drama in the English Classroom*. London: Methuen.

Caine, G. & Caine, R. (2010) *Strengthening and Enriching Your Professional Learning Community: The Art of Learning Together*. Alexandria, VA: ASCD.

Caine, R. N., & Caine, G. (1991, 1994). *Making Connections: Teaching and the Human Brain*. Menlo Park, CA: Addison-Wesley.

Canale, M. & Swain, M. (1980) Theoretical Bases of Communicative Approaches to Second Language Teaching and Testing. Applied Linguistics, 1, 1–47. http://dx.doi.org/10.1093/applin/I.1.1.

Carbonell J., (1998) *The Use of MMR, Diversity-Based Reranking for Reordering Documents and Producing Summaries*. SIGIR '98: Proceedings of the 21st Annual International ACM SIGIR Conference on Research and Development in Information Retrieval.

Center for Curriculum Redesign. (2015). Skills for the 21st Century: What Should Students Learn?

Chance, J. E. (1965). *Internal Control of Reinforcements and the School Learning Process*. Paper presented at Society for Research in Child Development Convention, ERIC.

Corbett, P. (2015) *Pie Corbett Storytelling and the Arts Project 2015–16* (with Patrice Baldwin) for The Wroxham Transformative Teaching Alliance.

Coyle, D. (1999). Supporting Students in Content and Language Integrated Learning Contexts: Planning for Effective Classrooms. In J. Masih (Ed.), Learning through a Foreign Language: Models, Methods and Outcomes, 46–62. CILT (Centre for Information on Language Teaching and Research).

Coyle, D., Marsh, D. & P. Hood. (2010) *Content and Language Integrated Learning*. Cambridge University Press. https://abdn.pure.elsevier.com/en/publications/content-and-language-integrated-learning.

Cozolino, L. (2014) *The Neuroscience of Human Relationship. Attachment and the Developing Social Brain*. New York, London: W. W. Norton & Company.

Craig, P. & Bloomfield, L. (2006) *An Experience with Conducting a Role-Play in Decision Making for a Food and Nutrition Policy Course*. Proceedings of the 23rd Annual Conference of the Australasian Society for Computers in Learning in Tertiary Education, University of Sydney.

Crandall, V. C., Katkovsky, W. & Crandall, V. J. (1965) Children's Beliefs in Their Control of Reinforcements in Intellectual Academic Achievement Behaviours. Child Development, 36, 91–109.

Culham, C. (2002) Coping with Obstacles in Drama-Based ESL Teaching: A Nonverbal Approach. In Bräuer, G. (Ed.), *Body and Language*. Westport, CT: Ablex Publishing, 95–112.

Curby, T. W., LoCasale-Crouch, J., Konold, T. R., Pianta, R., Howes, C., Burchinal, M., et al. (2009) The relations of observed pre-k classroom quality profiles to children's academic achievement and social compe-tence. Early Education and Development.

Dance and Drama: Creative Community in the Time of COVID (2020), Re-opening Schools in Ontario in September 2020. The Council of Ontario Drama and Dance Educators (CODE). https://www.code.on.ca/files/inline-files/code_plan_for_school_re-opening.pdf

Darn, S. (2006) Content and Language Integrated Learning (CLIL): A European Overview, ERIC online, Number: ED490775. EuroCLIC - www.euroclic.org.

Davila, S. (2016). 21st Century Skills and the English Language Classroom.

Deci, E. L. & Ryan, R. M. (1985) *Intrinsic Motivation and Self-Determination in Human Behavior*. New York: Plenum Press.

Dede, C. (2010) Comparing Framework for 21st Century Skills. In Bellanca, I. and Brandt, R. (Eds.), *21st Century Skills*. Bloomington, IN: Solution Free Press.

Dornyei, Z. & Murphey, T. (2003) *Group Dynamics in the Language Classroom*. Cambridge University Press.

Dornyei, Z., Csizer, K., The Internal Structure of Language Learning Motivation and Its Relationship with Language Choice and Learning Effort. First published: February 16, 2005. https://doi.org/10.1111/j.0026-7902.2005.00263.x.

Dudley-Evans, Tony (1998). *Developments in English for Specific Purposes: A Multi-disciplinary Approach*. Cambridge University Press.

Eaton, S. E. (2010). *Global Trends in Language Learning in the 21st Century*. Onate press.

Edwards A., (2005). *Relational Agency: Learning to be a Resourceful Practitioner*. International Journal of Educational Research.

Eggen, P. & Kauchak, D. (2004) *Educational Psychology: Windows on Classrooms*. 6th edn. Upper Saddle River, NJ: Pearson Prentice Hall.

Ehrman, M. E., Leaver, B. L. & Oxford, R. (2003). *A Brief Overview of Individual Differences in Second Language Learning*. System, 31 (3), 313–30.

Ernest P. (1995) The One and the Many. In L. Steffe and J. Gale (Eds.), *Constructivism in Education*. New Jersey: Lawrence Erlbaum Associates, Inc, 459–86.

Exploring Talk in School (2008) Ed. by: Neil Mercer – University of Cambridge, UK, The Open University. Steve Hodgkinson - Brighton University, UK, SAGE Publications Ltd. Voice 21 https://www.voice21.org/

Falconer, L. (2011) *Metaxis: The Transition between Worlds and the Consequences for Education*. Presented at Innovative Research in Virtual Worlds.

Fleming, M. (2006) Drama and Language Teaching: The Relevance of Wittgenstein's Concept of Language Games. Humanising Language Teaching, 8 (4), 97–110. http://www.hltmag.co.uk/jul06/mart01.htm

Fosnot See C. (1996) Constructivism: A Psychological Theory of Learning, [in:] Constructivism: Theory, Perspectives, and Practice, ed. C. Fosnot, Teachers College Press, New York, 8–33.

Frederickson, N., & Cline, T. (2002) *Special Educational needs, Inclusion and Diversity: A text book*. Berkshire: Open University Press.

Gałązka A. (2008) *Motywacyjna rola dramy w glottodydaktyce*. IMPULS. https://cyfroteka.pl/ebooki/Motywacyjna_rola_dramy_w_glottodydaktyce-ebook/p02010089i020.

Gałązka A. (2018). Attachment-Based Teaching through Drama in ELT Classroom. Edulearn18. Proceedings Pages: 7118–25 Publication year: 2018. ISBN: 978-84-09-02709-5ISSN: 2340–1117.

Gałązka A. (2018). Building Teacher's Psychological Resilience and Well-being through Drama. ICERI2018 Proceedings, 11th International Conference of Education, Research and Innovation November 12th–14th, 2018—Seville, Spain, ISBN: 978-84-09-05948-5, s. 373-383, DOI: 10.21125/iceri.2018.

Gałązka A., (2020) *Positive Education and Well-Being in the ELT Classroom*. Humanising Language Teaching April 2020 Issue 2, ISSN 1755-9715.

Gałązka, A. & Jarosz, J. (2019) Life Coaching as a Remedy in Building Teachers' Psychological Resilience and Well-Being. EDULEARN19 Proceedings ISBN: 978-84-09-12031-4.

Gałązka A. and Trinder M., *Creating a "Positive Environment" through Drama in the EFL Classroom Creating a "Positive Environment"* through Drama in the EFL Classroom: The New Educational Review 2018/4 DOI: 10.15804/tner.2018.54.4.17.

Gilbert, P. (2009) *The Compassionate Mind*. London: Constable.

Halliday, M. A. K. (1978). *Language as Social Semiotic: The Social Interpretation of Language and Meaning*. London: Edward Arnold.

Halverson, A. (2018) 21st Century Skills and the "4Cs" in the English Language Classroom.

Hamre, B.K. & Pianta, R.C. (2001) Early Teacher-child Relationships and the Trajectory of Children's School Outcomes through Eighth Grade. Child Development, 72(2), 625–38.

Heathcote, D. & Bolton, G. (1995) *Drama for Learning*. Portsmouth, NH: Heinemann.

Heathcote, D. & Bolton, G. (1995) *Drama for Learning: Dorothy Heathcote's Mantle of the Expert Approach to Education*. Portsmouth, NH: Heinemann Press.

Herrmann, E. (2015) The 4 C's of 21st Century Learning for ELLs: Critical Thinking. http://exclusive.multibriefs.com/content/the-4-cs-of-21st-century-learning-for-ells-critical-thinking/education

Hillyard S. (2012) *Drama and CLIL: The Power of Connection*. Humanizing Language Teaching, 12.

Hillyard, S. (2016) English through Drama—Creative Activities for Inclusive ELT Classes. Helbling Languages.

Holden, S. (1981) *Drama in Language Teaching*. Harlow: Longman.

Hornbrook, D. (1989). *Education and Dramatic Art*. Oxford: Blackwell.

Horwitz M. & Cope J. (1986) Foreign Language Classroom Anxiety. The Modern Language Journal, 70 (2), 125–32.

Hsieh, P.-H. P., & Schallert, D. L. (2008). Implications from Self-Efficacy and Attribution Theories for an Understanding of Undergraduates' Motivation in a Foreign Language Course. Contemporary Educational Psychology, 33 (4), 513–32.

Hutchinson, T. & Waters, A. (1987). *English for Specific Purposes: A Learner-Centered Approach*. Cambridge University Press.

Hymes, D. H. (1972). On Communicative Competence. In J. B. Pride, & J. Holmes (Eds.), *Sociolinguistics: Selected Readings*. 269–93. Harmondsworth: Penguin.

Immordino-Yang, M. H. (2016) *Emotions, Learning and the Brain: Exploring the Educational Implications of Affective Neuroscience*. New York: W. W. Norton & Company.

James, F. Lee (1999) Tasks and Communicating in Language Classrooms. McGraw-Hill Humanities/Social Sciences/Languages.

Johns, A. M. & Dudley-Evans, T (1991) *English for Specific Purposes: International in Scope*, Specific *in Purpose*. TESOL Quarterly, 25 (2), 297–314.

Joyce, S., Shand, F., Tighe, J., Laurent, S. J., Bryant, R. A., & Harvey S. B. (2018). Road to Resilience: A Systematic Review and Meta-analysis of Resilience Training Programmes and Interventions. BMJ Open, 8 (6). https://pubmed.ncbi.nlm.nih.gov/29903782/.

Kabat-Zinn, J. (1994). *Wherever You Go, There You Are: Mindfulness Meditation in Everyday Life*. New York: Hyperion.

Kagan, S. & McGroarty, M. (1993) Principles of Cooperative Learning for Language and Content Gains. In Holt, Daniel (Ed.), *Cooperative Learning: A Response to Linguistic and Cultural Diversity*, 47–64. McHenry, IL: Delta Systems, Inc.

References

Kao, S-M. (1995), From Script to Impromptu: Learning a Second Language through Process Drama. In Taylor, P. and Hoepper, C. (Eds.), *Selected Reading in Drama and Theatre Education: The IDEA '95 Papers* (2nd, Brisbane, Australia, July 1995). NADIE Research Monograph Series, 3. Brisbane: IDEA Publications.

Kao, S-M. & O'Neill, C. (1998). *Words into Worlds: Learning a Second Language through Process Drama*. Stanford: Ablex Publishing.

Kao, S-M & C. O'Neill. 1998. *Words into Worlds*. Stamford, CT: Ablex Publishing.

Kormos, J., & Csizér, K. (2008). *Age-Related Differences in the Motivation of Learning English as a Foreign Language: Attitudes, Selves, and Motivated Learning Behavior*. Language Learning.

Kramsch, C., (1993) *Context and Culture in Language Teaching*. Oxford University Press.

Krashen S. (1982) *Principles and Practice in Second Language Acquisition*. Oxford: Pergamon Press. Inc.

Kuhl, P. (2003). *Born to Learn, Language, Reading and the Brain of the Child*. Paper presented at the Colorado Early Learning Summit, Denver, Colorado.

Language Teaching http://journals.cambridge.org/LTAAdditional services for Language Teaching:Email alerts: Click hereSubscriptions: Click hereCommercial reprints: Click hereTerms of use : Click here Zoltan Dornyei (1998). Motivation in second and foreign language learning. Language Teaching 31(3), 117–335. DOI: 10.1017/S026144480001315X, Published online: June 12, 2009.

Lewis C. (1996) *Aspects of Human Development*, British Psychological Society, Leicester.

Lloyd P. (1995) *Cognitive and Language Development*. Leicester: British Psychological Society.

Lunenberg F. C. (1998) Constructivism and Technology: Instructional Designs for Successful Education Reform, Journal of Instructional Psychology, 1998 (2).

Mackey, A. & Gass, S. (2006). Introduction to Special Issue on New Methods of Studying L2 Acquisition in Interaction. Studies in Second Language Acquisition, 28 (2).

Maley, A. & Duff, A. (2009) [1978]. *Drama Techniques*, 3rd ed., 4th print. Cambridge: Cambridge University Press.

Marks, H.M. (2000). Student Engagement in Instructional Activity: Patterns in the Elementary, Middle, and High School Years. American Educational Research Journal.

Mercer, N. (2008) Talk and the Development of Reasoning and Understanding, Human Development, 51 (1), 90–100.

Mercer, N. & Mannion, J. (2018) *Oracy across the Welsh Curriculum*, EAS, Welsh Government.

Zoltan Dornyei (1998). Motivation in second and foreign language learning. Language Teaching 31(3), 117–35. DOI: 10.1017/S026144480001315X, Published online: June 12, 2009.

Muszyńska A. (2012) *Drama Method in CLIL: The Power of Motivation. An Example of Practical Application on the Secondary School Level*. Servicio de Publicaciones. Universidad de Navarra.

Muszyńska, A. Carmen, Guercia U, & Gałązka, A (2016) *Teacher Education through Drama. CLIL Practice in Spanish Context in ESE*: Estudios sobre educación, ISSN 1578-7001, N°. 32, 2017, page: 179–95.

Neelands, J. (1990) *Structuring Drama Work: A Handbook of Available forms in Theatre and Drama*. Cambridge: Cambridge University Press.

Neff K. D. (2011). Self-Compassion, self-Esteem, and Well-Being. Social and Personality Compass 5/1 (2011), 1–12, 10.

New Vision for Education, 2016 Geneva, Switzerland: World Economic Forum.

Nunan, D & Wong, Lillian L. C (2011). The Learning Styles and Strategies of Effective Language Learners. An International Journal of Educational Technology and Applied Linguistics, 39(2), 144–63.

Norwich, B. (2008) Dilemmas of Difference, Inclusion and Disability: international perspectives, European Journal of Special Needs Education, 23 (4), 287–304.

Olssen M. (1996) Radical Constructivism and Its Failings: Anti-realism and Individualism, British Journal of Educational Studies, 1996 (3).

O'Neill, C. (1995) *Dramaworlds: A Framework for Process Drama*. Portsmouth, NH: Heinemann.

O'Toole, J. & Dunn, J. (2002) *Pretending to Learn*. Sydney: Pearson Education.

Partnership for 21st Century Skills. (2008) Teaching and Learning for the 21st Century: Report and Recommendations of the Arizona Summit on 21st Century Skills. Washington, DC.

Pinol, J. (2007) *La influencia de la confirmacion del professor en el aprendizaje de ingles en la Educacion Secundaria Obligatora*, Unpublished MA thesis, University of Sevilla.

Prescott T. (2010) Why Is Progress a Controversial Issue in Coaching? International Journal of Evidence Based Coaching and Mentoring, Special Issue no. 4, 21–36.

Puchta, H. (1999) Creating a Learning Culture to Which Students Want to Belong: The Application of Neuro-linguistic Programming to Language Teaching. In Arnold, J. (Ed.). *Affect in Language Learning*, 246–60. Cambridge University Press.

Puchta, H. & Williams, M. (2014) Teaching Young Learners to Think ELT-Activities for Young Learners Aged 6-12. Helbling.

Reasoner, R. (1982) *Building Self-Esteem: A Comprehensive Program for Schools*. Palo Alto: Consulting Psychologists Press, Inc.

Rimm-Kaufman, S. E., La Paro, K. M., Downer, J. T., & Pianta, R. C. (2005) The Contribution of Classroom Setting and Quality of Instruction to Children's Behavior in Kindergarten Classrooms. The Elementary School Journal, 105(4).

Rotter, J. B. (1966) Generalised Expectancies for Internal versus External Locus of Control of Reinforcement. Psychological Monographs, 80, 489–93.

Ryan, R. & Deci, E. (2001) On Happiness and Human Potentials: A Review of Research on Hedonic and Eudaimonic Well-Being. Annual Review of Psychology 52(1), 141–66.

Ryff, C. D. & Keyes, C. L. M. (1995) The Structure of Psychological Well-Being Revisited. *Journal of Personality and Social Psychology*, 69 (4), 719–72.

Ryff, C. D. & Singer, B. (1998) The Contours of Positive Human Health. Psychological Inquiry, 9 (1), 1–28. https://www.tandfonline.com/doi/abs/10.1207/s15327965pli0901_1.

Sayers, R. (2014) *Drama Research: International Journal of Drama in Education (Volume 5, No 1)*. National Drama.

Schewe, M. & T. Scott. (2003) Literatur verstehen und inszenieren—Foreign Language Literature through Drama. A Research Project. GFL—German as a Foreign Language, 2003 (3), 56–83. http://www.gfl-journal.de/3-2003/schewe_scott.pdf

Schewe, M. (2007) Drama und Theater in der Fremd- und Zweitsprachenlehre: Blick zurück nach vorn. Scenario, 1 (1), 154–69. publish.ucc.ie/scenario/2007/01/schewe/08/de

Scott, C. (2012) *Teaching English as an Additional Language, 5–11: A Whole School Resource File*. London: Routledge.

Shapiro B. L. (1994) *What Children Bring to Light. A Constructivist Perspective on Children's Learning in Science*. New York: Teachers College Press, 1994, 3.

Skinner, E. A. & Belmont, M. J. (1993) Motivation in the classroom: Reciprocal Effects of Teacher Behavior and Student Engagement across the School Year. Journal of Educational Psychology, 85 (4), 571–81. https://doi.org/10.1037/0022-0663.85.4.571.

Sondra H. Birch & Gary W. Ladd, GW (1997), The Teacher-Child Relationship and Children's Early School Adjustment, Journal of School Psychology.

Stern, H. H. (1983) *Fundamental Concepts of Language Teaching*. Oxford, England: Oxford University Press.

Stevick, E. W. (1980) *Teaching Languages: A Way and Ways*. Rowley, MA: Newbury House.

Swartz R. & Parks, S. (1994) Infusing the Teaching of Critical and Creative Thinking into Content Instruction, Critical Thinking Books and Software, Pacific Grove, CA, (1994) The Modern Language Journal, 70 (2) (Summer, 1986).

Valdes, J.M. (1986) *Culture Bound: Bridging the Cultural Gap in Language Teaching*. Cambridge University Press, Cambridge.

Von Glasersfeld E. 1989 Abstarction, Representation, and Reflektion. In Steffe, L. P. (Ed.), *Epistemological Foundations of Mathematical Experience*. New York: Springer. https://files.eric.ed.gov/fulltext/ED306120.pdf.

Vygotsky, L. S. (1980) *Mind in Society: The Development of Higher Psychological Processes*. Cambridge, MA: Harvard University Press.

Wagner, B. J. (1979) *Dorothy Heathcote: Drama as a Learning Medium*. London: Hutchinson.

Way, B. (1967) *Development through Drama*. London: Longmans.

Wertsch J. V. (1998) *Mind as Action*. Oxford University Press.

Wertsch J. V. (1997) *Vygotsky and the Formation of the Mind*. Cambridge.

Wentzel, K. R. (1998). Social relationships and motivation in middle school: he role of parents, teachers, and peers. Journal of Educational Psychology, 90(2), 202–9.

White, M. A., & Kern, M. L., (2018). Positive education: Learning and teaching for wellbeing and academic mastery. International Journal of Wellbeing, 8(1), 1–17.

WHO (2001d) *Strengthening mental health promotion*. Geneva, World Health Organization (Fact sheet no.220).

Wilkinson, A. (1965) The Concept of Oracy. Educational Review, 17 (4), 11–15.

Wilkinson, J. A. (2000) The Power of Drama in English Language Learning. The Research Evidence. CEQ World Wellness Inc. The Ontario Institute for Studies in Education of the University of Toronto.

Williams, M., Mercer, S. & Ryan, S. (2015) *Exploring Psychology in Language Learning and Teaching*: Oxford University Press.

Williams, M. & Burden, R. (1997) *Psychology for Language Teachers*. Cambridge: Cambridge University Press.

Wilson, K. (2008) *Drama and Improvisation*. Oxford, UK. Oxford University Press.

Woolley, Michael E., Kol, Kelli L., & Bowen, Gary L. The Social Context of School Success for Latino Middle School Students: Direct and Indirect Influences of Teachers, Family, and Friends. First Published November 24, 2008. https://journals.sagepub.com/doi/abs/10.1177/0272431608324478.

Yates, T. M., & Masten, A. S. (2004). Fostering the Future: Resilience Theory and the Practice of Positive Psychology. In P. A. Linley & S. Joseph (Eds.), *Positive psychology in practice*, 521–39. John Wiley & Sons, Inc.

Index

Active Storytelling 70–1, 109, 122, 128
agility 33–4
   cognitive 34
   innovation 34
   interpersonal 34
   intrapersonal 34–5
   product-oriented 34
Alexander, R. J. 18
American Psychological Association 37
analyzing skill 28–9
applying skill 28

Baldwin, P. 21
Bloom, B. S. 27
Boal, A. 11, 60, 73
Bolton, G. 8
bullying 15, 73, 77–82
Burden, R. 13

child and social learning 14
Choral Speaking 79
classroom
   L2 20
   second language 8, 29
cognitive agility 34
collaboration 27, 30–1
Collective Role 20, 53, 54, 56, 66, 90, 106, 111, 121
Collective Voice 106
Commission Model 13, 15
communication 17–18, 27, 30
Conscience Alley 20, 23, 36, 45, 51–3, 54, 62–3, 96, 98, 111, 120
Conservation/Change 100–7
content integrated language learning (CLIL) 2, 9, 16–17, 47, 58
contrasting images 60
Corbett, P. 21, 70
Coyle, D. 16
Cozolino, L. 1
creativity 27, 29–30
critical thinking 27–9, 31, 32
cultural learning 18
curriculum
   cognition 16
   communication 16
   content 16
   culture 16
cyber-bullying 32
cyber-mobbing 32

Decision Alley. See Conscience Alley
Dialogic Talk 18
Discussion 92
distance 20
divergent (lateral) thinking 29
drama. See also Process Drama
   as communication 17–18
   contract 19–20, 41–3
   in education 8–9
   games 43
   and language 18

   moving the 45
   pausing the 45
   in second language teaching 8
   and self 12–13
   for talk 18–19
   thought and talk 23
   for writing 21–31
Drama Balloon 43

Eavesdropping 20, 51, 52, 53, 65–6, 80, 88, 105, 111, 120
education 8–9, 25
efficiency 36
Ehrman, M. E. 13
embodied learning 10
emotion 11–12
English as a second language (ESL) 2, 15
English for specific purposes (ESP) 15–16
equal status role 56
Essence Machine 71–2
evaluation 29
Exploratory Talk 18
Eyewitness 89

flexibility 33–5
FLIPSI (flexibility, leadership, initiative, productivity, social skills, interpersonal and intrapersonal skills) 26, 33–7
foreign language 15, 18, 39
   anxiety 12
Forum Theater 32, 36, 51, 73, 82
4Cs
   curriculum 16
   learning skills 27
Freeze Frame 45, 51, 59–60, 62, 63, 66, 86, 95, 107, 114

Great Fire of London 31, 44, 45, 47, 56, 58, 71, 84–90

Heathcote, D. 8, 11, 13, 15, 33, 38, 57–8
high-status role 56, 57
Hornbrook, D. 8
Hot-Seating 20, 36, 52, 53, 54, 66–8, 90, 93, 119

Improvisation 20, 53, 54, 80, 87, 88, 90, 93–6, 106, 111, 114, 120, 121–2
information literacy 31–2
infusion approach 17
initiative 35–6
innovation agility 34
intermediary role 56–7
interpersonal agility 34
intrapersonal agility 34–5
intrapersonal skills 36–7

Kabat-Zinn, J. 39

landscapes and settings 70
language 15, 18. See also second language
   foreign 12, 15, 18, 39
   teachers 2–4, 9, 10, 14–15, 17, 18, 26, 27–8, 31, 38, 44, 51, 72, 77, 100

leadership 35
learning
    cultural 18
    embodied 10–11
    rote 11
    skills 26–7
    social 14
Learning to Learn skill 30
lessons 46–7
life skills 26, 33–40
listening 19
literacy skills 26, 31–3
locus of control (LOC) 13
low-status role 56, 57

"Making Sense" of the Moment 112
Mantle of the Expert 13, 15, 20, 35, 54, 57–8, 103–4
Mapping 104
media literacy 32
memory 11
Mercer, N. 18
Mime 88, 103, 109
mindfulness 39
Move If … 92

neuroscience 11

Occupational Mime 86, 102
O'Neill, C. 57
opening activity 44
Overheard Conversations. See Eavesdropping

Parks, S. 17
Passing Thoughts 45, 51, 64, 119
Performance Carousel 47, 54, 61–2, 80, 82, 93, 107, 115, 124
personification 70
Poem 92
Presentations 104
private writing 22
Process Drama 9–10. See also twenty-first-century skills
    CLIL and 16–17
    and collaboration 27
    and communication 27
    and creativity 27
    and critical thinking 27
    and language 15
    lesson 10, 11, 13, 14–16, 22, 30, 36, 44
    performance 23–4
    as social learning 14
productivity 36
product-oriented agility 34
Proxemics 97, 107
Puchta, H. 29

questioning 67

real image 59
real life and fiction 14–15
Reasoner, R. 13
Refugees 91–9
remembering skill 28
resilience 37–8
role 20–1
Role on the Wall 28, 52, 63, 66, 67–9
rote learning 11
rounding off activity 46–7
Rumors 54, 64–5, 87, 94, 104, 110, 121

Scott, C. 31
scribe 22–3
sculpting images 60
second language 12, 67

classroom 8, 29
communication 30
learners 13, 42, 67–8
teaching 8, 17, 66, 117
second language acquisition (SLA) 1–2, 8, 12, 15, 25, 28, 33, 38, 40, 70
"self" 12–13, 34–5
self-compassion 39
self-confidence 13
self-efficacy 13
self-esteem 12, 13, 22, 46
self-image 13
Shared and Guided Writing 97
Small Group Playmaking 18, 21, 30, 34, 46, 53–4, 60–1, 81, 107, 123
social
    constructivism 1
    interaction 30
    learning 14
    media 36
    skills 36
sociocultural theory 1
Sound Collage and Voice Collage 72
Soundscape 62, 72
speaking 19
Stern, H. H. 18
Still Image 20, 55, 59–60, 63, 78, 79–80, 92–3, 110, 114–15, 123
Storytelling 114
summing up activity 46–7
sustainable development skills 26, 39–40
Swartz, R. 17

Tableau 59–60, 78, 86, 102, 110, 122
Talk for Writing approach 21–2, 70
talking 18–21, 23, 41–3, 50, 52–3
Talking Objects 54, 67, 69–70, 79, 89, 112
teacher
    as co-participants 51
    deviating 45
    drama contract 19–20, 41–3
    drama games 43
    drama lesson 44
    L2 14, 21, 27
    lessons and 46–7
    moving the drama 45
    opening activity 44
    ownership and responsibility 46
    pausing the drama 45
    scribe/cowriter 22–3
    time limits 46
    working groups 46
Teacher as Narrator 87
Teacher as Storyteller 45, 54, 70, 103, 122–3
Teacher in Role 20, 22, 44, 51, 53–4, 55–7, 81, 83, 87, 90, 94, 97, 98, 103, 105, 111, 112, 119, 121, 122, 124
technology literacy 33
Thinking about Thinking skill 30
thinking frames 23, 27, 52
Thought Collage 47, 51, 64
Thought-Tracking 55, 63–4, 88, 93, 95
Thought Walks 20, 47, 53, 55, 64
time limits 46
Total Physical Response (TPR) 70
twenty-first-century skills 1–4, 16, 25–7, 29, 31, 33, 75
    collaboration 30–1
    communication skills 30
    creativity 29–30
    critical thinking 27–9
    learning skills 27
    life skills
        flexibility 33–5
        initiative 35–6

intrapersonal skills 36–7
   leadership 35
   mindfulness and self-compassion 39
   productivity 36
   resilience 37–8
   social skills 36
   well-being 37
  literacy 31
   information 31–2
   media 32
   technology 33
  sustainable development 39–40

understanding skill 28

Visualization 78
Voice Collage 20, 47, 51, 52, 54, 64, 72, 87–8, 113
Vygotsky, L. S. 14

Warm-Up Activity 109
Way, B. 8
well-being 37
whole class circle 50
whole class drama 46
Whoosh! 50, 71
Williams, M. 13, 29
working groups 46
writing 21–2, 53–5
Writing in Role 97, 105, 121

www.ingramcontent.com/pod-product-compliance
Ingram Content Group UK Ltd.
Pitfield, Milton Keynes, MK11 3LW, UK
UKHW050024310126
467534UK00005B/128